Get Started in Beginner's English

Cindy Cheetham

D0011767

First published in Great Britain in 2016 by Hodder and Stoughton.
An Hachette UK company.

This edition published in 2016 by John Murray Learning

British Library Cataloguing in Publication Data: a catalogue record for
this title is available from the British Library.

Library of Congress Catalog Card Number: on file.

9781473612143

1

Typeset by Cenveo® Publisher Services.

Printed and bound in Great Britain by CPI Group (UK) Ltd., Croydon,
CR0 4YY.

John Murray Learning policy is to use papers that are natural, renewable
and recyclable products and made from wood grown in sustainable
forests. The logging and manufacturing processes are expected to
conform to the environmental regulations of the country of origin.

Carmelite House
50 Victoria Embankment
London EC4Y 0DZ
www.hodder.co.uk

**Also available
in ebook**

Contents

About the author

I have worked in English as a foreign language teaching for over 30 years, as a teacher, trainer, trainer of trainers, examiner, assessor and materials writer.

My first teaching job was in Spain and I have since worked in Portugal, Brazil and the UK. I have taught all levels, from complete beginners to advanced, and to a very wide range of students. I have taught ten-year-old children, teenagers, university students, factory workers, company directors, retired bankers and senior politicians. One of my favourite levels is beginners. For a teacher, it is very rewarding to see the dramatic progress that beginners can make.

I am also a teacher trainer and so I teach people how to teach as well as helping experienced teachers in schools and colleges. I have always written my own materials and some have been published but this is my first title for the Teach Yourself series.

I studied French and Spanish at school and learnt Portuguese while I was living in Portugal and Brazil, so I understand the difficulties of learning a new language. I believe that learning vocabulary, and not just individual words but whole phrases, is just as important as learning grammar rules. I hope the emphasis on vocabulary in this book helps you make progress more quickly. I also think it is really important to keep things as simple as possible, particularly if you are learning without a teacher. English, like many languages, can be complicated but if things get too complicated, people often give up and I don't want you to give up!

I really hope this book helps you learn English and you find it simple and easy to use. There are so many things you can read and listen to when you understand some English. It is all very exciting!

Good luck!

Cindy Cheetham

How the book works

Who is *Get Started in Beginner's English* for?

I can't speak English very well	**beginners**	Don't worry! The book is very simple.
	people who studied English at school but have forgotten their English	The book is a good way to remember and study again.
	business people	You have help with reading and writing emails, meeting people and introducing yourself, travelling, socializing and making arrangements.
	tourists and people going to the UK on holiday	You learn phrases to use in hotels, restaurants, tourist information centres, when travelling, sightseeing or shopping.
	studying alone	All the information is in the book. The explanations, the exercises and the answers. You are the student **and** the teacher!
	studying with a tutor	All the information you need is in the book, but it's great if you have someone to help you when you have a question and correct you when you make a mistake.
	studying in a class	The book can give you extra help and practice with vocabulary, grammar, listening, speaking, reading and writing.

	people who like English	There are a lot of words for you to learn and activities for you to do.
	teachers of English	There are a lot of resources you can use in class or as homework to supplement your course book (topic-based vocabulary exercises, activities and exercises to focus on and practise specific grammar and language points, reading, listening and writing practice, speaking tasks, tests and information about life in the UK). You can also use it as a course book – everything you need is included.

Why choose *Get Started in Beginner's English*?

▶ It has everything you need – vocabulary, grammar, pronunciation, listening, speaking, reading, writing and review units for revision.

▶ The material is simple to use so you can find what you want easily.

▶ You can use the different sections separately: for example, you can use just the listening and speaking material, or just the vocabulary material.

▶ You can use the culture sections to learn about life, customs and traditions in the UK and compare it with life, customs and traditions in your country.

▶ You can decide how often to study (every day? once a week?) and how long to study for (ten minutes every morning? half an hour after work? two hours in the morning at the weekend?). The course can fit in to your life.

▶ The material is in short sections, so you can make good use of whatever time you have, even if it is just ten minutes.

▶ The audio gives you pronunciation practice, conversations and other things to listen to.

▶ Full listening audioscripts and a language summary list for each unit can be downloaded for free from the Teach Yourself Library app (for Android and iOS) or www.library.teachyourself.com.

How to use the book for self-study

THE DISCOVERY METHOD

Everyone can learn another language but it is sometimes difficult and there are a lot of different ways to learn. This course uses the 'Discovery method'. The 'Discovery Method' helps people learn and remember languages better and more easily. If you are active in learning and do things for yourself, you remember things more easily so in this book, we don't **tell** you the grammar rules. You look at examples in a conversation, answer questions and find out (or **'discover'**) the grammar rules for yourself. With this book, you are the student and the teacher!

THE MATERIAL

There are ten units in the book and each unit has these sections:

Aims of the unit

This describes what you learn.

 ### Culture

Each unit has a topic (for example, Unit 4 is about sport and free time; Unit 10 is about shopping). At the start of the unit there is a short text about the topic.

 ### Vocabulary

In each unit there are vocabulary exercises to help you learn the key words and expressions for that topic. There is an audio for you to learn how to pronounce all the words and usually an exercise to practise using the words.

 ### Language discovery

This is where you learn the grammar or phrases. First you hear a conversation and answer some questions to check you understand it. Then you have some 'discovery' questions. These questions help you look at the grammar or phrases and understand when and how you can use them. You also learn the pronunciation and then practise using the language.

 ### Listening practice

You practise listening in each unit and listen to typical things for the topic, for example, listening to airport announcements or understanding tourist recommendations. The listening also gives you more practice with the vocabulary and grammar.

Speaking practice

You practise speaking in each unit with typical and useful tasks, for example, ordering food in a restaurant, enrolling on a language course or complaining in a hotel.

Pronunciation practice

You hear the vocabulary and grammar and then practise saying the words and phrases. There is a lot of work on pronunciation to help you have a good British English accent. There is a guide to British English pronunciation at the start of the book. It's a good idea to look at this after one or two units when you have a little more English.

Reading practice

You practise reading in each unit and read typical things for the topic, for example, reading a social media post, reading tourist information leaflets or reading a hotel review.

Writing practice

You practise writing in each unit with typical and useful tasks, for example, writing an email, writing a review of a restaurant, booking a room or filling in a form.

Test yourself

These exercises at the end of each unit help you check how much you know and understand.

There are two review units. Review unit 1 checks you understand the grammar and vocabulary from Units 1–5. Review unit 2 checks you understand the grammar and vocabulary from Units 6–10. At the end of the course, there is an Answer key, with all the answers to all the exercises. Finally, you can download a language summary from the Teach Yourself Library app or www.library.teachyourself.com. The language summary lists all the grammar, phrases and vocabulary from each unit. There is also a list of UK/US vocabulary. Most words in British English and American English are the same, but there are some differences, for example, in the UK we say *taxi*, but in the US they say *cab*.

HELPING YOU LEARN – A FEW SUGGESTIONS AND IDEAS

▶ Start with Unit 1 and do the units in the book in order (Unit 1, Unit 2, Unit 3, …).

▶ Make sure you are confident with the language in one unit before you start the next.

- ▶ Don't do all the vocabulary or all the grammar exercises together. Do a different vocabulary or grammar exercise each day.
- ▶ Do the exercises again and again. It helps you remember.
- ▶ Test yourself on the vocabulary and grammar and see how much you can remember.
- ▶ Repeat the conversations as many times as you can … try to memorize them and say them quietly to yourself.
- ▶ Listen to the conversations as many times as you can … and listen when you are doing something else (when you are walking home, waiting for a bus …).
- ▶ Find a study friend. You can test each other and help each other and it is great to have someone to practise with.
- ▶ Read the section 'Learning to learn: how to be a good language learner'.
- ▶ Don't forget:

Learning = understanding + remembering

Before you start

Learn the vocabulary you need for the book

For the answers to these exercises, see the end of this section.

1 Complete the table. Put ✎ the word in the correct (✓) place, a–i.

> word ~~phrase~~ sentence
> conversation picture question
> answer table text

a phrase	No problem!
b _____	My name is Ana.
c _____	What's your name?
d _____	
e _____	
f _____	
g _____	
h _____	I live in London.
i _____	English

2 Put the words in the correct (✓) place, a–l.

fill in   check   practise saying
read   listen to   ~~write~~   look at
choose   match   repeat   find   put

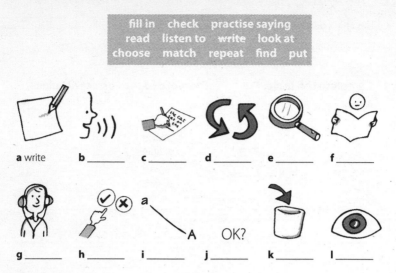

a write   **b** _____   **c** _____   **d** _____   **e** _____   **f** _____

g _____   **h** _____   **i** _____   **j** _____   **k** _____   **l** _____

3 Use the words to complete the tables. Put one word in each space a–h.

questions   gaps   true   no
words   read   correct   order

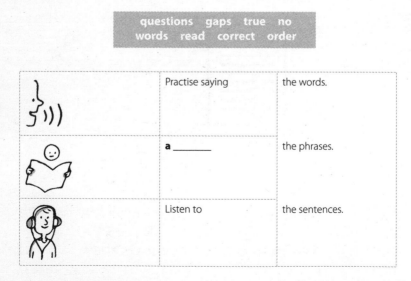

	Practise saying	the words.
	a _____	the phrases.
	Listen to	the sentences.

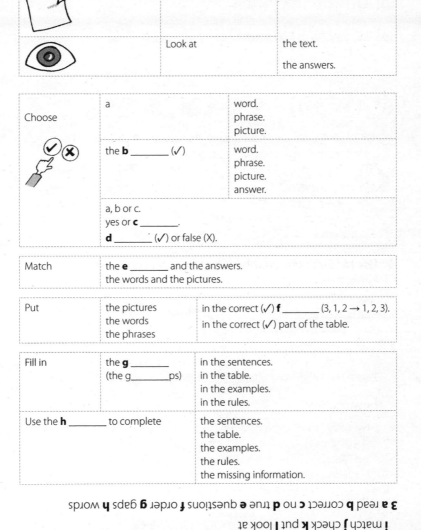

	Write	the conversation.
	Look at	the text. the answers.

Choose	a	word. phrase. picture.
	the **b** _____ (✓)	word. phrase. picture. answer.
	a, b or c. yes or **c** _____. **d** _____ (✓) or false (X).	

Match	the **e** _____ and the answers. the words and the pictures.	

Put	the pictures the words the phrases	in the correct (✓) **f** _____ (3, 1, 2 → 1, 2, 3). in the correct (✓) part of the table.

Fill in	the **g** _____ (the g_____ps)	in the sentences. in the table. in the examples. in the rules.
Use the **h** _____ to complete	the sentences. the table. the examples. the rules. the missing information.	

Before you start: Answers to exercises

1 b answer c question d conversation e text f table g picture h sentence
i word

2 b practise saying c fill in d repeat e find f read g listen to h choose
i match j check k put l look at

3 a read b correct c no d true e questions f order g gaps h words

Learning to learn: how to be a good language learner

1 MAKE LEARNING A HABIT

▶ Study a little every day.
▶ It's better to study every day for ten minutes than once a week for an hour.
▶ If you study for more than an hour, have a break.
▶ Have somewhere calm and quiet where you can study.
▶ Have a well-organized notebook with different sections for vocabulary, grammar, writing and pronunciation.
▶ Have short-term goals (for example 'today I want to learn 10 new words' or 'this week I want to finish Unit 3' or 'I want to get 80% in Review 1').
▶ Look back and revise often.
▶ Remember, you need two things to learn a new language: a lot of **time** and **practice**.

2 READ, LISTEN TO, WRITE AND SPEAK AS MUCH ENGLISH AS POSSIBLE

▶ Listen to English language radio and British or American music.
▶ Watch films and TV programmes in English.
▶ Go on the internet in English.
▶ Read English magazines and newspapers.
▶ If you have a hobby or interest, read about it in English.
▶ Follow the news in your language and then in English.

3 VOCABULARY

▶ Have a vocabulary notebook with a page for each topic.
▶ Read, listen, say and write the words again and again.
▶ Keep lists on your phone and look at them – often!
▶ Make a word cloud for each topic (type 'word + cloud + free + English' in a search engine on the internet) and put it on a wall at home.

- Make a mind map and use it to remember words.

- Make flash cards and look at them every time you have five minutes free.
- Keep the flash cards in different boxes: Box 1 – 'words I know'; Box 2 – 'words I nearly know'; Box 3 – 'words I don't know'. Try to move some cards from Box 3 to Box 2 and Box 2 to Box 1 every day!
- Try to find more words to add to the topics in the book.

4 GRAMMAR
- Compare English and your language – how different is it?
- For each pattern you learn (for example, *love* + verb + *ing*: *I love reading*), make a list of examples, as many as possible with different words.
- When you read, look for more grammar patterns or examples of patterns you know.

5 PRONUNCIATION
- Do the pronunciation exercises more than once.
- Record yourself and compare to the original.
- Write a list of words or sounds you find difficult.
- Use the internet to hear how to make the sounds or words you find difficult.
- Practise those sounds or words more.
- Repeat the conversations in the book line by line and copy the pronunciation.
- Try to remember the whole conversation.
- Remember about word stress, sentence stress, weak forms, linking and intonation.

6 LISTENING AND READING
- When listening or reading, try to concentrate on the main idea. Understanding every word is sometimes difficult but you can get a lot of information from the main idea.

- You can also imagine the situation and guess what people are going to say (for example, in a café, people talk about food).
- Don't panic if you don't understand and don't stop listening – try to guess what they are saying and keep following the conversation.
- Don't worry about individual words and try to guess key words. Check in a dictionary later.

7 SPEAKING

- Try to change a few words in the dialogues in the book (for example, the phrase *I love swimming* can change to *I like swimming*, *I like running*, *I quite like cycling*).
- Talk to yourself in English.
- Take every chance to speak English – the best way to improve your speaking is to speak.
- If you don't know a word, describe it or use gesture or mime – but don't stop the conversation.
- If you are learning English in your country, imagine doing everyday things in English (for example, going to a shop or asking for directions).

8 LEARN FROM YOUR MISTAKES

- Some people get very worried about mistakes and only say something if they are sure it is correct. This stops you learning and making progress and makes it difficult to have a conversation.
- Don't worry about making mistakes (it's normal)!
- Most mistakes aren't important – people can usually still understood you (for example, if you say 'my sister live in London' or 'I don't like go to the cinema', these sentences are not correct but everyone can understand them).
- If possible, remember your mistakes and later, try to learn the correct version.

9 DON'T WORRY IF YOU ARE NOT SURE OR DON'T UNDERSTAND

- If you are reading or listening and don't understand, don't worry. Keep reading and listening, you might understand more later.
- Don't use your dictionary for every new word. Try to guess the meaning. If you can, read or listen to it again.
- If you still don't understand and it is an important word, check it in a dictionary.
- You can also just ask someone! ('Sorry, excuse me … What does X mean?')

Key points about English pronunciation

SOUNDS

It is sometimes difficult to know how to pronounce an English word. English spelling and English pronunciation are not always the same.

 1 00.01 **Look at the highlighted letters. Is it the same sound in both examples? Choose Yes or No.**

Example sentence 1	Example sentence 2	Same sound?
a **Choose** the correct answer.	It's **Tues**day today.	Yes/No
b **No**, I don't.	I don't **know**.	Yes/No
c That's **right**.	**Write** the answer.	Yes/No
d I've got s**o**me money.	Have you got any h**o**mework?	Yes/No
e I h**a**te swimming.	Yes, I h**a**ve.	Yes/No
f I g**o** to work at nine o'clock.	I d**o** my homework after dinner.	Yes/No

Some words have a similar spelling but a different pronunciation. Some words have a different spelling but the same pronunciation. Because of this, phonetic symbols are a useful way to show how to pronounce a word and we sometimes use them in the book.

 2 00.02 **There are 26 letters in the alphabet but 44 sounds. Listen to the sounds (vowel sounds, diphthongs and consonant sounds) and note the symbols we use to represent them. Listen again and repeat the sounds and examples.**

Vowel sounds

ʊ put, look	æ bank, man	ɪ it, big	ə above, cinema	ʌ cup, up	ɒ hot, stop
u: blue, two	ɑ: car, father	i: me, eat	ɜ: her, learn	ɔ: more, four	e ten, men

Diphthongs

ɪə near, here	eɪ say, eight	aɪ five, my	əʊ go, home
ʊə Europe, tourist	eə where, their	aʊ now, out	ɔɪ boy, noisy

Consonant sounds

p pen, put	b big, book	t tea, get	d do, good
f five, if	v very, five	θ think, thank	ð this, the
k can, look	g go, get	s speak, this	z zoo, please
tʃ choose, check	dʒ July, juice	ʃ she, wash	ʒ Asia, television
m man, make	n no, ten	ŋ morning, thing	h how, hello
l look, love	r red, right	w what, where	j yes, you

Don't worry if it is difficult to remember the symbols. When we use the symbols in this course, we give you a lot of examples and there are usually some symbols that are easy to read because they look similar to letters in the alphabet. This can help you.

3 00.03 **Can you read these words?**
   a /wʌt/
   b /neim/
   c /gɪv/
   d /frɛndli/
   e /ʌmbrɛlə/

Listen and check.

If you want more practice, look in a good dictionary, and you can see words in phonetics.

STRESS

The word *France* has one syllable. The word *London* has two syllables. The word *America* has four syllables. A syllable is part of a word with a vowel sound.

 4 00.04 **How many syllables are in these words? Listen and answer.**
- **a** English
- **b** bye
- **c** understand

When a word has two or more syllables, one of the syllables has more emphasis than the others. It is **stressed**.

 5 00.05 **Look at the words. Listen and note the stressed syllable. Which syllable is stressed?**
- **a** London
- **b** Australia

This is word stress. You can check word stress in a dictionary. It doesn't change.

In phrases and sentences, one or more of the words (or syllables) has more emphasis than the others. It is **stressed**.

 6 00.06 **Look at the phrases. Listen and note the stressed words (or syllables). Which word (or syllable) is stressed?**
- **a** Good morning.
- **b** How are you?
- **c** My name's Cindy.

This is sentence stress. You can't check sentence stress in a dictionary. It changes depending on the situation. We usually stress the important or information words.

 7 00.07 **What are the information words in these sentences?**
- **a** I live in Rome.
- **b** I come from Spain.
- **c** I don't know.

Listen and note the stressed words. They are the information words.

CONNECTED SPEECH

When we say two or more words together, the way we say some words sometimes changes, and the beginning and endings of words sometimes change.

The way we say some words – weak forms

 8 00.08 **Look at the highlighted words. Is it the same pronunciation in both examples? Choose Yes or No.**

Example sentence 1	Example sentence 2	Same sound?
a Does she speak English?	Yes, she **does**.	Yes/No
b Can you swim?	I **can** speak French.	Yes/No
c Yes I **can**.	She **can** speak Arabic.	Yes/No
d I'd love **to**.	I'm going **to** France.	Yes/No
e There **are** two chairs.	How **are** you?	Yes/No
f Are there any more?	Yes, there **are**.	Yes/No

 9 00.08 **Listen again and note the stressed words (or syllables). Which word (or syllable) is stressed? What do you notice?**

Some words in English have two different pronunciations. All the words in the box have two different pronunciations, a strong pronunciation (when the word is stressed) and a weak pronunciation (when the word isn't stressed). We often say the weak form. The weak form of these words has the sound /ə/.

a, an, of, at, from, for, to, and, does, was, were, can, am, are, have, has, there

The beginning and endings of words – linking

 10 00.09 **Listen to this sentence. What happens between the words where you see ?**

My name is Marta.

When one word ends in a consonant sound (in this sentence, /m/) and the next word starts with a vowel sound (in this sentence, /i/) we link the words together. It sounds like one word: My /neimiz/ Marta.

 11 00.10 **Look at these sentences. Note where one word links to the next word.**
   a I live in China.
   b Get started in English!

INTONATION

12 00.11 **Listen to two people saying *hello*. Which person sounds friendly? Choose Person A or Person B.**

Our voice can go up and down or stay flat. This is intonation (or the music of our voice). Intonation is very important in English because it shows how we feel. We use intonation to be friendly and polite and to show if we are interested or not. If our voice doesn't go up and down but stays flat, we sound unfriendly or rude or not interested. Is intonation important in your language?

13 00.12 **Listen to more sentences. Are the people friendly, polite and interested – or not?**

	Friendly, polite, interested 🙂 〜〜〜	Not friendly, rude, not interested ☹ --------
a Hello		
b Good morning		
c How are you?		
d Thank you		
e Sorry		
f Excuse me		
g OK		

14 00.12 **Listen again and copy the pronunciation of the friendly people.**

In this course there are exercises to help you with pronunciation. There are exercises on sounds, word stress, sentence stress, weak forms, linking and intonation.

1 Hello! Where are you from?

In this unit you will learn how to:
▶ *greet people.*
▶ *give and find out personal information.*
▶ *use polite and friendly phrases.*
▶ *fill in a simple form.*
▶ *say the letters of the alphabet.*
▶ *read email and web addresses.*

CEFR: (A1) *Can introduce himself and ask and answer questions about personal details. Can recognize and produce simple phrases and sentences to describe where he or she lives. Can use basic greeting and leave-taking expressions.* **(A2)** *Can fill in forms of personal details.*

US and UK cities

1   Match the cities to the letters on the maps.

London, Washington D.C., San Francisco, Manchester, Glasgow, New Orleans, Los Angeles, Birmingham, New York, Belfast

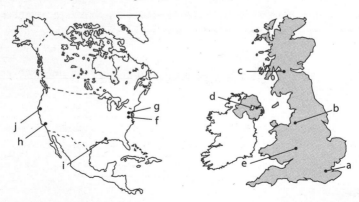

2 01.01 **Listen and repeat. Note the stressed syllable, for example,** _London_, **New** _York_. **Practise saying the words.**

V Vocabulary builder

VOCABULARY 1: GREETINGS

1 Complete the table. Put the greetings in the correct part of the table.

Bye	See you later	Hello
Hi	Good afternoon	~~Bye bye~~
Good night	Hi there	See you tomorrow
~~Good morning~~	Goodbye	Good evening

	INFORMAL	FORMAL
		Good morning
	Bye bye	

2 01.02 **Listen and repeat. Note the stressed syllable, for example, Good _morn_ing, Hel_lo_. Practise saying the words.**

VOCABULARY 2: COUNTRIES

1 Match the countries to the letters on the map.

Japan	Russia	Spain	Indonesia
Canada	Korea	Australia	Brazil
France	China	Germany	Egypt
The United States	India	South Africa	The UK

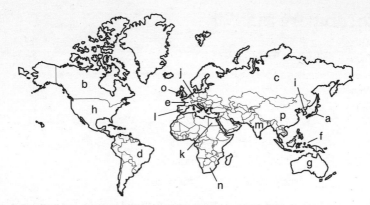

2 Label the map of the United Kingdom a–e.

United Kingdom   England
Scotland   Wales   Northern Ireland

 3 01.03 Listen and repeat. Note the stressed syllable, for example, *Indonesia*, *Australia*. Practise saying the words.

Conversation 1: *What's your name? Where are you from?*

 1 01.04 Tom and Anita meet for the first time. Read and listen to the conversation. Choose the correct name, *Tom* or *Anita* and put it next to the flag.

Tom	Hello.
Anita	Hi.
Tom	My name's Tom. What's your name?
Anita	My name's Anita. Where are you from?
Tom	I'm from England. And you?
Anita	I'm from India.

2 **What do they say? Fill in the gaps.**

My _____ Tom. I'm _____ England.

_____ name's Anita. _____ from India.

3 01.05 **Listen and repeat. Note the stressed words, for example, _My name's Tom_. Practise saying the sentences.**

4 **Complete sentences for three other people. You choose the names. Use the countries in Vocabulary 2. Then write about you.**

My _____ (Name). I'm _____ (Country).

_____ _____ _____

5 **What's the question? Fill in the gaps.**

Question:	Answer:
A: What's _____ _____?	**B:** My name's Paulo.
A: Where _____ _____ _____?	**B:** I'm from Brazil.

6 01.06 **Listen and repeat. Note the stressed words, for example, _What's your name?_ Practise saying the questions.**

VOCABULARY 3: NATIONALITIES

1 **Complete the missing countries and nationalities.**

COUNTRY	NATIONALITY
India	Indian
	German
	French
The United States	
	Spanish
	Brazilian
	Egyptian

	Indonesian
	English
	Welsh
Russia	
	South African
	Canadian
	Japanese
	Korean
Australia	
	Chinese
	Portuguese
	Irish
	Scottish
	British

 2 01.07 **Listen and repeat. Note the stressed syllable, for example,** *Chi<u>nese</u>, A<u>me</u>rican.* **Practise saying the words.**

Conversation 2: *I'm + nationality*

 1 01.08 **Read and listen to the conversation. What extra words do Tom and Anita say? Fill in the gaps.**

Tom	Hello!
Anita	Hi.
Tom	My name's Tom. What's your name?
Anita	My name's Anita. Where are you from?
Tom	I'm from England. I'm _____. And you?
Anita	I'm from India. I'm _____.

2 01.09 **Listen and repeat. Note the stressed words, for example,** *My name's <u>Tom</u>.* **Practise saying the sentences. Say sentences about you.**

3 **Complete the table. Make sentences for the people.**

Example: a *My name's Ali. I'm from France. I'm French.*

6

	COUNTRY	NATIONALITY
Ali	France	French
Nelson	Brazil	Brazilian
Sarah	South Africa	
Yuki		Japanese
Natasha	Russia	

 4 01.10 **Listen and check your answers to Exercise 3. Write sentences about you.**

5 **Complete the conversations. Use the information from Exercise 3.**

Ali	Hello!
Anita	Hi.
Ali	My name's Ali. _____ _____ _____?
Anita	My name's Anita. Where are you from?
Ali	_____ _____ _____. I'm _____. And you?
Anita	I'm _____ _____. I'm Indian.
Nelson	Hello!
Sarah	Hi.
Nelson	_____ _____ _____. What's _____ _____?
Sarah	_____ _____ _____. Where _____ _____ _____?
Nelson	_____ from _____. I'm _____. And you?
Sarah	_____ _____ South Africa. _____ _____ _____.

6 **Write a conversation for Yuki and Natasha.**

7 **Write a conversation for you and a friend.**

Vocabulary builder

VOCABULARY 4: LANGUAGES

> **LANGUAGE TIP**
>
> We often use the same word for language and nationality, but not always.

1 Complete the table.

COUNTRY	LANGUAGE	NATIONALITY
Spain	Spanish	Spanish
Germany	German	
	Portuguese	Brazilian
England		English
The United States		American
China	Chinese	
France		French
Egypt	Arabic	
		Russian
		Japanese
		Korean
	Hindi, Bengali	Indian

 2 01.11 **Listen and repeat. Note the stressed syllable, for example,** *Portuguese*, *Arabic*. **Practise saying the words.**

 3 What are the two usual endings for language and nationality words?

4 What languages do people speak? Here are the top ten, but they are not in order. What do you think? Put them in order. Then check the answer in the Answer key.

Japanese	Portuguese
German	Bengali
Russian	Mandarin Chinese
English	Spanish
Arabic	Hindi

5 What are the top ten languages on the internet? What do you think? Write your top ten. Then check the answer in the Answer key.

Conversation 3: *Where do you live? Do you speak English?*

 1 01.12 **Read and listen to Mike and Sally. Fill in gaps a–f in the table. Use one word in each gap.**

Mike	Hello.
Sally	Hi!
Mike	My name's Mike. What's your name?
Sally	My name's Sally. Where are you from?
Mike	I'm from the UK. I'm British. And you?
Sally	I'm from the UK too. I'm British but I live in Canada.
Mike	Do you speak French?
Sally	No, I don't. I speak English but I don't speak French. And you? Where do you live?
Mike	I live in France.
Sally	Oh! Do you speak French, Mike?
Mike	Yes, I speak a little French.

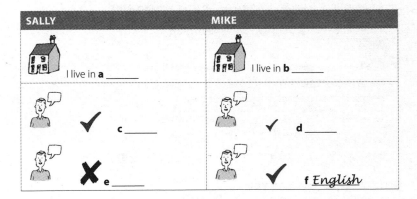

2 What do they say? Fill in the gaps.

Sally: I _____ _____ Canada. I _____ English. I _____
               _____ French.

Mike: I _____ _____France. I _____ _____ _____
               French.

3 Look at the table and fill in the missing words.

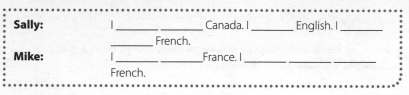

Canada	English ✔	French ✔	Chinese ✗
a I _____ _____ Canada.	**b** I _____ English.	**c** I speak a little French.	**d** I _____ _____ Chinese.

4 01.13 Listen to the sentences in Exercise 3 and repeat. Note the stressed words, for example, I _live_ in _Canada_. Practise saying the sentences.

5 Make more sentences.

Example: *I live in Brazil. I speak Portuguese.*

Example: Brazil	Portuguese
a India	Bengali
b Egypt	Arabic
c Hong Kong	Chinese

Write a sentence about you.

6 Make more sentences.

Example: *I speak English. I speak a little French. I don't speak Chinese.*

✔	🗨 ✔	🗨 ✗
Example: English	French	Chinese
a Spanish	Arabic	English
b Russian	Portuguese	Bengali
c German	English	Korean

Write a sentence about you.

7 What's the question? Fill in the gaps.

Where _____ _____ _____? I live in England.

_____ you _____ French?   No, I don't/Yes, a little.

8 01.14 Listen and repeat. Note the stressed words, for example, _Where_ do you _live_? Practise saying the sentences.

Conversation 4: Polite phrases

1 01.15 Look at the pictures. Read and listen to Conversations 1 and 2. Choose 1 or 2 for each picture.

> **Conversation 1**
>
> **A:**   Excuse me … excuse me … excuse me?
> **B:**   Yes?
>
> **Conversation 2**
>
> **A:**   Ow!
> **B:**   Oh I'm sorry! Are you OK?

2 Look at the pictures a–d. Choose *Excuse me* or *Sorry!* for each picture.

a 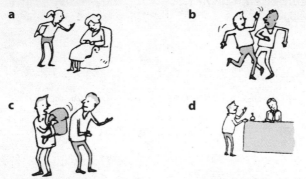 b

c d

3 01.16 **Read and listen to a conversation at passport control. Put the pictures a–e in the correct order.**

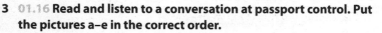

Immigration officer	Good morning.
Traveller	Good morning.
Immigration officer	Can I see your passport, please?
Traveller	I'm sorry, I don't understand. Can you speak more slowly, please?
Immigration officer	Can I see your passport, please?
Traveller	Here you are.
Immigration officer	Thank you. Enjoy your stay.

a b c

d PASSPORT CONTROL e

4 Look at the sentences. What is the difference? What word do we use to be polite and friendly?

Can I see your passport?   Can I see your passport, please? 🙂

What name is it?   What name is it, please? 🙂

Can you speak more slowly?   Can you speak more slowly, please? 🙂

5 When do we say *please*? When do we say *thank you*? Complete the conversations.

a   b   c   d   e

6 01.17 Listen and repeat. Note the stressed syllable, for example, _thank_ you. Practise saying the words and phrases.

Listening, speaking and pronunciation

LISTENING: MEETING PEOPLE

1 01.18 Listen to the conversation. Which picture shows the conversation?

a

b

2 01.18 Listen to the conversation again. Complete the table.

	NATIONALITY		
Claudia	German		
Rama			

3 01.19 **Listen to the conversation with Fatima and Sofia.**
Read the sentences. Choose Fatima or Sofia.

	FATIMA	SOFIA
I'm from Russia.		
I'm from Pakistan.		
I live in Dubai.		
I live in London.		
I speak Russian.		
I speak English.		
I speak Arabic.		

PRONUNCIATION 1: GREETING PEOPLE AND SOUNDING FRIENDLY

1 01.20 **Listen to the people saying *hello* and *good morning*. Are they friendly 😊 or not friendly 😠?**

a _____   d _____
b _____   e _____
c _____

Listen again and copy the pronunciation of the friendly people.

SPEAKING: MEETING PEOPLE

1 Look at the conversation. Fill in the gaps about you.

Dieter	Good morning. Welcome to Business Solutions. My name's Dieter.
You	Good morning. My name's _____.
Dieter	Pleased to meet you. Where are you from?
You	I'm from _____. I live in _____.
Dieter	You speak English very well.
You	Thank you. _____ _____ _____ from?
Dieter	I'm from Berlin, Germany.
You	Where _____ _____ _____?
Dieter	I live in Dubai. And you?
You	Oh I live in _____.

2 01.21 **Listen to the conversation with Dieter. Say your answers in the gaps.**

Close your book, listen again and have the conversation.

PRONUNCIATION 2: LETTERS OF THE ALPHABET, SPELLING

 **1** 01.22 **Listen to these sounds.**

/ei/   /i:/   /e/   /ai/   /eu/   /u:/   /a:/

2 01.23 **Now listen to the letters of the alphabet. Put the letters in the correct part of the table.**

/ei/	/i:/	/e/	/ai/	/eu/	/u:/	/a:/
A, H	B, C	F, L				

3 01.24 **Listen to the spelling and complete the words.**

Names, countries, nationalities and languages all start with a CAPITAL LETTER.

Example: the **U**nited **K**ingdom, **F**rench, **H**indi.

   a _ mer _ ca
   b Ne _ _ ork
   c Un _ ted _ _ ngd _ m
   d Q _ _ b _ c
   e E _ rop _ _ _
   f Ital _ _ _
   g _ _ _ tral _ _
   h N _ w _ _ _ land
   i   _ _ _ _ _ _ _
   j   _ _ _ _ _ _ _

4 01.25 **Practise spelling these city names, then listen and check your answers.**

New Orleans   Manchester   San Francisco   Birmingham

PRONUNCIATION 3: SAYING EMAIL AND WEB ADDRESSES

1 01.26 **Look at and listen to these website and email addresses.**

www.bbc.co.uk
www.tourist-information-uk.com
www.discoverlosangeles.com
www.learnenglish.britishcouncil.org/en/
attractions@visitengland.org

2 01.27 **Look at the parts of email addresses. What do we say? Listen and match a–h with the parts of email addresses in the box.**

> . @ .com / .org .co.uk - www

a double u double u double u
b dot
c at
d dot com
e slash
f dot org
g dot co dot uk
h dash

3 01.26 **Practise saying the addresses in Exercise 1. Then listen again and check your answers.**

4 01.28 **Listen to four addresses and write them down.**

Reading and writing: Personal forms

1 Choose the correct word for each picture.

> married single
> children date of birth address

a _____

b _____

c _married_

d _____

e _____

2   Put the words in the correct part of the table.

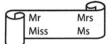

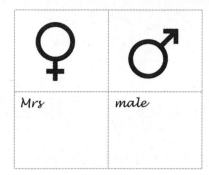

Mrs	male

3   01.29 Look at how we write titles and then listen to how we say them.

Mr	Mrs
Miss	Ms

/mɪstə/	/mɪs/
/mɪsɪz/	/məz/

Are the sentences correct (✓) or not correct (✗)?

a Mrs Jones is married.

b Miss Jones is not married.

c We don't know if Ms Jones is married or not.

4   01.30 Listen to the titles. Practise saying the words.

1 Read Tom's visa application form. Which picture shows Tom and his family?

a

b

c

d

Given name(s) as shown in your passport	Tom
Family name	Mitcham
Sex	male/~~female~~
Date of birth	07/11/1978
Place of birth	San Francisco
Country of birth	The United States
Nationality	American
Marital status	~~single~~/married
Full name of spouse/partner	Amélie Lafayette
Spouse/partner's date of birth	03/09/1981
Spouse/partner's nationality	French
Do you have any children?	yes/~~no~~
Details of children (name and date of birth)	Marie Lafayette 28/04/2011
Your full residential address and postcode	8924, Boulevard Lazare, Montreal, QC H2A, Canada
Email address	tom.mitcham@ canadamail.com
Home (landline) telephone number	+1 438 0956054
Mobile telephone number	07896 1293455

WRITING 1: COMPLETING A VISA APPLICATION FORM

Complete the visa application about you. Use Tom's form to help you.

Given name(s) as shown in your passport	
Family name	
Sex	male/female
Date of birth	
Place of birth	
Country of birth	
Nationality	
Marital status	single/married
Full name of spouse/partner	
Spouse/partner's date of birth	
Spouse/partner's nationality	
Do you have any children?	yes/no
Details of children (name and date of birth)	
Your full residential address and postcode	
Email address	
Home (landline) telephone number	
Mobile telephone number	

WRITING 2: COMPLETING A WEBSITE REGISTRATION FORM

Look at Tom's registration forms. Add your details to the forms.

Registering with AmazingIdeas.com

	YOU	TOM
My name is		Tom Mitcham
My email address is		tom.mitcham@canadamail.com
Confirm email address		tom.mitcham@canadamail.com
My mobile phone number is		07896 1293455
Choose a password		passwordtom0711
Confirm password		passwordtom0711

Creating a Findit account

	YOU	TOM
Name (first and last)		Tom Mitcham
Choose your user name		tom.mitcham@gmail.com
Choose a password		passwordtom0711
Confirm your password		passwordtom0711
Birthday		07/11
Gender		I am male/~~female~~
Your current email address		tom.mitcham@canadamail.com

 Test yourself

1 How many greetings can you remember? Fill in the table.

	INFORMAL	FORMAL
		Good morning
	Bye bye	

2 Complete the table.

		NATIONALITY
	English	English
France		
The United States		
Saudi Arabia		Saudi (Arabian)
Germany		
China		
Spain		

3 Fill in the questions and complete the answers for you.

a What's _your_ name?	My _____ _____.
b Where _____ _____ from?	I'm _____ _____ (country). I'm _____ (nationality).
c Where _____ _____ live?	I _____ in _____ (city/country).
d _____ you _____ English?	No, I _____. _____ I do./a little. I speak _____ (language). I speak a little _____ (language). I _____ speak _____ (language).

4 01.31 Can you spell out these words? Practise, then listen and check.

> **language speak listen read write**

5 01.32 How do you say these web and email addresses? Practise, then listen and check.
  a www.learnenglishteens.britishcouncil.org
  b www.bbclearningenglish.com
  c anna.brown51@btinternet.co.uk

SELF CHECK

I CAN ...
... greet people.
... give and find out personal information.
... use polite and friendly phrases.
... fill in a simple form.
... say the letters of the alphabet.
... read email and web addresses.

2 Family and friends, jobs and home

In this unit you will learn how to:
▶ *talk about your family.*
▶ *talk about jobs and workplaces.*
▶ *talk about where you live.*
▶ *describe people and places.*

CEFR: (A1) *Can introduce himself and ask and answer questions about personal details. Can recognize and produce simple phrases and sentences to describe where he or she lives and people he or she knows.* **(A2)** *Can use phrases and sentences to describe family, other people, living conditions and job.*

Family life and homes in the UK

Look at the questions. Do you know the answers? Choose a, b or c.

1 **How many people live in the UK?**
 a 54,000,000 (54 million)
 b 64 million
 c 74 million

2 **How many people live in London?**
 a 7 million
 b 10 million
 c 4 million

3 **What kind of home do most people in the UK live in?**

a
b
c

4 What kind of home is most popular in London?

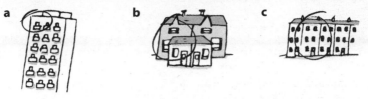

a   b   c

5 How many people are there in most families in the UK?

  a 2
  b 3
  c 4

**Read the text on family life and homes, and check the answers.
Use your dictionary for any words you are not sure of.**

FAMILY LIFE

There are about 64 million people in the UK and most live in England
(54 million). Five million people live in Scotland, three million people live
in Wales and two million people live in Northern Ireland. There are 18.2
million families. Most of these families are married couples (with or without
children) but there are two million single parents living with children. 20%
of people with children live together but are not married. Most families have
two children but nearly one million families have three or more children.

HOMES

Most people in the UK live in towns and cities. Seven million people
live in London. The other big cities are Birmingham, Leeds, Glasgow,
Sheffield, Bradford, Edinburgh, Liverpool, Manchester and Bristol. The most
popular type of house is a semi-detached house, but people also live in
flats, terraced houses and detached houses. 27% of people live in semi-
detached houses. In London, 50% of people live in flats.

Vocabulary builder

1 Fill in the gaps in the table. Use the family words in the box.

> grandmother sister ~~son~~ husband
> children grandparents father

grandfather		
	mother	parents
son	daughter	
brother		
	wife	

2 Complete the family tree. Use the [img] **and** [img] **family words.**

	Prudence (*grandmother*) + Hamish (grandfather)	
	Jean (_____) + Bryan (_____)	
Ruby (_____)	ME! ☺ + Michael (*husband*)	Julian (brother)
	Ellie (_____) Paul (_____)	

3 Look at the family tree and fill in the names.

   a *Hamish* is my grandfather and _____ is my grandmother.

   b _____ is my mother and _____ is my father.

   c _____ is my husband, _____ is my sister and _____ is my brother.

   d _____ and _____ are my children.

Draw your family tree. Write sentences about your family.

> **LANGUAGE TIP**
> People (and children) sometimes use informal words to talk about people in their family.

4 Look at the informal words in the table. What do the words mean? Put the correct words from Exercise 1 in the table.

	INFORMAL WORDS
a *mother*	mum
b	dad
c	kids
d	granny
e	grandpa

LANGUAGE TIP
When we talk about more than one, we usually add *s* to the noun, for example, *one girl, two girls*. We make most plurals like this. If the noun ends in a consonant + *y* or *fe* the spelling rules are different.

 5 Look at the three rules. Put them in the correct part of the table, 1, 2 or 3.

fe → v + es

y → i + es

+ s

1	2	3	IRREGULAR PLURALS
girl – **girls**	family – **families**	wife – **wives**	child – **children**
son – _____	baby – _____	life – _____	_____ – **men**
daughter – _____			_____ – **women**
brother – _____			person – _____
sister – _____			
boy – _____			

LANGUAGE TIP
Some nouns have an irregular plural.

6 Fill in the missing irregular plural nouns in the table in Exercise 5.

 7 02.01 Listen and repeat. Note the stressed syllable, for example, *grandmother, parents*. Practise saying the words.

VOCABULARY 2: JOBS AND WORKPLACES

1 Match the places to the pictures.

I work …
- **a** … in a factory <u>4</u>
- **b** … in an office
- **c** … in a school
- **d** … in a shop
- **e** … in a hospital (two pictures)
- **f** … at home

Look up more workplaces in a dictionary and add them to your list.

2 Match the jobs to the pictures in Exercise 1.
- **a** I'm a nurse. I work in a hospital.
- **b** I'm a businesswoman. I work in an office.
- **c** I'm a factory worker. I work in a factory.
- **d** I'm a teacher. I work in a school.
- **e** I'm a doctor. I work in a hospital.
- **f** I'm a computer programmer. I work at home.
- **g** I'm a shop assistant. I work in a shop.

3 02.02 Listen and repeat. Note the stressed syllable, for example, *I'm a <u>nurse</u>. I <u>work</u> in an <u>office</u>.* Practise saying the sentences.

4 Talk about what you do. Use the words from Vocabulary 2 to make sentences.

Conversation 1: *Have got; a, an* and *any*

1 02.03 **Listen to Steve and Bob talking about their families. Which picture is Bob and his family? Which picture is David (Bob's brother) and his family?**

a   b   c

Steve	Tell me about your family. Have you got any children?
Bob	Well, I'm married and we've got three children, two boys and a girl.
Steve	That's great. And have you got any brothers and sisters?
Bob	I've got a sister and a brother. My sister is married but she hasn't got any children.
Steve	What about your brother?
Bob	His name's David. He lives in Berlin with his family. He is married and they've got two little boys. His wife is German but she speaks English. David speaks a little German but their children speak English and German very well. David's got a very good job. He is a computer programmer.

2 02.03 **Listen again and fill in the gaps.**

Have you got _**any**_ children?

We've _____ three children.

I'_____ _____ a sister and a brother.

My sister hasn't got _____ _____.

They'_____ _____ two children.

David'_____ _____ a very good job.

3 **Look at the conversation. How do we use *have got*? Fill in the gaps in the table.**

+	–	?
I/you/we/they _**have**_ **got**	I/you/we/they _____ **got**	**Have** I/you/we/they _____?
He/she/it _____ **got**	He/she/it hasn't _____	_____ he/she/it _____?

4   When do we say *a*, *an* and *any*? Look at these sentences:

My sister hasn't got **any** children.

I've got **a** sister.

Put the rules in the correct part of the table.

▶ with singular nouns
▶ ~~with singular nouns that begin with a, e, i, o, u~~
▶ with plural or uncountable nouns in a question or a negative sentence

A	AN	ANY
	with singular nouns that begin with a, e, i, o, u	
window job car *garden*	iPod	brothers or sisters children free time

5   Look at the nouns. Choose 'countable' or 'uncountable' for each noun. Put them in the correct part of the table in Exercise 4.

umbrella   questions   iPhone   house
garden   job   friends   grandparents

6 02.04 **Read the conversation and fill in the gaps. Then listen and check your answers.**

Mary	Tell me about your family.
Joanna	Well, I am married and we *'ve got* three children, two girls and _____ boy. I'_____ _____ two sisters and _____ brother. My brother is married but he _____n't _____ _____ children.
Mary	What about your sisters?
Joanna	My older sister _____n't _____ _____ children. She isn't married. She'_____ _____ a very good job. She's _____ engineer. My other sister is married and they'_____ _____ two children, _____ boy and _____ girl.

7 What about you? Have you got …

a car?

a job?

an iPod?

any brothers or sisters?

any children?

any grandparents?

any free time?

MY, HIS, HER, ETC.

Look at these sentences.

Tell me about **your** family.

My brother is married.

Now look at more words like *your* and *my* in the table.

my		Joe
your		?
his	name is	Paul
her		Susan
our		Stevens
their		Johnson
our	names are	Ravi and Nina
their		Anna and Bob

1 **You meet Joe Stevens. Use the words from the table to fill in the gaps in the conversation.**

Hello! What's your name?

Hello! **a** _My_ name is Joe. This is my brother. **b** _____ name is Paul.

This is my sister. **c** _____ name is Susan. This is my mother and this is my father. **d** _____ names are Anna and Bob. **e** _____ family name is Stevens.

 2 02.05 **Listen and repeat.**

 3 **Write about your family. Use Bob's sentences in Conversation 1 and Joanna's sentences in Exercise 6 to help you.**

Conversation 2: Questions and answers about *he* or *she*

 1 02.06 **Tom shows Peter some photos. Who is in the photos? Listen and choose the two correct answers.**

   a his sister

   b his wife

   c his daughter

2 02.06 **Listen again and complete the table.**

		Nationality	Lives in	
Amélie	*wife*		Canada	
Louise		American		

3 Read the conversation. Fill in the gaps in the table.

Peter	Who's this?
Tom	This is my wife. Her name's Amélie.
Peter	Where is she from?
Tom	She's from France, she's French.
Peter	Does she speak English?
Tom	Yes, she does. She speaks English very well. And this is my sister.
Peter	What's her name?
Tom	Her name's Louise. She's an English teacher.
Peter	Where does she live?
Tom	She lives in Brazil.
Peter	Does she speak Portuguese?
Tom	No, she doesn't. She speaks Spanish but she doesn't speak Portuguese.

QUESTIONS	ANSWERS
What's *her* name?	Her _____'_____ Amélie. (name)
Where _____ _____ from?	_____'_____ _____ France. (country) _____'_____ French. (nationality)
Where _____ _____ live?	_____ _____ in Brazil. (city/country)
_____ _____ speak English? (language)	No, _____ _____. Yes , _____ _____.
What about Spanish and Portuguese?	_____ _____ Spanish but _____ doesn't _____ Portuguese.

4 **Look at these sentences from Vocabulary 2.**

I work in an office. I am a businesswoman.

Change *I* to *she*. How do the verbs change?

She _____ in an office. She _____ a businesswoman.

5 **Write about two people in your family. Talk about languages, work and where he/she lives.**

VOCABULARY 3: DESCRIBING YOUR HOME

1 **Match the words and the pictures.**

   a a terraced house   *3*
   b a town
   c a detached house
   d a semi-detached house
   e a city
   f a flat (apartment)
   g a village

1  **2** **3**

4 **5** **6**

7

2 02.07 **Listen and repeat. Note the stressed syllable, for example,** *a de<u>tach</u>ed <u>house</u>.* **Practise saying the words.**

3 02.08 **Here are some sentences to say where you live.**

					PLACE
		in			England
I	live	in the	North West East South	of	France Japan Germany
		in a		near 10 miles from	London Manchester

Listen and repeat. Note the stressed syllable, for example, _I live in France_. Practise saying the sentences.

Conversation 3: _Where do you live? What's it like?_

 1 02.09 **Steve and Bob talk about their homes. Listen to and read their conversation. Where does Bob live? Choose the correct picture.**

a   **b**   **c**

Steve	…. and where do you live, Bob?
Bob	We live in a new terraced house in a very small village in the north of England. It is about 10 miles from Manchester.
Steve	What's it like?
Bob	Well, Steve, it's a very typical English village. There are a lot of beautiful, old houses and there is a lovely pub but there aren't any shops and there isn't a bank. The young people think it is quite boring but I think it is nice and quiet! The people are very friendly. It's a really great place to live.

VOCABULARY 4: DESCRIBING PEOPLE AND PLACES

Read Conversation 3 again. The highlighted words are all adjectives.

> **LANGUAGE TIP**
>
> Some adjectives describe places; some describe people; some describe people and places. Look at the table.
>
> | PLACES | PLACES AND PEOPLE | PEOPLE |
> |---|---|---|
> | small, big, typical, new | lovely, nice, friendly, boring, old, quiet, great | serious, kind |

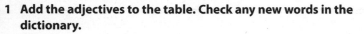

1 Add the adjectives to the table. Check any new words in the dictionary.

beautiful

noisy

important

modern

hard-working

funny

young

interesting

2 Look at the words in Exercise 1. Fill in the missing opposites in the table.

OPPOSITES	
small	*big*
new (places) young (people)	
	noisy
funny	
	interesting

34

3 **Look at the words. One is negative 😞. Which one?**

> lovely kind funny nice
> friendly boring great
> beautiful hard-working

4 **Look at all the words in Exercises 1–3. Which words describe the place where you live? Which words describe people in your family? Write the names next to the words, for example:**

hard-working   *My sister, Sarah*

young   *My daughter, Jane*

serious   *My friend, Tom*

beautiful   *My village, Hampton*

LANGUAGE TIP

We can change the meaning of adjectives with the words *really*, *very* or *quite*.

---

5 **Use the words and phrases to complete the table.**

> very small/really small
> very big/really big
> quite small quite big

	a *very small / really small*	
My car is	**b**	
	c	
	d	

6 02.10 **Listen and repeat. Mark the stressed syllable, for example,** *typical*. **Practise saying the adjectives.**

ADJECTIVES WITH *TO BE*

1 Look at Bob's sentences from Conversation 3. What are the missing words?

It _____ nice and quiet!   The people _____ very friendly.

2 With adjectives, we use the verb *to be*. Fill in the gaps in the table with the correct form of the verb *to be*.

	+	**–**	**?**
I	I *am* (I'm)	I'm not	_____ I?
you we they	you _____ (you're) we _____ (we're) they _____ (they're)	you aren't we aren't they aren't	_____ you? _____ we? _____ they?
he she it	he _____ (he's) she _____ (she's) it _____ (it's)	he isn't she isn't it isn't	_____ he? _____ she? _____ it?

3 Look at the sentences. Correct the mistakes.
   a London very beautiful.   *London is very beautiful.*
   b It is very big?
   c She is funny?
   d They nice and friendly.
   e I hard-working.

4 Steve asks two questions about where Bob lives. Look at Conversation 3 again and complete the questions.

Where _____ _____ live?   _____ _____ like?

Answer his questions about where you live.

I live in _____.   It's _____.

USING *THERE IS, THERE ARE*; ARTICLES

1 Anna is on holiday. Read her postcard to James. Is her holiday good?

Dear James,
I am on holiday in a very small village, five miles from a town called Buxton in the north of England. Buxton is lovely. There are a lot of shops and places to visit and there's a really good market.
There aren't any nightclubs but the pubs are great. At the house there isn't any Wi-Fi or mobile reception but it's beautiful here and I am having a lovely time!
See you soon
Love Anna
xx

James Smith
4563 Pillsbury Avenue
Minneapolis
MN 53120-4193
United States

2 What does Anna say? Complete the sentences.

There are   a lot of shops in Buxton √√√

_____   a lot of places to visit. √√√

_____   a really good market in the town. √

_____   any nightclubs √√√

_____   any Wi-Fi or mobile reception at the house. √

3 How do we use *there is* and *there are* to describe the things in a place? Look again at Exercises 1 and 2. Put the examples in the correct place a–c in the table.

mobile reception

internet cafés, banks, people

a gym, a nightclub, a post office

	+	-	?
singular nouns for example: **a** _____ uncountable nouns for example: **b** _____	**There is** **a** hotel **a** pharmacy Wi-Fi	**There isn't** **a** cinema **any** Wi-Fi	**Is there** **a** dentist? **any** Wi-Fi?
plural nouns for example: **c** _____	**There are** **two** cinemas **some** restaurants **a lot of** shops	**There aren't** **any** internet cafés **any** tourists	**Are there** **any** restaurants? **any** pubs?

4 Look at the sentences. Find the mistakes and write the sentences correctly.

a There is hotel. *There is a hotel.*

b There is a mobile reception.

c There is some pub.

d There isn't any cinema.

e There isn't 3G coverage.

f There are banks.

g There are some hotel.

h There are a lot of supermarket.

i There are mobile reception.

j There aren't some post office.

k There aren't shops.

5 Look at the table. Read the sentences about the village. Choose T (true) or F (false).

	VILLAGE	TOWN	CITY
a hotel	no	yes	yes, a lot
a pub	yes	yes, some	yes, a lot
a cinema	no	no	yes, some
an internet café	no	yes, a lot	yes, a lot
a bank	no	yes, some	yes, a lot

a post office	yes	yes	yes, some
a supermarket	no	yes, some	yes, a lot
a market	no	yes	yes, some
a shop	yes	yes	yes, a lot
mobile reception	yes	yes	yes
3G/4G coverage	no	yes	yes
Wi-Fi	yes	yes	yes

a In the village there's a pub.   T/F
b In the village there's a post office and a cinema.   T/F
c In the village there is mobile reception.   T/F

6 02.11 **Use the information in the table in Exercise 5, and complete the text about the town.**

In the town, *there is* a hotel and _____ _____ some pubs. _____ _____ a cinema but _____ _____ a lot of internet cafés. _____ _____ a market and _____ _____ some supermarkets.

7 Write about what there is in the city.

In the city, there is _____

8 Write about your village, town or city.

I live in _____. It's _____.
There's a _____. There isn't a _____. There are _____.

Listening, pronunciation and speaking

LISTENING: DESCRIBING FAMILY AND WHERE YOU LIVE

1 02.12 **Listen to the conversation. Put a, b, or c in the gap.**

Michael and his family live here.   _____
Christina and her family live here.   _____

a   b   c

2 02.12 Listen again. Look at the pictures a–d. For each picture, choose M (Michael's family), C (Christina's family) or L (Louise's family).

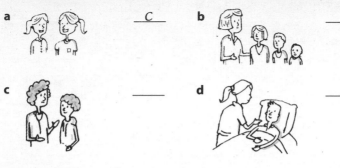

a _____C_____ b _____

c _____ d _____

PRONUNCIATION: WEAK FORMS AND LINKING – PREPOSITIONS AND ARTICLES

1 02.13 Listen to these sentences. Note the stressed syllables.

How do we pronounce the words *a* and *an*?

What happens between the words where it is highlighted?

There's a café.

There isn't a shop.

There isn't any Wi-Fi.

There aren't any tourists.

Is there a hotel?

Are there any shops?

I've got a cat.

He's got a car.

She hasn't got an umbrella.

We haven't got a garden.

Have you got an iPhone?

> **LANGUAGE TIP**
>
> We usually pronounce *a* and *an* as /ə/ and /ən/ and stress the noun.
>
> When one word ends with a consonant sound (for example /s/ or /t/ or /r/) and the next word begins with a vowel sound (for example /ə/ or /iː/), we usually say them together and it sounds like one word, for example *gotanumbrella* and *gotanIphone*.

40

2 Listen again and practise saying the sentences.

SPEAKING: DESCRIBING FAMILY AND WHERE YOU LIVE

 1 02.14 Listen to the first part of Christina and Michael's conversation again. Fill in the gaps.

Christina	Is this your family, Michael?
Michael	Yes. It's not a very good photo but this *is my wife,* Helen, and _____ _____, Harry. _____'_____ _____ three children. This is a good photo, my wife with Harry and next to Harry is _____, Paul and _____ _____, Anna.
Christina	Is this where you live?
Michael	Yes. It's a small _____ _____ in a very beautiful _____ _____ the south _____ England. It's about 50 miles _____ London. It's very quiet and _____ _____n't a lot to do, but we like it. _____ _____ a shop and a pub but _____ _____n't _____ restaurants or cafés and _____ _____n't a bank or a post office. What about you, Christina? Where do you live?

 2 02.15 You are Michael. Listen to the conversation and answer Christina's questions.

 3 02.14 Listen to Michael and Christina again and check your answers to Exercise 2.

4 Michael asks you about where you live and your family. Complete the conversation for you.

Michael	Tell me about your family. Do you have any brothers and sisters? Where do they live and work?
You	_____
Michael	Do you have any children?
You	_____
Michael	Where do you live? What's it like?
You	_____

Reading and writing

READING 1: PERSONAL DETAILS

1 Read Tom's visa application form again, in Unit 1, Reading 1. Answer the questions.

  a Where is Tom from?   *He's from The United States.*

  b What's his wife's name?

  c Where is his wife from?

  d Have they got any children?

  e Where does Tom live?

READING 2: DESCRIBING YOUR HOME

1 Read the description. Choose the correct picture.

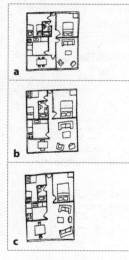 **a**	This is a big, modern flat in Notting Hill. It's very near Ladbroke Grove tube station and quite near a very big shopping centre. There are also a lot of lovely restaurants and cafés and the great Portobello Market is near the flat.
b	There is a big living room with two windows and a really big sofa. There is one big and one small bedroom and a bathroom with a bath and a shower. There is a new kitchen with an oven, a microwave, a fridge-freezer and a washing machine but there isn't a dishwasher. There is a dining table with chairs in the living room. There is Wi-Fi but there isn't a phone or a TV. There isn't a garden and there isn't a lift.
c	

2 Read the description again. What is there in the flat? Note the correct pictures.

a   **b**   **c**  **d**

Look at a house rental website for more words to describe homes.

1 Look at the pictures. Complete the description of the flat for the house rental website.

There is a big living room with a _____ and a _____. There _____ _____ bedrooms, one with a single bed and one with a double bed. There _____ a bathroom with a _____ but there isn't a _____. In the kitchen, there is an _____ and a _____ but _____ _____ a microwave. There is _____ in the flat but there isn't a _____. _____ _____ _____ garden.

Write the description again. Choose positive words from the box and put them in your description.

beautiful lovely noisy nice
modern boring great new old
really very

2   **Now write a description of your home for the house rental website website.**

WRITING 2: INTRODUCING YOURSELF AND YOUR FAMILY

You ask a new friend to your house for a few days. Choose some photos and write to her. Introduce your family and describe where you live.

Dear Sarah

I am very happy that you can stay with us for the weekend. Let me tell you a little about my family and where we live. Here are some photos.

Say who is in the photo (your wife/husband or your children or your brothers and sisters or your parents).

Say their names.

Say what they do or where they work.

Say what kind of house you live in (flat/house…).

Say if you live in a village/town/city and in the north/south/east/west and say which country.

Say how far it is from a big city (and which city).

Say what it is like (quiet/modern/big . . .).

Say what there is/isn't and what there are/aren't.

Have a good journey and see you in two weeks.

Best wishes

1 Fill in the gaps.

a Tom is my father. I am his 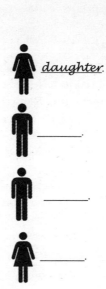 *daughter*.

b Gemma is my wife. I am her _____.

c Mary is my mother. I am her _____.

d Peter is my brother. I am his _____.

2 Correct the spelling mistakes in these plurals.

a mens *men*

b womans _____

c childs _____

d brotheres _____

e lifes _____

f babys _____

g persons _____

h familys _____

3 Fill in the gaps.

a I am *a* nurse. I work in a _____.

b I am a t_____ I work in _____ school.

c I am _____ computer programmer. I work at _____.

d My sister is a businesswoman. She _____ in _____ office.

e My grandmother hasn't got a job. She _____ work.

4 Correct the mistakes.

a This ~~are~~ *is* my sister.

b She name Susana.

c She live in Spain.

d She speak Spanish.

e She not speak French.

f She from Australia.

g She Australian.

h She work in hospital.

i She a nurse.

j She very kind.

k She got two children.

l She not got a car.

5 Look at these sentences. Write the questions.

a *Where does he live?*   He lives in France.

b _____   He is from Germany. He is German.

c _____   His name's Johan.

d _____ English?   No, he speaks French and German.

e _____ city?   No, he lives in a town.

f _____   It's a very modern town.

g _____ Yes, he's got two sons.

h _____ in his town? Yes, there are three hotels.

6 Look at the words. Make sentences about the village.

a The village/very old   *The village is very old*

b It/quite small   _____

c It/very boring   _____

d The people/really friendly   _____

e √ √ beautiful old houses   _____

f √ lovely pub   _____

g X shops   _____

h X café   _____

i X Wi-Fi in the pub.   _____

7 Look at the adjectives. Choose three adjectives for each part of the table. Note the positive adjectives 😊.

> beautiful lovely serious kind
> noisy nice modern boring great
> new old funny interesting young

PLACES	PEOPLE AND PLACES	PEOPLE
	beautiful	

SELF CHECK

I CAN ...

⬤	... talk about my family.
⬤	... talk about jobs and workplaces.
⬤	... talk about where I live.
⬤	... describe people and places.

Numbers, times and dates

In this unit you will learn how to:
▶ *say numbers.*
▶ *talk about the date and the time.*
▶ *ask and answer questions about dates and times.*

CEFR: (A1) *Can handle numbers and time. Can ask and answer questions and fill in forms about personal details.*

Festivals, celebrations and important dates

1 **Match the festivals with the 2016 dates. Put the festivals in part A of the table.**

~~Jewish New Year (Rosh Hashana)~~

Muslim Festival of Eid al-Adha

Chinese New Year

Diwali, Hindu Festival of Lights

Jewish Feast of Passover

Christian festival of Christmas

Muslim Ramadan

Christian festival of Easter

A	B	C
Festival	2016	2017
	8 February	
	25–8 March	
	22–30 April	
	6 June–5 July	
	11 September	

Jewish New Year (Rosh Hashana)	2–4 October	
	30 October–3 November	
	25 December	

2 What are the festival dates in 2017? Look on the internet and complete part C of the table.

3 Look at the inventions (new ideas) a–h. Match the inventions to the dates.

Example: a *1876*

a

b

c

d

1817 1876 1885 1901

e

f

g

h

1903 1927 1943 1973

Vocabulary builder

VOCABULARY 1: NUMBERS

1 Complete the table with the words in the box.

> three eighteen one six
> thirteen four seven
> nineteen nine sixteen
> eleven five twelve
> fifteen seventeen ten

1		6		11		16	
2	two	7		12		17	
3		8	eight	13		18	
4		9		14	fourteen	19	
5		10	*ten*	15		20	twenty

2 Choose the correct numbers.

89   100   64   23   48   75   97   32   56

a twenty-three   <u>23</u>
b thirty-two   —
c forty-eight   —
d fifty-six   —
e sixty-four   —
f seventy-five   —
g eighty-nine   —
h ninety-seven   —
i a hundred   —

3 Match the numbers and the words.

200
202
220
2,000
~~2,002~~
2,200
2,022

a Two thousand and two   <u>2,002</u>
b Two hundred   ____
c Two thousand two hundred   ____
d Two hundred and twenty   ____
e Two thousand   ____
f Two hundred and two   ____
g Two thousand and twenty-two ____

4 03.01 When do we use the word *and* in numbers?

a Find three more that are NOT correct.

Twenty and two X

One hundred and two

One thousand and two

One thousand and twenty

One thousand and twenty and two

One thousand and twenty two

One thousand and two hundred

One thousand two hundred

> **LANGUAGE TIP**
>
> We use *and* after 100: *One hundred **and** four, one hundred **and** sixty-nine.*
> After 1,000, we use *and* only before numbers 1–99: *One thousand **and** three; One thousand **and** thirty-one; one thousand four hundred.*

b Now listen to the correct numbers. How do we pronounce the word *and*?

5 03.02 **Listen and repeat.**

6 03.03 **Listen to the numbers and write them down.**

5, 11, _____

VOCABULARY 2: DAYS, MONTHS, SEASONS

1 Complete the list. Put the days of the week in the correct order.

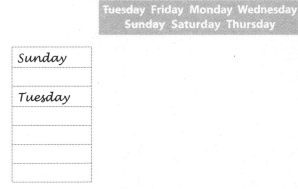

> Tuesday Friday Monday Wednesday
> Sunday Saturday Thursday

Sunday
Tuesday

2 Look at the first letter of the months of the year. Put the months in the correct order.

> December June March
> October April February
> May January August
> September November July

January	July
F	A
M	S
A	O
M	N
J	D

> **LANGUAGE TIP**
>
> In the UK, there are four seasons.
>
> Months are sometimes abbreviated (we just write the first part). For example, *Jan* instead of *January*.
>
> Days of the week are sometimes abbreviated too. For example, *Mon*, *Weds* instead of *Monday*, *Wednesday*.

3 Match the seasons with the pictures.

> autumn (US fall) spring
> winter summer

a

spring

b

_____

c

_____

d

_____

4 Look at the abbreviated months in the table. Complete the seasons.

a	spring	b	c
Dec	Mar	June	Sep
Jan	Apr	July	Oct
Feb	May	Aug	Nov

 5 03.04 **Listen and repeat. Note the stressed syllable, for example, _Monday_. Practise saying the words.**

6 Answer these questions.
   a What month is it now? For example, _May_
   b What month is your birthday? For example, _July_
   c What season is your birthday in? For example, _winter_
   d What day is it today? For example, _Tuesday_

VOCABULARY 3: DATES

1 Look at the dates (A) and notice how we say them (B). Four of the dates in B are NOT correct. Write the correct date.

A	B
7/11	the seventh of November
12/4	the twelfth of April
3/1	the third of September
5/6	the fifth of June
25/11	the twenty-fifth of December
1/1	the first of January
3/5	the third of May
31/7	the thirty-first of July
4/4	the fourth of August
21/4	the twenty-first of April
30/3	the thirtieth of March
22/9	the twenty-second of September
8/10	the eighth of December
2/10	the second of October
20/3	the twentieth of March

LANGUAGE TIP

When we say the date we use ordinals, not numbers. We say the *first* of January 😊 NOT the *one* of January 😞.

 2 **Complete the table with the correct ordinal words. Look at Exercise 1 to help you.**

1st		11th	eleventh	21st	twenty-first
2nd	second	12th		22nd	
3rd		13th	thirteenth	23rd	twenty-third
4th		14th	fourteenth	24th	twenty-fourth
5th		15th	fifteenth	25th	
6th	sixth	16th	sixteenth	26th	twenty-sixth
7th		17th	seventeenth	27th	twenty-seventh
8th		18th	eighteenth	28th	twenty-eighth
9th	ninth	19th	nineteenth	29th	twenty-ninth
10th	tenth	20th		30th	thirtieth
				31st	

Most ordinals are the number + *th* (*4th, 15th, 28th*). Some are different. Look at the table again. Which ordinals have a different ending?

 3 03.05 **Listen and repeat. Note the stressed syllable, for example, *twenty-second*. Practise saying the words.**

 4 03.06 **What else do you notice about how we say the date? Listen to the examples.**

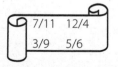

7/11 12/4
3/9 5/6

The seventh of November   The twelfth of April
The third of September   The fifth of June

Listen again and repeat. Stress the ordinal and the month.

5 03.07 **Listen and repeat. Then listen again and write the dates in numbers, for example 7/11.**

6 03.08 **How do you say these dates?**

   a 1/1

   b 23/11

   c 4/10

   d 15/4

   e 22/3

   f 31/7

Listen and check your answers.

7 **Match these dates to the dates in Exercise 6. Then add *th*, *rd*, *nd* or *st* after the numbers.**

   a 15 April   *d 15th April*

   b 23 November

   c 1 January

   d 31 July

   e 4 October

   f 22 March

What's the date today?

When is your birthday?

> ┌─────────────────┐
> │ **LANGUAGE TIP** │
> └─────────────────┘
> To say years, we usually separate them into two numbers.
>
> For 1819 we say *eighteen nineteen* (think 18, 19).
>
> For 1963 we say *nineteen sixty-three* (think 19, 63).
>
> For 2010 we say *twenty ten* (think 20, 10) or *two thousand and ten* (think 2,010).
>
> For 2011 we say *twenty eleven* or *two thousand and eleven*.
>
> BUT for 2001–9 we always say *two thousand and one* (think 2,001), *two thousand and two*, etc.

 8 03.09 **Listen and complete the years.**

    a *1591*

    b _____

    c _____

    d _____

    e _____

    f _____

    g _____

    h _____

9 03.10 **Some years are different. Listen and read. Complete the years in numbers next to the words.**

    a Nineteen oh one   *1901*

    b Nineteen hundred   _____

    c Seventeen oh two   _____

    d Two thousand   _____

    e Two thousand and one   _____

    f Two thousand and nine   _____

What year is it now?

Conversation 1: Using numbers in questions and answers

 1 03.11 **Telma is in a language school, talking to the receptionist. Listen to the conversation. What kind of English course does Telma want?**

    a a course of 15 hours a week

    b a conversation course of ten hours a week for four weeks

    c a conversation course of ten hours a week for one week

Receptionist	Good morning.
Telma	Good morning. I am looking for an English course.
Receptionist	We've got a lot of courses. There are courses for 15 hours a week or 20 hours a week. And we've got a conversation class which is ten hours a week, that's two hours each day.
Telma	Great. The conversation class sounds good. How much is it?
Receptionist	There are different prices. You can do a course for one week, or for four weeks. Here is some information.
Telma	Thank you. Yes, four weeks looks good, I'll do the four-week conversation course, please. Can I start next week?
Receptionist	Yes, of course. You just need to complete this form. We can do that now if you like?
Telma	Great.
Receptionist	So, what's your name?
Telma	Telma Silva – that's T-E-L-M-A S-I-L-V-A.
Receptionist	Thanks. And your date of birth? What's your date of birth?
Telma	Sorry, I don't understand.
Receptionist	Oh, um, when were you born?
Telma	Oh, I was born on 5 April 1993.
Receptionist	And what's your address?
Telma	My address is 19, Scott Street, Wellbridge.
Receptionist	And what's your postcode?
Telma	WB14 7JR.
Receptionist	Lovely. And what's your home phone number?
Telma	01723 453123.
Receptionist	And have you got a mobile number?
Telma	Yes, the number is 07396 213431.
Receptionist	Just one more thing – have you got an email address?
Telma	Yes, it's telmasilva@gnet.com.
Receptionist	Lovely. Thank you. See you Monday.
Telma	Yes, see you Monday!

2 03.11 **Look at the language school enrolment form. Listen again and read the conversation. Complete the form with information about Telma.**

London City Language
School – enrolment form

Family name	Silva
Given names	**a** *Telma*
Date of Birth (DD/MM/ YYYY)	**b**
Address	**c** *, Scott Street, Wellbridge*
Postcode	**d**
Home phone	**e**
Mobile phone	**f**
Email	*telmasilva@gnet.com*

3 Look at the information in the table and complete the questions.

a What's _your_ date of birth? **b** When _____ you _____?	Date of birth (DD/ MM/YYYY)	05/04/1993
c What'_____ _____ address?	Address	19, Scott Street, Wellbridge
d What'_____ _____ postcode?	Postcode	WB14 7JR
e What'_____ _____ phone number?	Home phone	01723 453123
f What'_____ _____ mobile number?	Mobile phone	07396 213431

Answer the questions about you.

> **LANGUAGE TIP**
> We use *were* or *was* with *born* to talk about our date of birth.

4 The receptionist asks Telma *When were you born?* What does she answer?

Can you complete the table?

Question _____ ?	Answer .
a When were you _____?	**c** I was _____ in 1989.
When was he born?	**d** He _____ _____ _____1972.
b When was your daughter _____?	**e** She _____ _____ in the first year of the 21st century, in 2000!

5 When was he born? Choose 1, 2 or 3.

a Elvis Presley was born …
1 in 1925   **2** in 1945   **3** in 1935 √

b Pablo Picasso was born …
1 in 1881   **2** in 1901   **3** in 1891

c Ghandi was born …
1 in 1899   **2** in 1849   **3** in 1869

d Albert Einstein was born …
1 in the eighteenth century   **2** in the nineteenth century
3 in the twentieth century

e William Shakespeare was born …
1 in the fifteenth century   **2** in the sixteenth century
3 in the seventeenth century

f Leonardo da Vinci was born …
1 in the fourteenth century   **2** in the fifteenth century
3 in the sixteenth century

Make sentences for you.

I was born on _____ (date).

I was born in _____ (month).

I was born in _____ (year).

I was born in _____ (century).

I was born in _____ (season).

PHONE NUMBERS

 1 03.12 **Listen to the phone numbers. Then complete the missing numbers in the Language Tip box.**

    a 01725 839721
    b 0161 455 6792
    c 0113 601 9765
    d 0223 538021
    e 0845 349 2341
    f 01349 563341

> **LANGUAGE TIP**
>
> For telephone numbers we say single numbers (so for example, *four five three one two three* not *forty-five twelve twenty-three*)
>
> For _____ we usually say *oh* not *zero*.
>
> For _____ we say *double five*.

 2 03.12 **Read aloud the phone numbers in Exercise 1. Then listen again to check your answers.**

3 **Complete the table with the correct numbers.**

453123	four five three one two three
	oh one nine two five
	two one three four three one
	oh seven three double two
	double six four oh double one

THE TIME

1 **Look at the questions. Which is the most polite?**

Excuse me. Could you tell me what time it is, please?

Excuse me. What time is it, please?

What time is it?

2 Match the times with the clocks.

a It's one o'clock

b It's six o'clock

c It's midnight

d It's eleven o'clock

e It's midday

f It's four o'clock

3 Complete the table with the times in numbers.

(MINUTES) PAST (THE HOUR)		(MINUTES) TO (THE HOUR)	
6.05	It's five past six	6.35	It's twenty-five to seven
6.10	**a**	6.40	**d**
6.20	**b**	6.50	It's ten to seven
6.25	**c**	6.55	**e**

4 **There are two ways of saying times. Put the sentences in the correct part of the table.**

It's quarter to seven.

It's six fifteen.

It's half past six.

a It's quarter past six	6.15	
b	6.30	It's six thirty
c	6.45	It's six forty-five

> **LANGUAGE TIP**
> People say the time both ways …
>
> It's ten to seven
> It's 6.50 (six fifty)

5 03.13 **Listen to the times. Note the stressed syllable, for example, *It's <u>one</u> o'<u>clock</u>, It's <u>ten</u> to <u>seven</u>. Practise saying the times.**

6 03.14 **Listen to the conversations a–h. Draw the time on the clocks.**

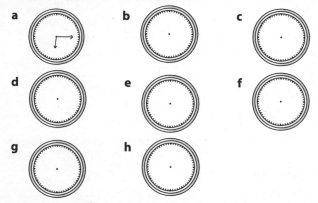

7 **We usually write the time with numbers. But how do we know if it is morning or afternoon?**

▶ We use *a.m.* (= morning) or *p.m.* (= afternoon or evening): *6.20 a.m., 6.20 p.m., 8.15 a.m., 8.15 p.m.*

▶ We use the 24-hour clock (*06:20* = morning, *18:20* = afternoon). We often see these 24-hour clock times on digital clocks, on computers and in travel information.

Complete the table with the missing 24-hour times.

MORNING		AFTERNOON		EVENING		NIGHT	
6 a.m.	9 a.m.	2 p.m.	4.30 p.m.	7.45 p.m.	9 p.m.	11 p.m.	2 a.m.
06.00					21.00		

What time is it now?

Say and write the time – can you do it in two different ways?

Conversation 2: What time ...?

1 03.15 **Listen to the conversation in a tourist information office. What does the tourist want information about? Choose the three correct pictures.**

a

b

c

d

2 Listen again and fill in gaps a–e.

Tourist	Hello
Advisor	Good morning. Can I help you?
Tourist	Yes, please. Can you give me some information about the City Museum? What time does it open?
Advisor	**a** It _____ at _____.
Tourist	And what time does it close?
Advisor	**b** It _____ _____ _____.

Tourist	Thank you. And I think there's a tour of the city. What time does it start?
Advisor	Yes, the tour is very interesting. **c** _____ _____ at _____.
Tourist	And what time does it finish?
Advisor	**d** _____ _____ _____ _____.
Tourist	And can I do a tour of the castle?
Advisor	Yes, there is a tour at 10 o'clock and a tour at 2.30.
Tourist	And how long does it last?
Advisor	It lasts **e** _____ hours.
Tourist	Thank you. That's very helpful.

3 **Look at the four highlighted questions in the conversation. Complete the questions in the correct part of the table.**

the museum	What time does it open?	**a** What...?
the tour of the city	**b** What...?	What time does it finish?

4 **Which things start and finish? Which things open and close? Use your dictionary to find any new words. Add them to the correct part of the table in Exercise 3.**

> the museum   the football match
> the tour of London   the bank
> the park   the film   the post office
> the TV programme
> the art gallery   the English class
> the concert   the shop
> the tour of the city

Ask questions about:
- **a** the post office
- **b** the English class
- **c** the tour of London
- **d** the bank
- **e** the film
- **f** the art gallery

5 The advisor says *It lasts two hours*. What question does the tourist ask?

Tourist _____ _____ _____ _____ _____?

Ask and answer the same question for the things in the table.

	Start time	Finish time	
film	7 p.m.	9 p.m.	**a** *How long does it last? It lasts two hours.*
TV programme	6 p.m.	7 p.m.	**b**
concert	8 p.m.	11 p.m.	**c**
tour of London	0900	1400	**d**

PREPOSITIONS OF TIME

1 Look at the information about Tom and his family. Read sentences a–f.

Four sentences are NOT correct. Find and correct these four sentences.

Given name(s) as shown in your passport	*Tom*
Family name	*Mitcham*
Sex	*male/~~female~~*
Date of birth	*07/11/1978*
Place of birth	*San Francisco*
Country of birth	*The United States*
Nationality	*American*
Marital status	*~~single~~/married*
Full name of spouse/partner	*Amélie Lafayette*
Spouse/partner's date of birth	*03/09/1981*
Spouse/partner's nationality	*French*
Do you have any children?	*yes/~~no~~*
Details of children (name and date of birth)	*Marie Lafayette 28/04/2011*
Your full residential address and postcode	*8924, Boulevard Lazare, Montreal, QC H2A, Canada*

Email address	tom.mitcham@ canadamail.com
Home (landline) telephone number	+1 438 0956054
Mobile telephone number	07896 1293455

a He was born on the seventh of November nineteen seventy-six.
b He was born in the nineteenth century.
c His wife was born in nineteen eighty-one.
d His wife was born in September.
e His daughter was born in May.
f His daughter was born in winter.

2 Read these sentences about shops and banks in the UK. Choose T (true) or F (false).

a	Shops in the UK open at ten o'clock in the morning.	T/F
b	Some shops in the UK close on Sunday.	T/F
c	Post offices in the UK close at Christmas.	T/F
d	Some banks in the UK close at lunchtime.	T/F
e	All shops in the UK close at night.	T/F
f	Banks in the UK close in the evening.	T/F
g	Tourist offices in the UK close at the weekend.	T/F

3 Look again at sentences a–f in Exercise 1 and a–g in Exercise 2. Find the prepositions *in*, *on* and *at*.

Now look at the words in the box. Put the words in the correct part of the table.

> night dates festivals
> the weekend months
> the evening years days
> centuries time seasons

IN	ON	AT
the morning the afternoon *months*		*festivals*

4 Now look at the examples in the box. Put them in the correct part of the table.

> January dinnertime
> autumn 2012 Monday Christmas
> 8 o'clock 21 July Friday 1999
> March Easter
> spring 7.30 10/11/14
> the 20th century lunchtime

IN	ON	AT
January		

5 Complete the sentences with the correct prepositions.

a He was born _on_ the tenth of May nineteen eighty-four.

b He was born _____ the 20th century.

c His wife was born _____ 1992.

d His wife was born _____ summer.

e His daughter was born _____ the 21st.

f His son was born _____ October.

g Shops in the UK open _____ 9 a.m.

h Some shops in the UK close _____ Sunday.

i Shops in the UK close _____ Christmas.

j Some shops in the UK close _____ lunchtime.

k Most shops in the UK close _____ night.

l Post offices in the UK close _____ the evening.

m Most banks in the UK close _____ the weekend.

PRONUNCIATION: WEAK FORMS OF *DOES, WAS, WERE, OF, AT, AND*

1 03.16 Listen to these phrases. Note the stressed (underlined) words.

What time does it open?

What time does it close?

When were you born?

I was born in June

The tenth of July

The fourteenth of August

at five thirty

at Christmas

two <u>hun</u>dred <mark>and</mark> <u>thir</u>ty

five <u>thou</u>sand <mark>and</mark> <u>for</u>ty

 Listen again. What do you notice about the pronunciation of the highlighted words? Practise saying the phrases. Remember, don't stress the highlighted words!

Listening and speaking

LISTENING 1: A PHONE CONVERSATION ABOUT MEETING

 1 03.17 **Ellie, Ruby and Pete are friends. They want to meet next week.**

Listen to the conversation. Do they choose a day to meet?

 2 03.17 Listen again and fill in the phone numbers.

	MOBILE	HOME
Ellie	04596 310352	
Ruby	**a**	
Pete	**b**	**c**

What is the date next Tuesday?

LISTENING 2: UK AND US FESTIVALS AND CELEBRATIONS

1 Read the list of festivals. Match the words to the pictures.

Christmas Easter Mother's Day
US Independence Day Hallowe'en
Thanksgiving

a   **b**   **c**

d   **e**   **f**

Which festivals do you celebrate in your country?

What dates are Thanksgiving and Mother's Day this year?

 2 03.18 **Listen to someone talking about the festivals and celebrations. Two festivals are only in the US, not in the UK. Which ones?**

SPEAKING 1: ENROLLING FOR A COURSE

1 03.19 **Read the information in the form.**

London City Language School – enrolment form

Family name	*Costa*
Given names	*Maria*
Date of Birth (DD/MM/YYYY)	*07/11/1992*
Address	*4, Cross Street, Millchester*
Postcode	*SK38 5RR*
Home phone	*0161 458 6950*
Mobile phone	*07943 345 675*
Email	*mariacosta567@gmail.sp*
Nationality	*Spanish*

You are the student, Maria. Complete the answers to the receptionist's questions.

Receptionist	Hello, can I help you?
Student	Good morning. Can I enrol for the English conversation class?
Receptionist	Yes, of course. You just need to complete the enrolment form. We can do that now if you like. What's your name?
Student	**a** _____
Receptionist	And your date of birth? What's your date of birth?
Student	**b** _____
Receptionist	And where do you live?
Student	**c** _____
Receptionist	And what's your postcode?
Student	**d** _____
Receptionist	Fine. And what's your phone number?
Student	**e** _____

Receptionist	And have you got a mobile number?
Student	**f** _____
Receptionist	Just two more questions…have you got an email address?
Student	**g** _____
Receptionist	And where are you from, what's your nationality?
Student	**h** _____
Receptionist	Great. So if I could just take payment, that is all done and you can start on Monday.
Student	Lovely. Thank you very much.
Receptionist	See you Monday.

Now listen to the complete conversation and check your answers.

 2 03.20 **You are Maria. Listen to the receptionist and answer his questions.**

 3 03.20 **Play the audio again. Answer the receptionist's questions with information about you.**

SPEAKING 2: IN A TOURIST OFFICE

1 You are a tourist in a tourist information office. You want information about the times of an art gallery and a concert. Complete the questions a–e.

Advisor	Good morning. Can I help you?
Tourist	Yes, please. I'd like some information about the City Art Gallery.
	a _____ _____ _____ _____ _____ ?
Advisor	Ten o'clock in the morning.
Tourist	**b** And _____ _____ _____ _____ _____ ?
Advisor	Seven thirty in the evening.
Tourist	Thank you. And there is a concert today in the Royal Albert Hall.
	c _____ _____ _____ _____ _____ ?
Advisor	Six o'clock.

Tourist	**d** Great, and _____ _____ _____ _____
	_____?
Advisor	About two hours.
Tourist	**e** _____ _____ _____ _____ finish?
Advisor	About eight thirty. There's an interval of about 30 minutes.
Tourist	Thank you.

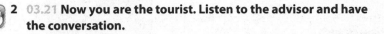

2 03.21 **Now you are the tourist. Listen to the advisor and have the conversation.**

Reading and writing

READING: TOURIST POSTERS

1 **You are in the tourist information office. Look at the posters and leaflets. What information is there? Choose *Yes* or *No*.**

    a The opening times of local libraries   Yes/~~No~~

    b Film times at a local cinema   Yes/No

    c The opening times of a zoo   Yes/No

    d The opening time of an art exhibition   Yes/No

    e The start time for a firework display   Yes/No

2 **Is there information about New Year's Day (Thursday 1 January)? Choose *Yes* or *No*.**

    a The Rex cinema poster   ~~Yes~~/No

    b The firework display poster   Yes/No

    c Cheshire libraries poster   Yes/No

    d Chester Zoo poster   Yes/No

The Rex Cinema
Cheshire Leisure Park
www.rex_cinemas.com
Films for
Fri 2 until Thurs 8 January
Summer of Love
2.50 p.m., 6.10 p.m., 9.10 p.m.
Shrek
12.20 p.m. (Sunday only)
The End of Time
Late show: 11.30 p.m. Sat 3
Book now • 08712 231 231

Buxton Town Council
New Year's Day
FIREWORK DISPLAY
Doors open 6 p.m.; fireworks at
7.30 p.m.

Hot food stalls Live music

Adults £5 Children £3

Family tickets £12 (2 adults and
2 children)

Victoria Parade, Buxton

For tickets: call Susan Linford
on 01852 566430, Monday–
Saturday 9 a.m.–5p.m.

Cheshire library opening hours over New Year

For information or to renew your books outside of opening hours, please phone: 0845 148 0148

	MON 29 DEC	TUES 30 DEC	WED 31 DEC	THURS 1 JAN	FRI 2 JAN	SAT 3 JAN
Bilton	10 a.m.– 1 p.m. 2 p.m.– 5 p.m.	10 a.m.– 1 p.m. 2 p.m.– 5 p.m.	Closed	Closed	10 a.m.– 1 p.m. 2 p.m.– 5 p.m.	9.30 a.m.– 1 p.m.
Chester	9 a.m.– 7 p.m.	9 a.m.– 5 p.m.	9 a.m.– 3 p.m.	Closed	9 a.m.– 5 p.m.	9 a.m.– 4 p.m.

Chester zoo

	Opening time	Closing time
Mon 3 Nov to Tue 23 Dec	10 a.m.	4 p.m.
Wed 24 Dec	10 a.m.	3 p.m.
Christmas Day	Closed	Closed
Fri 26 Dec to Tues 30 Dec	10 a.m.	4 p.m.
New Year's Eve and New Year's Day	10 a.m.	3 p.m.
Fri 2 Jan to Sat 28 Feb	10 a.m.	4 p.m.

We're open every day from 10 a.m., except for Christmas Day, with FREE on-site parking.

Our opening hours change depending on the season and school holidays.

Don't forget – buy your tickets online and you can beat the queues with Fast Track admission.

3 Look at the information again and answer the questions.

a What day is the film 'Shrek'?   *Sunday*

b What time does 'Shrek' start?

c What day is the film 'Terminator'?

d What time does 'Terminator' start?

e What is the phone number for cinema tickets?

f What date is the firework display?

g What time does the firework display start?

h What is the phone number for tickets for the fireworks?

i What time does Chester library close on 29 December?

j What time does Chester library close on New Year's Eve?

k Does Bilton library open on New Year's Eve?

l What time does Bilton library close on 3 January?

m Does the zoo open on 25 December?

n Does the zoo open on 1 January?

o What time does the zoo close on 24 December?

p What time does the zoo open on 23 January?

q What time does the zoo close on 16 January?

WRITING 1: FESTIVALS AND CELEBRATIONS

Write about festivals and celebrations in your country.

Look at the audioscript from Listening 2 (download for free from the Teach Yourself Library app or www.library.teachyourself.com.) for ideas and help, then fill in the gaps.

Use the correct preposition – *in* + month or *on* + date.

Use capital letters for days and months.

Festivals and celebrations in _____ (your country)

The most important festivals and celebrations in _____ (your country) are probably _____ and _____ (the names of two important festivals). People also celebrate _____ and _____ (the names of two other festivals).

Some festivals happen on the same date each year. For example, _____ (name of the festival) is always on _____ (date)/in _____ (month).

The other festivals and celebrations happen on different dates each year. For example, this year, _____ (name of the festival) is on _____ (date). Last year, it was on _____ (date).

1 Look at the pictures of different festivals and celebrations.

What do we write on a greeting card for these festivals and celebrations? Match the phrases to the festivals.

Congratulations!   *Happy Birthday!*   *Happy Anniversary!*

Happy Mother's Day!   *Happy New Year!*   *Happy Diwali!*

Happy Thanksgiving!   *Merry Christmas!*

2 Look at the card. Choose a celebration or festival and write a card for a friend or someone in your family.

Happy Birthday mum hope you have a lovely time

Test yourself

1 Put the words in the correct part of the table.

> Tuesday January summer
> morning March Monday
> afternoon autumn Wednesday
> Thursday December spring
> night April August evening
> Friday October winter Sunday

Days of the week	Months of the year	Seasons	Parts of the day
Tuesday			

2 Write the numbers in order, small to big.

Five hundred, ...

Five thousand five hundred

Five thousand five hundred and fifty

Five hundred and fifty

~~Five hundred~~

Five thousand

Five thousand and fifty-five

Five thousand and five

Five thousand and fifty

Five hundred and five

Five hundred and fifty-five

3 Read the sentences. The prepositions are not correct! Note the correct prepositions.

a He was born at <u>*on*</u> the 7th November 1986.

b His wife was born on _____ 1981.

c His daughter was born at _____ May.

d His daughter was born at _____ summer.

e Shops in the UK open on _____ ten o'clock.

f Shops in the UK open in _____ Sunday.

g Shops in the UK close on _____ night.

h Banks in the UK close on _____ the weekend.

4 Put the times in the correct part of the table.

> quarter past four   16.00
> twenty past five   5 p.m.
> ~~twelve o'clock~~   four thirty
> four in the morning   four fifty

midnight	*twelve o'clock*
4 a.m.	
five o'clock in the afternoon	
half past four	
five twenty	
four o'clock in the afternoon	
ten to five	
4.15	

5 Write the dates in numbers and put them in order.

> 12th June   31st October
> ~~4th January~~   19th April
> 2nd December

4/1, …

6 Fill in the gaps.
   a What time _____ it open?
   b How long does it _____?
   c When _____ you born?
   d What'_____ your phone number?

SELF CHECK

I CAN ...

○ ... say numbers.

○ ... talk about the date and the time.

○ ... ask and answer questions about dates and times.

4 Everyday life, sports and free time

In this unit you will learn how to:
▶ *speak and write about everyday routines and free time activities.*
▶ *speak and write about likes and dislikes.*
▶ *speak and write about ability using* can.

CEFR: (A1) *Can ask and answer questions about personal details. Can get an idea of the content of simpler informational material and short simple descriptions.* **(A2)** *Can use a series of phrases and sentences to describe daily routines. Can explain what he or she likes or dislikes.*

Popular sports in the UK and the US

1 Which sports are popular in the UK? Which sports are popular in the US? What do you think? Look at the sports and complete the table.

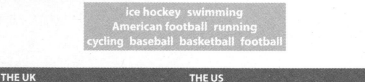

ice hockey swimming
American football running
cycling baseball basketball football

THE UK	THE US

2 Read the text and check your answers.

Sport is very popular in the United Kingdom. The number one sport is swimming, then running, then cycling and then football. About 25% of the UK population and over 50% of young people (16–25 years old) play sport once a week, but about 50% don't play any sport. A lot of people watch sport on television. People like watching football, rugby and tennis best. People all over the world watch English football with famous teams like Manchester United, Liverpool and Arsenal. 46% of English people watch football on television. Tennis is also popular. Wimbledon is the most famous tennis competition. It happens every year in June and nearly a quarter of people in the UK watch the final. In 2012 the Olympics were in the UK and 90% of the UK population watched some of it on television (51.9 million people). In the United States, the most popular sport is American football, then baseball, then basketball and then ice hockey. Not many people play these sports in the United Kingdom.

3 Complete the sentences with the correct numbers.

In the UK …

a _25%_ of people play sport once a week.

b Over _____% of young people (16–25 years old) play sport once a week.

c About _____% of people don't play any sport.

d _____% of English people watch football on television.

e _____% of people in the UK watch the Wimbledon final.

f _____% of the UK population watched some of the 2012 Olympics on television.

 04.01 **Listen and check your answers.**

Vocabulary builder

VOCABULARY 1: SPORTS

1 04.02 **Listen and repeat. Mark the stressed syllable, for example, _football_. Practise saying the words.**

football   cricket   jogging   basketball   hockey   swimming

tennis   volleyball   baseball   rugby   golf   cycling

2 Read the text on popular sports in the UK and the US again.

a What is the most popular sport in the UK?   _swimming_

b What is the most popular sport in the US?

c What is the most popular sport in your country?

> **LANGUAGE TIP**
> We say _play football_, _play cricket_, _play basketball_, _play hockey_, but three sports in the list use a different verb. Which verb?

3 Complete the table. Match the sports with the correct verb.

play	football, _cricket, basketball, hockey_ …
go	

VOCABULARY 2: OTHER LEISURE ACTIVITIES

1 Match the words to the pictures.

watch TV/television

go out with friends

listen to music

go shopping

~~read~~

go on the internet

go on social media

play computer games

go to the cinema

go to a museum/an art gallery

read

 2 04.03 Listen and repeat. Note the stressed syllable, for example, *watch T<u>V</u>.* **Practise saying the words.**

What do you do in your free time?

Conversation 1: *Like/love/hate* + verb + *ing*

1 04.04 **Tom and Sandra are talking about free time. Listen to the conversation. Who has lots of free time?**

Sandra	So Tom, what do you do in your free time?
Tom	Well, I work every day and I don't have much free time during the week, but I spend the weekend relaxing. I love going to the cinema and I also like going out with friends. I don't like going to museums or art galleries but I love watching TV, particularly football. In the evenings, I am usually quite tired but I quite like reading and listening to music. I also like going on the internet but I hate playing computer games and I don't like using social media. What about you?
Sandra	I don't work and so I have a lot more free time. I love going out with friends and family and I also quite like going to museums and art galleries. I like watching television but I don't like reading or listening to music. I have a new computer and I like going on the internet. I love going on Facebook™.

2 04.04 **Listen to the conversation again.**

What do they like doing? ♡

What do they not like doing? ✕

Put ♡ or ✕ in the table.

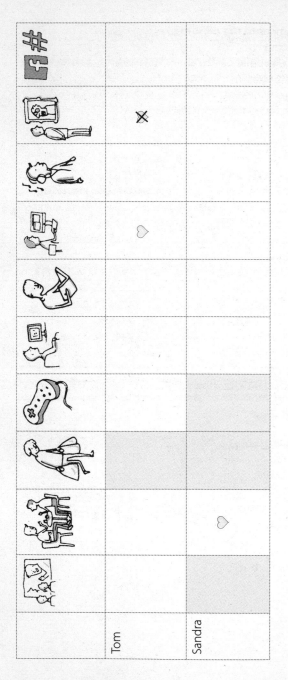

3 Match the sentences to the pictures.

a ~~I quite like reading~~
b I hate playing computer games.
c I don't like using social media.
d I like going on the internet.
e I love going on Facebook™.

♡♡♡   _____

♡♡   _____

♡   *a I quite like reading*

✗   _____

✗✗   _____

4 Look at the sentences in Exercise 3. What do we use after *love/like/hate*?

	love	
I	like	verb + *ing*
	hate	

04.05 **Look at the information in the table. Complete sentences a–g for Tom. Write sentences h–l for Sandra. Then listen and check your answers.**

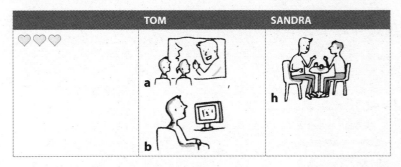

	TOM	SANDRA
♡♡♡	a	h
	b	

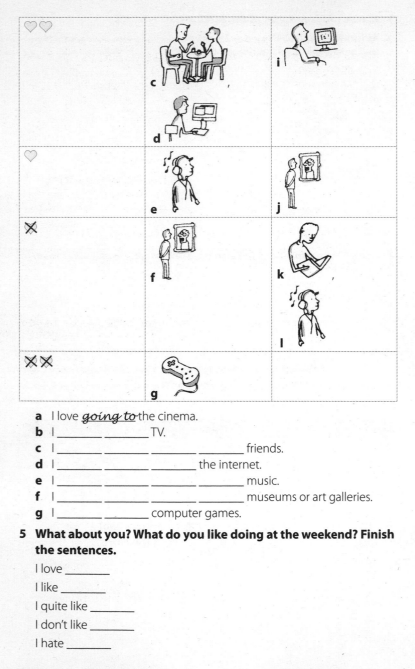

a I love *going to* the cinema.
b I _____ _____ TV.
c I _____ _____ _____ _____ friends.
d I _____ _____ _____ the internet.
e I _____ _____ _____ _____ music.
f I _____ _____ _____ _____ museums or art galleries.
g I _____ _____ computer games.

5 What about you? What do you like doing at the weekend? Finish the sentences.

I love _____

I like _____

I quite like _____

I don't like _____

I hate _____

VOCABULARY 3: EVERYDAY VERBS AND NOUNS

1 **What do you do every day? Put the verbs in the correct part of the table for your days. Check any words you are not sure of in the dictionary.**

~~get up~~

have a shower

get dressed

have breakfast

do the housework

have dinner

do the washing up

do the washing

go to bed

go to work

have lunch

do the cleaning

go out

do the shopping

get home

MY DAYS		
every day	on working days	on days off (not working days)
get up		

Write the words in the every day column in the correct order for you.

2 **Match the times to the phrases.**

01.30 06.30 20.30 ~~10.00~~

get up early		go to bed early	
get up late	*10:00*	go to bed late	

3 04.06 **Listen and repeat. Note the stressed syllables, for example, _have_ a _shower_. Practise saying the words.**

4 **Cover the words in Exercise 1. Can you remember the verbs? Put the correct verb with each list in the table.**

		get	
the housework	a shower	up	to work
the cleaning	breakfast	dressed	out
the shopping	lunch	home	to bed
the washing	dinner	up early	to bed early
the washing up		up late	to bed late

5 **Describe a typical day for you.**

VOCABULARY 4: HOW OFTEN?

Mon	Tues	Wed	Thurs	Fri	Sat	Sun
play tennis	do yoga		go to the gym	go out with friends	go to the cinema	watch football
Mon	**Tues**	**Wed**	**Thurs**	**Fri**	**Sat**	**Sun**
play tennis	do yoga		go to the gym	go out with friends	go out for lunch	
Mon	**Tues**	**Wed**	**Thurs**	**Fri**	**Sat**	**Sun**
	do yoga	play tennis	go to the gym	go out for lunch	go to the theatre	visit Mum and Dad
Mon	**Tues**	**Wed**	**Thurs**	**Fri**	**Sat**	**Sun**
play tennis	do yoga		go to the gym	go out with friends	visit Mum and Dad	go out for lunch

1 **Look at the calendar. Read the sentences. One is NOT true. Which one?**

a I go out with friends three times a month.

b I play tennis once a week.

c I go out for lunch twice a month.

d I always go to the gym on Thursday.

e I usually play tennis on Monday.

f I sometimes play tennis on Wednesday.

g I never play tennis on Friday.

2 **How do we say *one time* in a week? How do we say *two times* in a month? Complete the table.**

_____ (one time)		day
_____ (two times)	a	week
three times		month

3 **Put the words in the correct part of the table.**

usually never always sometimes

	✓	✓	✓	✓
usually	✓	✓	✓	X
	✓	✓	X	X
	X	X	X	X

 4 **04.07 Listen and repeat. Note the stressed syllables. How do we pronounce the word *a* in *once a month*? Practise saying the words.**

5 **Which sentences are correct English? Use the table to help you.**
  a I **always** cook dinner.
  b I cook dinner **always**.
  c I am **always** late.
  d I **always** am late.

	verb *to be*	always	adjective
I	am/is/are	usually	
You		sometimes	
He		never	late
She	always	**verb**	early
We	usually	cook/cooks dinner	
They	sometimes	go/goes to the gym	
	never	do/does the shopping	

4 Everyday life, sports and free time **91**

6 Look at the table in Exercise 1. Complete the sentences.

a I go to the gym _once_ a _week._

b I visit my parents _____ _____ _____.

c I _____ do yoga on Tuesday.

d I _____ go out with friends on Friday.

e I _____ go to the gym on Sunday.

f I _____ go out for lunch on Friday.

7 Complete sentences about you.

a I _____ once a day.

b I _____ twice a week.

c I _____ three times a day.

d I _____ once a month.

e At the weekend, I always _____.

f I never _____.

g I usually _____.

h I am sometimes _____.

Conversation 2: Present simple third person (*he* or *she*)

1 04.08 **Listen to the conversation about Joanna. Is it about a school day? Decide *Yes* or *No*.**

Tom	Tell me about Joanna's typical day.
Sandra	Well, she lives in London and she goes to school. She gets up early, at seven o'clock, and she goes to school at eight o'clock. She usually has lunch at school but sometimes she has lunch in a café. She gets home at about four o'clock.
Tom	What does she do when she gets home?
Sandra	Well, she often has a lot of homework and she usually finishes her homework before dinner. She never cooks dinner but she sometimes does the washing up. After dinner, she watches television or goes on the internet. She always goes on Facebook™. She usually goes to bed at about ten o'clock.
Tom	Does she like listening to music?
Sandra	Oh yes, she listens to music all the time and she plays the piano quite well.

2 **04.08 Listen to the conversation again. Read the sentences and choose T (true) or F (false).**

Example: She goes to school at seven o'clock.　　　T̶/F

- **a** She always has lunch at school.　　　T/F
- **b** She has a lot of homework.　　　T/F
- **c** She doesn't cook dinner.　　　T/F
- **d** She finishes her homework after dinner.　　　T/F
- **e** She doesn't listen to music.　　　T/F
- **f** She goes to bed at eleven o'clock.　　　T/F

3 **Sandra tells us about Joanna's typical day. Read Sandra's sentences and find all the verbs. Use the correct verbs to complete spaces a–j in the table.**

I YOU WE THEY	HE SHE + _____	I YOU WE THEY	HE SHE + _____	I YOU WE THEY	HE SHE + *irregular verb*
play	**a**	watch	**f**	have	**j**
listen	**b**	finish	**g**		
live	**c** *lives*	do	**h**		
cook	**d**	go	**i**		
get	**e**				

4 **How do we change verbs when we write about _he_ and _she_? Put the rules in the correct place and complete the table in Exercise 3.**

verb + *s*　　verb + *es* (if the verb ends in *ss*, *x*, *ch*, *sh* or *o*)　　i̶r̶r̶e̶g̶u̶l̶a̶r̶ ̶v̶e̶r̶b̶

5 **Fill in the table with more _he_ or _she_ verb forms.**

I/YOU/WE/THEY	HE/SHE	I/YOU/WE/THEY	HE/SHE
use		say	
live		choose	
speak		know	
read	*reads*	decide	
write		see	
look		start	
practise		give	
put		help	

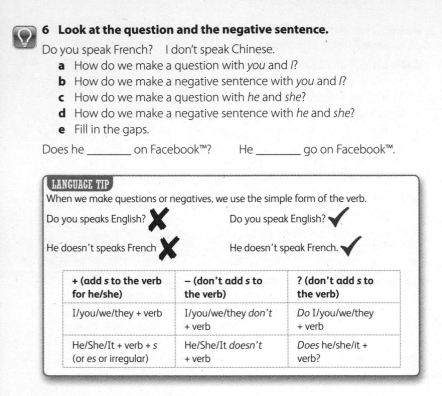

6 Look at the question and the negative sentence.

Do you speak French?   I don't speak Chinese.

- **a** How do we make a question with *you* and *I*?
- **b** How do we make a negative sentence with *you* and *I*?
- **c** How do we make a question with *he* and *she*?
- **d** How do we make a negative sentence with *he* and *she*?
- **e** Fill in the gaps.

Does he _____ on Facebook™?   He _____ go on Facebook™.

LANGUAGE TIP

When we make questions or negatives, we use the simple form of the verb.

Do you speaks English? ✖   Do you speak English? ✔

He doesn't speaks French ✖   He doesn't speak French. ✔

+ (add *s* to the verb for he/she)	– (don't add *s* to the verb)	? (don't add *s* to the verb)
I/you/we/they + verb	I/you/we/they *don't* + verb	*Do* I/you/we/they + verb
He/She/It + verb + *s* (or *es* or irregular)	He/She/It *doesn't* + verb	*Does* he/she/it + verb?

---

7 Correct these sentences.

- **a** He don't watch television.
- **b** He doesn't listens to music.
- **c** Do he use the computer?
- **d** Does he goes to work early?

8 Look at the text. Change *I* to *she* and then change all the verbs.

I **get** up early and **go** to the gym at seven o'clock. I **have** a shower and breakfast and then I **go** to work. I **start** work at nine o'clock and **finish** at five thirty. I usually **have** lunch in a café near work. I **don't like** staying in the office for lunch. I sometimes **do** the shopping before I **go** home. I **get** home at about seven o'clock and **cook** dinner. In the evening, I usually

watch television or **use** the computer. I **like** going on the internet. I don't **go** to bed late but I often **read** before I **go** to sleep.

Write some sentences about a friend or a person in your family.

1 Match the activities to the pictures a–i.

drive

ride a bike

sing

speak French

play the guitar

swim

cook

use a computer

use Microsoft Excel

a *play the guitar*

b _____

c _____

'Bonjour'

d _____

e _____

f _____

g _____

h _____

i _____

2 04.09 **Listen to Tom talking about his free time. Look at the three activities a–c. Tom can do one activity. Is it a, b or c?**

a   b    c

3 04.09 **Listen to Tom again. Are the sentences true (T) or false (F) about Tom?**

Example: He can drive.   ~~T~~/F

a He can't play the guitar.   T/F

b He can't cook.   T/F

c He can use a computer.   T/F

4 Match the two sentences to the pictures.

> I can't do it.
>
> I can do it.

a _____   b _____

5 Look at the sentences. Correct the mistakes. Use the sentences about Tom and the table in Exercise 6 to help you.

Example: I can ~~to~~ swim.

a He cans cook.

b He can speaks French.

c I not can speak French.

d He no can ride a bike.

e You can play the piano?

6 Complete the table. Use the corrected sentences from Exercise 5.

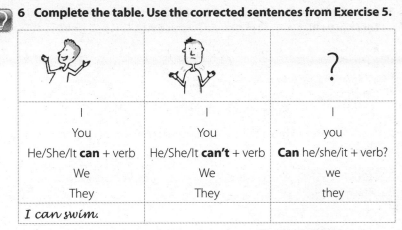

I You He/She/It **can** + verb We They	I You He/She/It **can't** + verb We They	I you **Can** he/she/it + verb? we they
I can swim.		

What activities can you do? Can you cook? Write sentences.

Listening, speaking and pronunciation

LISTENING: A JOURNALIST ASKS PEOPLE ABOUT THEIR EVERYDAY LIFE

1 04.10 **A journalist asks people about their everyday life for a TV programme. Listen to the conversations. Who doesn't work in the evening? Person 1, Person 2, or Person 3?**

2 04.10 **Listen to the conversations again. Read the sentences about Person 1 and Person 2. Choose T (true) or F (false).**

Person 1

a   She goes to the gym after work.   T/F
b   She finishes work at eight o'clock.   T/F
c   She cooks dinner every night.   T/F
d   She watches television in the evening.   T/F
e   She visits family at the weekend.   T/F
f   She loves going to the theatre.   T/F

Person 2

g   He gets up at four o'clock.   T/F
h   He finishes work at six o'clock.   T/F
i   His wife doesn't work.   T/F
j   His wife does the housework and the shopping.   T/F
k   He can play football well.   T/F
l   He loves listening to music and playing the guitar. T/F

3 04.10 **Listen to the conversations again. Complete the sentences for Person 3.**

Example: She works _two_ evenings a week.
a She starts work at _____.
b She finishes work at about _____.
c She usually goes out on a _____ and _____ evening.
d She _____ football.
e She _____ Facebook™.

SPEAKING: TELLING SOMEONE ABOUT YOUR DAILY LIFE

A journalist asks you about your daily life. Answer the journalist's question for you.

> We are asking people about their daily life. Can you tell me a little about yours?

PRONUNCIATION 1: THIRD PERSON SINGULAR VERB ENDINGS

1 04.11 **Listen to the pronunciation of these words:**

visits   plays   watches

How do we pronounce the final _s_?

2 04.12 **Listen to the verbs. Put them in the correct part of the table.**

reads watches visits
listens uses goes
takes gets finishes
stays starts plays

/S/	/Z/	/IZ/
visits	_plays_	_watches_

Practise saying the verbs.

PRONUNCIATION 2: *CAN* AND *CAN'T*

1 04.13 **Listen to the sentences. Which words are stressed?**

I can speak French but I can't speak Spanish. Can you?

Yes, I can, and I can speak Japanese. Can you speak Japanese?

No, I can't.

2 04.13 **Listen to the sentences again.**

How do we pronounce *can't*?

When do we pronounce *can* as /kæn/?

When do we pronounce *can* as /kən/?

Use the sentences to complete the table.

> No, I can't. I can speak French.
> ~~Can you?~~ I can't speak Spanish.
> Yes, I can.

affirmative		/kən/
question	*Can you?*	/kən/
negative		/ka:nt/
short answer negative		/ka:nt/
short answer affirmative		/kæn/

3 04.14 **Listen and repeat.**

PRONUNCIATION 3: QUESTIONS IN THE PRESENT SIMPLE

1 04.15 **Listen to the sentences. Which words are stressed?**

Where does he work?

What time does he start?

When do you go?

What do you cook?

2 04.15 **Listen to the sentences again.**

How do we pronounce *do* in questions?

How do we pronounce *does* in questions?

Practise saying the questions.

Put *do* and *does* in the correct part of the table.

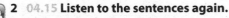

Question word	Do/does	Subject	Main verb
When	_____ /də/	you	go?
What			cook?
Where	_____ /dəz/	he/she	work?
What time			start?

3 04.15 **Listen and repeat.**

Reading and writing

1 Look at the questionnaire. Does the person do a lot of things in their free time?

Free time questionnaire – How do you spend your free time?					
How often do you do the following activities? Choose one answer for each question.					
	Every day	Three or more times a week	Once or twice a week	Once a month	Never
Watch television	✔				
Go shopping			✔		
Go to a museum or art gallery					✔
Read a book	✔				
Play a sport		✔			
Go out with friends		✔			
Go on the internet	✔				
Drive a car			✔		
Visit family				✔	
Go to the cinema				✔	

2 Look at the questionnaire again. Are the sentences true (T) or false (F)?

    a He plays a sport three or more times a week.   T/F

    b He never reads.   T/F

    c He watches television every day.   T/F

    d He plays sport every day.   T/F

    e He visits family once a month.   T/F

    f He goes to the cinema once or twice a week.   T/F

3 Fill in the questionnaire about you.

WRITING 1: FREE TIME

Use your answers to the free time questionnaire. Write five sentences about your free time.

READING 2: A PERSONAL PROFILE

1   **Tina is a student from Portugal. She wants an English-speaking penfriend. She finds three profiles on a penfriend website. Match the profiles with the pictures.**

a   b   c

Margaret

I live in London and I speak English. I want penfriends from the UK. I am retired and so I have a lot of free time. I love going out with friends and visiting family. I also love visiting museums and art galleries and going to the cinema. I don't like playing sports but I love watching sports, particularly tennis and athletics. I can't play the piano but I love listening to music. I can use a computer and I like going on the internet but I don't like using Facebook™.

Susan

I live in New York and work full-time for an IT company. I can speak German, English and Japanese but I can't speak French very well. I want to practise my French so I want a penfriend from a French-speaking country. I love going to the theatre and the cinema but I also like watching television in the evenings after work. I don't like cooking but I love going out with friends to restaurants. I listen to music every day and I love listening to jazz music in particular. I play tennis once a week and go swimming three or four times a week. I work with computers so when I come home I don't like using the computer or going on the internet.

Tracy

I live in Canada and I can speak English but I can't speak French. I want penfriends from all over the world. I love animals. I have a cat and a horse and I ride every day. I play lots of other sports, usually tennis and football and at the weekend I sometimes go fishing with my Dad. I love going on the internet and playing computer games but I don't really like watching television. I can't play the guitar very well but I love playing and listening to music.

2 Read the profiles again and complete the table.

	MARGARET	SUSAN	TRACY
♡	going out with friends		
✗			
			speak English
		speak French	

3 Who does Tina choose? Margaret, Susan or Tracy?

WRITING 2: A PERSONAL PROFILE

1 Write your personal profile. Use the examples for help and ideas. Write about what you love doing, what you like doing, what you don't like doing, what you can do and what you can't do.

2 Look online at a real penfriend website and register. Writing to a penfriend helps your English! Look at:

www.globalpenfriends.com

http://usa.ipfpenfriends.com/

www.penpalworld.com/

Test yourself

1 Correct the spelling mistakes in the sports.

a football
b criket
c joging
d basketbal
e hocky
f swiming

g tenis
h vollyball
i basball
j rogby
k gof
l cyclng

2 How many activities and everyday verbs can you remember? Fill in the table.

DO	HAVE	GET	GO
the washing	breakfast	home	jogging
_____	_____	_____	_____
_____	_____	_____	_____
_____	_____	_____	_____

3 Write the sentences in correct English.

Example: I get up usually at seven o'clock.   *I usually get up at seven o'clock.*

    a I am have breakfast at eight o'clock.
    b I go to English classes one time per week.
    c I never am late.
    d I love to learn English.
    e I not like do homework.
    f I can't to speak English very well.
    g My teacher help me a lot.
    h My girlfriend speak English very well.

4 Use the information in brackets. Complete the sentences. X = negative.

Examples: (She/watch) *She watches* television every evening.

(She/X go shopping) *She doesn't go shopping* on Mondays.

    a (She/go) _____ to the gym every day.
    b (He/have) _____ breakfast at eight o'clock.
    c (He/ X work) _____ in the evening.
    d I play tennis (two times/week) _____.
    e I (♡ go) _____ to the cinema.
    f He (✗ cook) _____ dinner.
    g He (♡ ♡ ♡ watch) _____ TV.
    h She (✗ go) _____ on Facebook™.

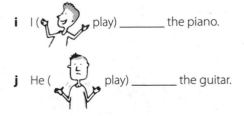

    i I (play) _____ the piano.

    j He (play) _____ the guitar.

I CAN . . .

○ . . . speak and write about everyday routines and free time activities.

○ . . . speak and write about likes and dislikes.

○ . . . speak and write about ability using *can*.

5 Going out

In this unit you will learn how to:
▶ *ask how people feel.*
▶ *say how you are.*
▶ *talk about plans and preferences.*
▶ *make and respond to suggestions and invitations.*

CEFR: (A1) *Can indicate time by such phrases as* next week. *Can get an idea of the content of simpler informational material.* **(A2)** *Can find specific, predictable information in simple everyday material. Can describe plans, arrangements. Can make arrangements to meet, decide where to go and what to do. Can explain what he or she likes or dislikes.*

Popular places for going out

1 When people go out, where do they go?

What do you think? Put pictures a–c in order from the most popular (1) to the least popular (3).

a  b  c

2 When people go to a pub or restaurant, what do they do?

What do you think? Read the sentences and choose T (true) or F (false).

a	People can smoke in British pubs.	T/F
b	Children can buy an alcoholic drink in a pub in the UK.	T/F
c	If the meal cost £40, people usually leave a tip of about £7.	T/F
d	People sometimes leave a tip in pubs.	T/F
e	People usually go out at about eleven o'clock at night.	T/F
f	People never have a meal at the pub.	T/F

3 Now read the text and check your answers.

A lot of people in the UK like going out with friends or family. The most popular activity is going to a restaurant. Going to a pub is very popular and going to the cinema is also quite popular. In the evening, people often go out at between 8 and 9 p.m. Many pubs and restaurants close at around 11 p.m. so this is often the time that people go home. If you have something to eat in a restaurant, you usually leave a tip of 10% of your bill. People don't always leave a tip in cafés or pubs. In pubs, cafés and restaurants in the UK, you can't smoke. You can't buy an alcoholic drink in a pub or restaurant until you are 18 years old. When people go to the pub they don't always have a meal. Sometimes they just have a drink.

Vocabulary builder

VOCABULARY 1: ASKING HOW PEOPLE ARE AND RESPONDING

1 Put the conversation in the correct order. Start with c.

  a Very well.
  b How are you?
  c Hello Amy!
  d Fine, thank you. How are you?
  e Hello.

2 A friend asks *How are you?*

Put ☺ or ☺ ☺ or ☺ ☺ ☺ for each answer.
  a Fine.   ☺ ☺

  b So-so.   _____
  c I'm good, thanks.   _____
  d Not bad.   _____
  e Very well.   _____
  f I'm OK.   _____

3 05.01 Listen to the question and the answers. Note the stress, for example, *How are you?* Practise saying the question and the answers.

What about you? How are you today?

VOCABULARY 2: SOCIAL ACTIVITIES

1 Match the activities and the pictures.

go to the pub

go to the cinema

go to the theatre

go to an art gallery

go to a restaurant or a café

go to someone's house for a meal

go to a concert

2 There are different ways to say some of the activities. Put four of the phrases from Exercise 1 next to the phrases with a similar meaning.

a go out for a meal/dinner/lunch/something to eat _____

b go round for dinner or lunch _____

c go and see a film _____

d go out for a drink _____

3 05.02 Listen and repeat. Note the stress, for example, _go to a concert_. Practise saying the words.

4 Correct the mistakes in the sentences.

a I like going to a cinema.   *I like going to the cinema.*

b He like going out for a dinner.

c She like going the theatre.

d I like going to pub.

e I like going to the restaurant.

f They like go out for meal.

When you go out, what do you like doing?

5 Cover the list of social activities in Exercise 1. Look at the pictures. Can you remember how to say them?

VOCABULARY 3: TIME PHRASES

1 Look at the tables. Fill in the gaps a–f.

today	Monday
a *yesterday*	Sunday
b	Tuesday
the day before yesterday	Saturday
the day after tomorrow	**c**

today	Friday
yesterday	**d**
e	Wednesday
tomorrow	**f**
the day after tomorrow	**g**

2 Today is Monday 10th July. Complete sentences a-c. Put one word in each gap. Use the table to help you.

a _____ Monday is 17th July.

b _____ Monday was 3rd July.

c _____ Thursday is 13th July.

last ←	Monday, Tuesday, Wednesday . . . weekend
this	week month
→ next	year

3   Today is Wednesday 3rd September. Put the missing dates in the table.

Last Monday	**a**
Next Monday	**b**
This Friday	**c**
Last Friday	**d**
Next Wednesday	**e**
This Thursday	**f**

4   05.03 Listen and repeat. Note the stress, for example, _yesterday_. Practise saying the words.

Conversation 1: Making, accepting and declining an invitation

1   05.04 Read and listen to three conversations. What do they decide to do and when? Fill in the table.

a Linda and Paula

Linda	Hi Paula. How are you?
Paula	I'm very well, thanks Linda. How are you?
Linda	I'm OK. Would you like to go to the cinema next weekend?
Paula	Yes, that would be great. When?
Linda	Is Friday evening any good?
Paula	I'm really sorry, I can't do Friday. Are you free on Saturday?
Linda	Yes, Saturday is fine.

b Sam and Pete

Sam	Hi Pete. How are you?
Pete	I'm good. And you?
Sam	Yes, very well. Do you fancy going to the pub sometime?
Pete	Yes, I'd love to. When?
Sam	How about tomorrow?
Pete	I'm afraid I can't. Tomorrow is no good. Are you doing anything the day after tomorrow?
Sam	Let's see, that's Friday. Yes, Friday's great.

c Maria and Susana

Maria	Hello Susana.
Susana	Hi Maria.
Maria	How are you?
Susana	Well. How about you?
Maria	Not bad. A bit tired. I had a really long day yesterday – and the day before yesterday!
Susana	Do you want to go for a coffee?
Maria	Yes, I'd love to. Now?
Susana	Yes. There's a really nice café near here. Are you ready?
Maria	Let's go!

		WHAT	WHEN
a	Linda and Paula	*go to the cinema*	
b	Sam and Pete		*Friday*
c	Maria and Susana		

2 05.04 **Listen again. How do Linda, Sam and Susana invite their friends to do something? Fill in the gaps.**

Linda	**a** _Would_ you like **b** _____ **c** _____ to the cinema?
Sam	**d** _____ you **e** _____ **f** _____ to the pub?
Susana	**g** _____ you want **h** _____ **i** _____ for a coffee?

3 Complete a–c in the table with either *to do* or *doing*.

a	Would		like _____	
b	Do	you	fancy _____	something?
c	Do		want _____	

4 Look at the different ways to invite people to do something in Exercise 3. Which one is the most polite? Which two are informal (with friends)?

5 05.05 **Listen to the invitations. Note the stress, for example,** *Would you <u>like</u> to go to the <u>cin</u>ema?* **Practise saying the invitations.**

6 **Invite a close friend. Complete the invitations with the missing words.**
  a _____ for a coffee?
  b _____ for dinner?
  c _____ and see a film?

7 **Now invite someone you don't know well (for example, a work colleague) to do the same activities. Complete the questions in Exercise 6.**

8 **How do people answer? Complete the conversations.**

SAYING *YES* 😃
Yes, _____ *would* _____ _____ . (Paula)
Yes, _____ _____ _____ . (Pete and Maria)

SAYING *NO* 😠
I'm _____ _____ , *I can't* . (Paula)
I'm *afraid* _____ _____ . (Pete)

	time/date
I _____ *do*	Friday next week eight thirty the morning April 4

time/date	
Thursday Next week Six o'clock The evening July 23	_____ _____ *good*

9 05.06 **Listen to the answers. Note the stress, for example,** *<u>Yes</u>, that would be <u>great</u>.* **Practise saying the answers.**

112

10 05.07 **Here is your diary. Listen to the different invitations and answer 😊. For example:**

You hear: Would you like to go for coffee on Sunday morning?

You look at the diary and say: Yes, I'd love to.

Tuesday 5 October English class 6-9 p.m.	**Friday 8 October** shopping in Manchester with Lucy.
Wednesday 6 October lunch with mum 12 p.m. theatre?	**Saturday 9 October** out for lunch? cinema 6 p.m.
Thursday 7 October coffee? English class 6-9 p.m.	**Sunday 10 October** p.m. art gallery?

11 Look at your diary again. Invite a friend to do different things. You already have some ideas (?) in your diary.

Then invite a colleague to go out. Use the ideas in your diary, or different ideas!

Vocabulary builder

VOCABULARY 4: USING *IT'S TOO* + ADJECTIVE

1 Can you remember these adjectives from Units 1–4? Fill in the missing letters.

Example: sm *all*

a n_c_

b q_ _ _t

c lov_ _y

d b_ _ _tiful

e gr_ _t

f n_w

g t_p_c_l

h n_ _sy

i b_g

2 **Complete the table with these adjectives.**

> bad expensive good cheap

| Cost or price | £££££££££££ **a** It's _____ | £ **c** It's _____ |
| In general | **b** It's _____ | **d** It's _____ |

3 **Look at these sentences. Which one is negative?**

> It's quite big. It's really big.
> It's very big. It's too big.

> **LANGUAGE TIP**
> *Too* + adjective has a negative (not good) meaning 😟.

4 **Look at the pictures. Finish the sentences using the adjectives:**

> noisy expensive small big

a It's too big.

b It's _____ _____.

c It's _____ _____!

d It's _____ _____.

5 05.08 **Listen to the adjectives and phrases. Note the stress, for example, *ex_pen_sive*, *_too big_*. Practise saying the words.**

Conversation 2: Making suggestions and arrangements

 1 05.09 **It's Saturday night and Janet and Martin are at home. Listen to the conversation and answer the questions.**

    a Does Janet go out?

    b Does Martin go out?

Janet	It's Saturday evening. I don't know what to do.
Martin	How about going out for a meal?
Janet	No, I'm not very hungry.
Martin	Why don't we go to the cinema?
Janet	No, it's too expensive.
Martin	Let's watch TV.
Janet	No, it's not very interesting.
Martin	How about a drink?
Janet	No, it's too noisy at the pub and I'm too tired.
Martin	Fine. You stay here. I'm going out on my own!

2 **Read the conversation. Note the phrases Martin uses to make suggestions. Fill in the gaps a–c with the words from the conversation.**

a *Why don't we*	go to the cinema?	**d** _____
b _____	going out for a meal? a drink?	**e** _____
c _____	watch TV	**f** _____

Now put the three different ways of making suggestions in the correct spaces d–f.

How about + verb + *ing* or noun?

Why don't we + verb?

Let's + verb

3 **Look at Units 1–4. Find positive adjectives and complete the gaps to say *yes*.**

That's a _____ idea. That sounds _____.

4 05.10 **Listen and repeat. Note the stress, for example, *<u>How</u> about going <u>out</u> for a <u>meal</u>?* Practise saying the suggestions and answers.**

5 **Correct the mistakes.**
   a Let's going out for lunch.
   b Why we don't meeting at the train station?
   c That's sounding great. Let's meet two o'clock.
   d Why not we go out for a drink?
   e How about meet in The King's Head at seven tomorrow?

6 **Make suggestions about going out.**
   a How about/go out for lunch
   b Let's/the Manchester Deli/one o'clock
   c Why don't we/film
   d How about/in front of the cinema/six o'clock

Conversation 3: Talking about preferences

1 05.11 **Listen to the conversation. Do they decide to go to a pub or to a café?**

2 05.11 **Listen to the conversation again and read the sentences. Choose T (true) or F (false).**
   a Kevin and Shona decide to go out for lunch.   T/F
   b Kevin is happy to have a meal.   T/F
   c Kevin is happy to go to The Coffee Shop.   T/F
   d Kevin likes the Downtown Deli more than The Coffee Shop. T/F

Kevin	Let's go out for lunch.
Shona	That's a good idea. Do you want to have a meal at the pub?
Kevin	I like the pub but it's too expensive. I'd prefer to have a sandwich at a café.
Shona	Yes, me too. There's a really lovely café near here.
Kevin	The Coffee Shop?
Shona	Yes.
Kevin	Mmm. It's OK but it's too busy. I'd rather go to the Downtown Deli. It's really nice and quiet.
Shona	OK. Let's go.

3 **Read the conversation again. Find two phrases for saying you want one thing more than another thing. Then complete these sentences.**

a The pub 🙂 is OK but I _____ _____ _____ go to a café 🙂 🙂.

b A meal 🙂 is OK but I _____ _____ _____ have a sandwich 🙂 🙂.

c The Coffee Shop 🙂 is OK but I _____ _____ go to the Downtown Deli 🙂 🙂.

4 **Look at the sentences. What do we say after *would prefer*? What do we say after *would rather*? Fill in the gaps in the table.**

> How about a meal at the pub?

I You He She We They	would 'd	prefer _____ _____ a sandwich.
		rather _____ a sandwich.

5 Read the sentences. Only one is correct. Find the correct sentence.

  a He rather to go to a café.

  b I would prefer go to the cinema.

  c They'd prefer to go in the evening.

  d I'd prefer to going on Monday.

 6 05.12 Listen and repeat. Note the stress, for example, *I'd prefer to go to the <u>cinema</u>*. Practise saying the sentences.

7 Make sentences using *prefer* and *rather*.

Example: A sandwich is OK but I'd rather have a meal.

😐	😊 😊
a a sandwich	a meal
b a glass of water	a glass of wine
c a restaurant	the pub
d a cup of coffee	a cup of tea
e the TV	the cinema

Conversation 4: Using the present continuous for plans

1 05.13 Listen to the conversation. What does Sam suggest?

Sam	Hi Linda. How are you?
Linda	I'm very well. How are you?
Sam	I'm good, thanks. Do you fancy going to the cinema sometime this week?
Linda	Yes, that would be great. When?
Sam	Are you doing anything on Friday?
Linda	I'm really sorry, I can't do Friday because my mum is coming to London for the day and we are going out for lunch. Is Saturday any good?
Sam	I can't do Saturday because I'm going to a concert with my brother. How about Sunday? Are you free on Sunday?
Linda	Sunday is great.

2 `05.13` **Listen again and read the conversation. Answer the questions.**

a Which day **can't** Linda go to the cinema?

b Which day **can't** Sam go to the cinema?

c Which day **can** they go to the cinema?

d What word do Linda and Sam use **just before** they say **why** they can't go out?

... _____ my mum is coming to London.

... _____ I'm going to a concert..

> **LANGUAGE TIP**
> Use the word *because* for an answer to the question *Why . . . ?*

3 `05.13` **Listen again. Answer the questions by filling in the gaps.**

a Why can't Linda go to the cinema on Friday? What does she say about her plans?

My mum _____ _____ to London for the day and we _____ _____ out for lunch.

b Why can't Sam go to the cinema on Saturday? What does he say about his plans?

I _____ _____ to a concert with my brother.

4 **Complete spaces a–f in the table.**

SUBJECT	VERB *TO BE*	VERB + *ING*	
My mum **g**_____ **h**_____	**a** _____	**b** _____	to London for the day.
We **i**_____ **j**_____	**c** _____	**d** _____	out for lunch.
I	**e** _____	**f** _____	to a concert with my brother.

Now complete spaces g-j by putting *he*, *she*, *you* and *they* in the correct place in the subject column.

5 **Look at the sentences about the grammar. Choose T (true) or F (false).**

a This is the present continuous tense. T/F

b We make it with *am*, *is* or *are* + verb + *ing* T/F

c We use it to talk about planned and arranged activities in the future. T/F

d Planned or arranged usually means other people know about it, or it is in our diary or on a calendar. T/F

6 05.14 **Listen and repeat. Note the stress, for example,** *My mum is* *coming to London.* **How do we pronounce the words** *am* **and** *are?*

We are /ə/ going out for lunch.

I am /əm/ going to a concert.

Practise saying the sentences.

7 **Look at the diary. We can use present continuous for most of the things but not all. Which activities can't we describe with present continuous and why?**

Mon 4	Fri 8
dentist 10 a.m.	London for the day with mum
lunch 2 p.m. Jackie	**Sat 9**
Tues 5	tennis 11 a.m.
work at home	Manchester Deli 5 p.m.
lunch with mum	then cinema with Paula
Wed 6	**Sun 10**
coffee with Sarah?	lunch with mum and dad 1 p.m.
cinema with Jackie	Paul football match 2 p.m.
Thurs 7	cinema with Sam?
doctor 11 a.m.	
lunch with Suzy?	

8 **Look at Linda's sentences about her plans and arrangements for next week. Correct the mistakes. There are two mistakes in each sentence.**

a On Tuesday I going to the dentist.

b On Wednesday I am work at home.

c On Tuesday I having lunch with dad.

d On Thursday Mum and I are go to London for the day.

e On Friday I meet Paula at the Manchester Deli.

f On Saturday morning we is going to the cinema.

g On Saturday I have lunch with mum and dad at one o'clock.

h On Monday afternoon Paul playing football at three o'clock.

9 **Complete the sentences about Linda's plans and arrangements for next week.**

a On Monday, she is _____ and she _____.

b On Wednesday, Jackie and Linda _____.

c On Thursday _____.

d On Saturday morning _____.

e On Sunday she _____.

10 Look again at Linda and Sam's conversation. Complete Sam's question.

a _____ anything on Friday?

Use the words in the box to make three more questions with a similar meaning.

> Friday Sunday Saturday free
> good about you any on

b Is _____?
c Are _____?
d How _____?

 11 05.15 Listen and repeat. Note the stress, for example, *Are you doing anything on <u>Fri</u>day?* Practise saying the questions.

Listening and speaking

LISTENING 1: PLANNING TO MEET

1 05.16 Listen to two friends, Jack and Rachel.

a What do they decide to do?
b When and where are they meeting?

2 Listen again and read the sentences. Choose T (true) or F (false).

a Rachel is very well. T/F
b Jack suggests going to see a film. T/F
c Jack is working on Tuesday and Thursday evening. T/F
d Rachel's brother is coming for dinner on Wednesday. T/F
e Jack can go to the cinema at the weekend but he would prefer to go on Monday. T/F
f Rachel is not free on Monday. T/F
g Jack doesn't want to spend too much money. T/F
h Jack suggests the Black Dog pub. T/F
i The Black Dog is cheap. T/F
j The café is cheap if you eat before six o'clock. T/F

LISTENING 2: PLANS AND ARRANGEMENTS

1 05.17 Listen to two friends (Simon and Paula).

a What do they decide to do?
b When and where are they meeting?

2 05.17 **Listen again and choose the correct answer.**

Example: Paula is **OK/~~good~~**.

a   Simon is **OK/good**.

b   Simon is free on **Tuesday/Wednesday**.

c   Paula is going out for lunch on **Tuesday/Saturday**.

d   Simon would rather go to the gallery **at the weekend/on Wednesday**.

e   Paula **is/isn't** free on Wednesday.

f   **Simon/Paula** doesn't want to spend too much money.

g   **Simon/Paula** doesn't like noisy places.

h   **Simon/Paula** suggests going to a café.

SPEAKING 1: YOUR FRIEND INVITES YOU OUT

1   You meet Susan and arrange to go out. Read the conversation and prepare your answers.

Susan	Hi. How are you?
You	**Reply and ask how Susan is.**
Susan	I'm very well. Hey, do you fancy going out sometime?
You	**Say yes and ask what she wants to do.**
Susan	How about going to the cinema? There's a really good film on at the moment.
You	**Say yes and ask when.**
Susan	Is this Thursday any good? I am working Tuesday and Wednesday evening but I am free on Thursday.
You	**Say no, explain why and suggest the weekend.**
Susan	Mmm, maybe, but tickets are more expensive at the weekend. I'd rather go during the week. How about next Monday? Are you free on Monday?
You	**Say yes, and suggest going out for something to eat.**
Susan	Great idea.
You	**Suggest Pizza House near the cinema, ask if Susan knows it.**
Susan	Yes, I do. It's very nice but it's quite expensive and too noisy.
You	**Agree and ask what she suggests.**
Susan	There's a really nice little café near the cinema called Dinner Time. I think it's really cheap if you eat before seven o'clock. I'd prefer to go there.

You	Agree.
Susan	How about meeting there at six?
You	Agree.

 2 05.18 **Listen to Susan and have the conversation.**

Then try to have the conversation without looking at the text.

SPEAKING 2: INVITING YOUR FRIEND TO GO OUT

1 **Now you meet Paul and arrange to go out. Read the conversation and prepare your answers.**

You	**Say hello and ask how Paul is.**
Paul	I'm OK thanks. How about you?
You	**Say how you are and ask if he wants to go out.**
Paul	Yes! That would be great. What do you fancy doing?
You	**Suggest going to an art gallery.**
Paul	That's a brilliant idea. I'd love to. When?
You	**Say you are working Monday and Wednesday and suggest Tuesday.**
Paul	I'm really sorry I can't, because I'm going out for lunch. How about Saturday?
You	**Say you would prefer to go next week, say why.**
Paul	No problem, which day is good for you?
You	**Suggest Wednesday.**
Paul	Wednesday is fine. How about going out for something to eat first? There's a really nice restaurant about five minutes away, Brad's Diner, do you know it?
You	**Say yes, you know it but say why you don't like it.**
Paul	Mmm, yes, maybe . . . So what do you suggest?
You	**Suggest the café in the gallery, say why you would rather go there.**
Paul	Yes, that sounds better.
You	**Suggest meeting at twelve.**
Paul	Great. See you then.

2 05.19 **Listen to Paul and have the conversation. Start by saying** *hello* **and asking Paul how he is. Practise until you can have the conversation with your book closed!**

5 *Going out*   123

Reading and writing

READING: A PARTY INVITATION

1 Match the words to the pictures of different types of celebration.

birthday wedding New Year

a   b   c

2 Look at the two invitations and the replies. Read the sentences and choose T (true) or F (false).

   a The invitations are for the same day.   T/F
   b The celebrations are in different towns.   T/F
   c Louise can go to the 40th birthday party and the wedding.   T/F
   d There is dinner at the 40th birthday celebration.   T/F
   e The wedding celebration is at a pub.   T/F
   f 'RSVP' means please reply and tell me if you are coming
         or not.   T/F
   g Louise is going to the birthday party.   T/F

> *Party*
> *Joanna is 40!*
> *Please come and celebrate my birthday!*
>
> *Drinks at The Swan Inn, Malmsbury*
> *on Saturday April 28*
> *From 9pm onwards*
> *RSVP*

> *Wedding!*
> *Robin and Alice*
> *are getting married*
> *on Saturday 28 April.*
> *Please come and celebrate*
> *with us*
> *at the Royal Ship Hotel, Telsford*
> *7pm for dinner at 8pm*
> *RSVP*

B I U Aa ✎ ☰ ☷ ☰◄ ►☰ ☰ ☰ ☰ ∞ ☺

Dear Joanna
Thank you for the invitation. I'd love to come
but I'm afraid I can't. I'm going to a wedding
party in Telsford that evening. I'm really sorry.
I hope you have a lovely birthday.
Best wishes
Louise

Dear Robin and Alice
Thank you very much for your kind invitation.
I would love to come and celebrate with you.
Congratulations and best wishes,
Louise

WRITING: EMAIL INVITATIONS: MAKING AND CHANGING PLANS

1 Read the emails.

a Who wrote the first email and who wrote the second email?

b What do Linda and Paula want to do?

c When do they arrange to meet?

Hi Paula. Good to hear from you 😊! **I'm very well.**
I'd love to go for a coffee. **I can't do Thursday** because I'm going to the dentist 😞
but Friday is great. Yes, I know Coffee City ... it's OK but it's quite expensive.
I'd prefer to go to the little café on New Street, The Tea Pot. **It's lovely.**
What do you think? **Why don't we meet at 11 on Friday?**
Linda

On 11 July 2016 at 19:54, Paula Johnson 'paulajohnson@me.com' wrote:

Hi there Linda
How are you? It seems ages since we met. **Do you fancy** a coffee sometime?
I am busy all this week but not next week. **Are you free on Thursday or
Friday? How about meeting at** that place in the city centre? Coffee City?
I'd rather go in the morning. **Is 11 any good?**
Paula

---

2 **There are some highlighted phrases in the emails. Re-write the emails. Change the highlighted phrases but <u>don't change</u> the meaning.**

Example: I'm very well: *I'm fine, thanks.*

How many different ways you can think of to say the same thing?

3 **Now write a reply to Paula's email (use Linda's email to help you).**
- ▶ Say you would love to go for coffee.
- ▶ Explain you can't do Friday (think of a different reason why).
- ▶ Agree to Thursday.
- ▶ Explain why you don't want to go to Coffee City (think of a different reason why).
- ▶ Suggest the new café next to the market, Central Stop, and say why.
- ▶ Explain you would prefer to go in the afternoon (think of a reason why).
- ▶ Suggest a time on Thursday afternoon.

4 **Write an email inviting a friend to go out. Use Paula's email to help you.**
- ▶ Ask how she is.
- ▶ Invite her for a drink.
- ▶ Explain you are working every day this week but not next week.
- ▶ Ask if she can meet on Tuesday or Wednesday next week.
- ▶ Suggest the pub near the train station, The Red Lion.
- ▶ Explain you would prefer lunchtime.
- ▶ Suggest 12 p.m.

 Test yourself

1 How many different answers can you remember to the question ***How are you?***

2 Look at the pictures. Complete the activities. Some (*) have more than one way of saying the same thing. Use the key words to help you.

a*  *go to the* cinema, *go to see* a film

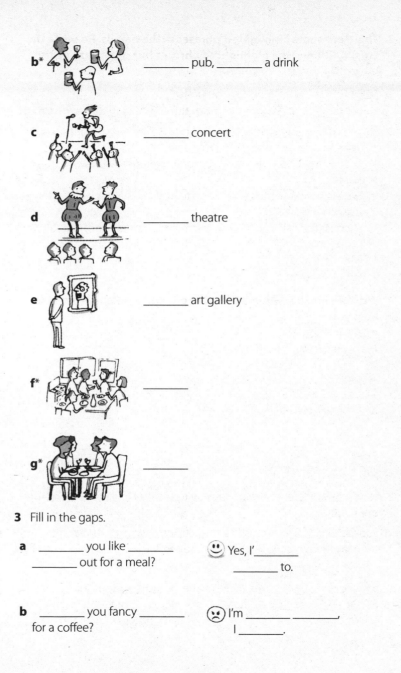

b* _____ pub, _____ a drink

c _____ concert

d _____ theatre

e _____ art gallery

f* _____

g* _____

3 Fill in the gaps.

a _____ you like _____
_____ out for a meal?

🙂 Yes, I'_____
_____ to.

b _____ you fancy _____
for a coffee?

🙁 I'm _____ _____,
I _____.

c Do you _____ to _____ to the cinema?

☺ Yes, _____ _____ _____ great.

d _____ you fancy a meal?

☹ _____ afraid I _____.

e Would you _____ a cup of tea?

_____ _____ have a cup of coffee.

f _____ _____ fancy a sandwich?

_____ _____ _____ have a meal.

g How _____ meeting on Friday?

☹ _____ _____ do Friday.

h _____ meet at six o'clock.

☹ Six o'clock _____ no _____.

i _____ _____ _____ meet at the train station?

☺ That's _____ _____ _____.

j How _____ a café?

☺ _____ _____ great.

k _____ meet in The Queen's Head.

☹ No, it's _____ noisy.

l _____ _____ The Red Lion?

☹ No, it's _____ expensive.

m _____ you_____ on Tuesday?

☹ _____

_____, I can't do Tuesday. _____' _____ meeting my dad.

n _____ you_____ anything at the weekend?

My brother _____ visiting us.

o _____ _____ Monday?

We _____ _____ out for dinner.

4 Look at the calendar. Today is Thursday 14th. Complete the table.

Mon	Tues	Weds	Thurs	Fri	Sat	Sun
4	5	6	7	8	9	10
11	12	13	(14)	15	16	17
18	19	20	21	22	23	24
25	26	27	28	29	30	31

a	Fri 15th
The day after tomorrow	**b**
Yesterday	**c**
d	Tues 12th
e	Mon 11th
This Saturday	**f**
g	Sat 23rd
Last Tuesday	**h**
This Friday	**i**
j	Fri 22nd

SELF CHECK

I CAN ...
... ask how people feel.
... say how I am.
... talk about plans and preferences.
... make and respond to suggestions and invitations.

Review 1

This Review tests the main vocabulary and language from Units 1–5. Each task has a number of points. Do all the tasks. When you finish, check your answers. How many points can you get? There is a table at the end of the test. It tells you your score.

1 Can you write five different ways to complete the sentence and say how you are?

Example: *fine*

I'm _____, thanks.

Points: _____/5

2 Complete the lists with the missing words.

Example: One, two, *three*, four, five, six

a Monday, _____, Wednesday, _____

b _____, today, tomorrow, _____

c March, April, May, June, _____

Points: _____/5

3 Make sentences: match the phrases.

Example: a *He is Russian.*

a	He is	too noisy.
b	I live in	Russian.
c	I live in a	tired.
d	It's	in a factory.
e	I am really	detached house.
f	He works	England.

Points: _____/5

4 How do we say these dates? Say and write the dates in words.

Example: 12/09/2001 *The twelfth of September two thousand and one*

a 01/02/1956

b 22/12/2002

c 05/01/1999

d 30/10/2010

e 14/08/2016

Points: _____/5

5 **Read the paragraph about when people were born. Fill in the gaps with the correct preposition: _in, on_ or _at_.**

I was born in London **a** _____ 1999. My mother says it was **b** _____ about four o'clock **c** _____ the afternoon. My daughter was born **d** _____ summer, on the same date as my father. Their birthday is **e** _____ 31st July. My son was born **f** _____ 3rd September. He was born **g** _____ night, at about 2 a.m. My mother was born **h** _____ December and she celebrates her birthday **i** _____ Christmas, because she was born **j** _____ 25th December!

05.20 **Listen and check your answers.**

Points: _____/10

6 05.21 **Listen to the sentences and fill in the times.**

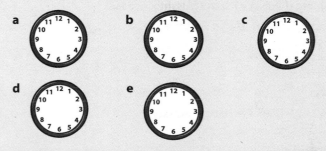

a **b** **c**

d **e**

Points: _____/5

7 **Write the plural of the underlined words in the sentences.**

a 255 <u>baby</u> are born every minute in the world.

b More <u>boy</u> are born than <u>girl</u>.

c 27% of the world's population is <u>child</u>.

d There are 18.2 million <u>family</u> in the UK.

e There are 51 <u>city</u> in England.

f There are 8.4 million <u>person</u> in London.

g There are more than 30 <u>country</u> in Europe.

h There are more <u>man</u> than <u>woman</u> in the world.

Points: _____/10

8 05.22 **Listen and note down the website and email addresses you hear.**

a _____

b _____

c _____

Points: _____/3

9 Spell the email addresses and websites.

a www.uktourist.org/advice

b mareko.yumi357@yahoo.com

05.23 **Listen to the audio to check your answers.**

Points: _____/2

10 Read the answers. Use the key words and write the questions.

Example: He's from Portugal.   from   *Where's he from?*

a It starts at five o'clock.   time

b It lasts about three hours.   last

c 28th April 1963.   born

d I am 52.   old

e 28th April   birthday

f 05694 340 865   number

g WR10 5CD   postcode

h 22, High Street, Wendon   what

i Jane Smith   your

j I'm from London.   where

k I live in Madrid.   you

l Miguel Silva   his

m He lives in London.   where

n No, he speaks Portuguese.   English

o Yes, two.   children

Points: _____/15

11 Make the sentences negative.

Example: I speak Spanish.   I *don't speak Spanish.*

a They live in New York.   They _____

b I like listening to music.   I _____

c He gets up early.   He _____

d She speaks Japanese.   She _____

e There are a lot of people. There _____

f He's from New Zealand. He _____

g It's very beautiful. It _____

h He can speak French. He _____

i He's got a car. He _____

j I've got a lot of free time. I _____

Points: _____/10

12 **Complete the sentences. Use the words in the box and the information in the table.**

> too
>
> there is/are
>
> there isn't/there aren't
>
> a/an/any
>
> a lot of
>
> quite/really

MY VILLAGE	
a café	no
a pub	yes
a bank	no
cinema	no
tourists	yes, a lot
a shop	yes, two
3G/4G coverage	no

I live in a village. It's **a** _____ small and **b** _____ beautiful ☺ but it's **c** _____ quiet ☹.

d _____ a pub and **e** _____ two shops but **f** _____ bank and **g** _____ cafés. In the summer, **h** _____ tourists. I love my village but I also like going to see films and **i** _____ cinema here. I like going on Facebook™ and the internet connection is quite good but **j** _____ 3G or 4G coverage ☹.

Points: _____/10

13 Read the conversation and fill in the gaps. Use one word for each gap.

Marilyn	Do you **a** _____ _____ out sometime?
David	I'd like **b** _____ _____ and see the new Bond film.
Marilyn	That's **c** _____ _____ _____.
David	How **d** _____ this weekend?
Marilyn	This weekend **e** _____ _____ good because **f** _____ _____ working all day Saturday and all day Sunday, so I'm afraid I can't.
David	**g** _____ _____ _____ next Monday?
Marilyn	Yes, Monday is good. Actually, I'd **h** _____ _____ go on Monday because it is quiet.
David	Yes, there are too many people at the weekend. Do you want **i** _____ _____ out for a meal first?
Marilyn	Well, food is a good idea but I'd **j** _____ have a sandwich in a pub or something.
David	Let's **k** _____ at five at the cinema. The Queen's Arms is two minutes from the cinema and it's a really nice pub and not too expensive.
Marilyn	The Queen's Arms **l** _____ perfect but five is **m** _____ early. I finish work at five thirty.
David	Oh, OK, so why **n** _____ _____ _____ at six?
Marilyn	Six sounds **o** _____ See you then.
Points: _____ /15	

14 Read about Mike and then write about him. Change the highlighted words. Start: *His name is Mike and he lives …*

My name is Mike and I live in Brazil. **a** I am a teacher and **b** I work in a language school in Sao Paulo. **c** I love living in Brazil. It's a beautiful country and the people are very friendly. **d** I've got a lot of friends and **e** I can speak Portuguese. **f** I love my job but **g** I haven't got any free time during the week and **h** I can't usually go out. The weekend is different. **i** I usually go to the beach in the morning and **j** play football with some friends and then **k** go home for lunch. **l** I often cook fish on the barbecue but **m** I don't like eating a lot when it is hot. In the afternoon **n** I sometimes go to the café or **o** I go round to a friend's house, but **p** I sometimes have homework to mark. In the evening,

q I usually **go** to a bar or the cinema. **r** I **stay** up quite late on Friday and Saturday but on Sunday **s** I **don't** go out. On Monday morning **t** I'm back at work!

Points: _____/20

15 Make sentences using the words and pictures.

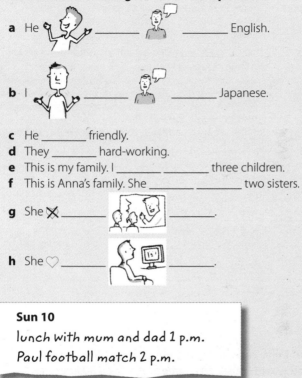

a He _____ _____ _____ English.

b I _____ _____ _____ Japanese.

c He _____ friendly.

d They _____ hard-working.

e This is my family. I _____ _____ three children.

f This is Anna's family. She _____ _____ two sisters.

g She ✗ _____ _____ _____.

h She ♡ _____ _____ _____.

Sun 10
lunch with mum and dad 1 p.m.
Paul football match 2 p.m.

i On Sunday I _____ _____ _____ with mum and dad.

j On Sunday Paul _____ _____ _____ at 2 o'clock.

Points: _____/10

Check your answers in the Answer key. How many points did you get?

Look at the table. Is your score excellent, very good, quite good or not too bad? Is it a good idea to do some more practice before you start Unit 6?

100–130	Excellent – congratulations! You are ready to start Unit 6.
80–99	Very good. You understand a lot of English and can use a lot of vocabulary and language from Units1–5. Note the things that are difficult. Practise them again.
60–79	Quite good. You understand some English and can remember some of the vocabulary and language from Units1–5. It is a good idea to look at the difficult points and practise them again, before you start Unit 6.
59 or less	Not too bad! English can be difficult to learn. It is a good idea to read Units 1–5 again and repeat some of the exercises for more practice. It is important to understand the vocabulary and language from Units1–5 before you start the next unit. When you feel more confident, do the test again and then start Unit 6.

6 Transport and directions

In this unit you will learn how to:
- ▶ *talk about travel and transport.*
- ▶ *buy tickets and ask about journey times and distance.*
- ▶ *understand simple instructions and announcements.*
- ▶ *ask for and give directions.*

CEFR: (A1) *Can follow short, simple directions.* **(A2)** *Can catch the main point in announcements. Can find specific, predictable information in simple everyday material. Can understand everyday signs and notices. Can ask about things and make simple transactions.*

Travelling around the UK by public transport

1 Read the text about travelling in the UK. Look at the pictures in Vocabulary 1. Find the three kinds of transport that are in the text.

People often use trains to travel around the UK. There are a lot of different train companies, but a good place to find information and buy a ticket for any journey is online at National Rail Enquiries. Train tickets can be very expensive but they can also be very cheap. For example, do you want to travel from London to Manchester? It is expensive when you travel first class, buy the ticket just before you go or travel early in the morning. It is often cheap when you travel standard class, buy the ticket a few weeks before you travel and leave after ten o'clock in the morning.

Travelling by coach is always a cheap way of travelling. It is possible to find very, very cheap tickets but the journeys take quite a long time.

How about travelling by plane? Some people use budget airlines for long journeys in the UK, for example when they travel from London to Scotland. It is sometimes cheap and the flight is very quick but the journey to the airport and check-in and security can take a lot of time.

2 **Read the text again and decide if the advice below is correct. Choose Yes or No.**

    a Find out information about train tickets online from National Rail Enquiries.   Yes/No

    b For cheap train tickets, buy your ticket a few weeks before you travel and don't leave early in the morning.   Yes/No

    c For a quick journey, travel by coach.   Yes/No

    d For a very cheap journey, travel by coach.   Yes/No

    e For a long journey, flying can be quick and cheap.   Yes/No

Vocabulary builder

VOCABULARY 1: TRAVEL AND PLACES

1 **Match the different forms of transport and the pictures.**

> train, underground
> (in London, 'tube'), bus,
> plane, coach, taxi (or minicab),
> car, ferry, bicycle (bike), foot

    a   **b**   **c**   **d**   **e**

plane

    f   **g**   **h**   **i**   **j**

2 **Where do we catch a plane? Match some of the different forms of transport with the correct places.**

> plane, ferry, train,
> bus, coach, taxi

    a airport

    b station

c taxi rank
d bus stop
e coach station
f ferry port   *ferry*

> **LANGUAGE TIP**
> We usually say *by* + a form of transport. For example, *I travel by car* or *I often go by bicycle.*

3 **We say *on* for one of the forms of transport in Exercise 1. Which?**

4 06.01 **Listen and repeat. Note the stress, for example, <u>*fer*</u>*ry*, <u>*coach*</u> *station*. Practise saying the forms of transport and places.**

5 **Answer for you. What forms of transport do you usually use . . .**
  a … when you go to work?
  b … when you go on holiday?
  c … when you go out at the weekend?

6 **Cover the words in Exercises 1 and 2 and look at the pictures. Can you remember the words?**

VOCABULARY 2: PUBLIC TRANSPORT

1 **Use words from the box to complete the sentences. Check the meaning of any words you don't know in a dictionary.**

> delayed cancelled check-in
> book gate passport leave arrive
> security boarding card
> hold luggage hand luggage
> single (ticket)
> return (ticket) platform

Example: You say hello when you *arrive* and goodbye when you *leave.*

  a You can _____ a ticket online. Do you want a _____ ticket or a _____ ticket?
  b A small suitcase can be _____ but a large suitcase is _____.
  c You go to an airport to catch a plane. First you go to _____ then to _____, then you go to a departure _____.
  d At check-in, you show your passport and they give you a _____.

e When you arrive in a different country, you usually have to show your _____.

f The 8.15 train is late. It's _____ and is now arriving at 8.45.

g The 10.30 coach is not going. It's _____.

h It's important to know which _____ your train is leaving from.

 2 06.02 **Listen and repeat. Note the stress, for example,** _delayed_**. Practise saying the words and phrases.**

VOCABULARY 3: PREPOSITIONS OF PLACE AND MOVEMENT

1 **Here are some announcements in a plane. Read the text and note the prepositions.**

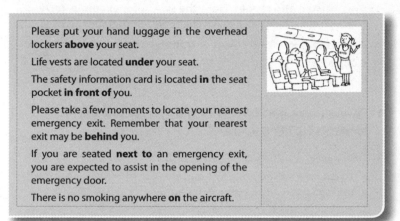

Please put your hand luggage in the overhead lockers **above** your seat.

Life vests are located **under** your seat.

The safety information card is located **in** the seat pocket **in front of** you.

Please take a few moments to locate your nearest emergency exit. Remember that your nearest exit may be **behind** you.

If you are seated **next to** an emergency exit, you are expected to assist in the opening of the emergency door.

There is no smoking anywhere **on** the aircraft.

2 **Match the prepositions to the correct pictures.**

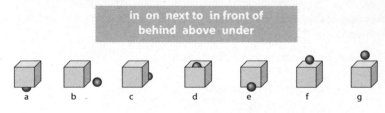

in on next to in front of
behind above under

a   b   c   d   e   f   g

 3 06.03 **Listen to the prepositions. Note the stress, for example** _behind_**. Practise saying the prepositions.**

4   **Look at the picture and complete the sentences.**

a   There are three people _____ the carriage.
b   A woman is _____ the window.
c   A man is _____ the woman.
d   A child is _____ the woman.
e   The suitcases are _____ the luggage rack _____ their heads.
f   There is a newspaper _____ the seat.

5   **Look at the sentences and the underlined verbs and prepositions. Are they correct? Note Yes or No.**
a   The train <u>arrives to</u> Liverpool <u>at</u> six o'clock.
b   The train <u>gets to</u> Liverpool <u>at</u> six o'clock.
c   We <u>leave to</u> Manchester tonight.
d   We are <u>going to</u> Scotland next week.
e   We are <u>going to home</u> tomorrow.
f   We are <u>flying to</u> New York the day after tomorrow.
g   We are <u>travelling to</u> Australia next month.
h   We are <u>visiting to</u> London next year.

6   **Look at the table. Put in the correct preposition *in* or *to* where necessary.**

a arrive _____			
b get _____			
c leave _____			
d go _____	+ place e.g. *London*	at	time
e fly _____			
f travel _____			
g visit _____			

PRONUNCIATION 1: SENTENCE STRESS, /ə/ FOR *A* AND *AN* AND LINKING

1 06.04 **Look at the sentences and listen to the pronunciation.**

Mark the stressed words and syllables. In English, we usually stress the most important words in the sentence.

Can you remember how to pronounce *a* and *an* in a sentence? Mark /ə/ next to *a* and *an*.

Note where one word links to the next word.

a Can I have a return ticket, please?
b I'd like to book a flight.
c The flight is cancelled.
d The train is delayed.
e Which platform is it?
f How much is a first class ticket?
g It's above the seat.
h I've got a single ticket.
i Quick! The flight is boarding!
j The train arrives in London at ten o'clock.

2 **Practise saying the sentences. Use the correct sentence stress, the weak forms of *a* and *an* and the linking between words.**

PRONUNCIATION 2: THE WORD *TO*

1 06.05 **Listen and notice how we pronounce the word *to*. Choose the correct answer, /tə/ or /tuː/.**

a get to London, fly to Spain, travel to Japan, go to China
In all these phrases do we say /tə/ or /tuː/?
b travel to Italy, get to Argentina, go to England, fly to Australia
In all these phrases do we say /tə/ or /tuː/?

When the word after **to** begins with a consonant sound, we usually say /tə/. When the word after **to** begins with a vowel sound, we usually say /tu:/.

2 **Look at the places, decide if we say /tə/ or /tu:/ and put the places in the correct part of the table.**

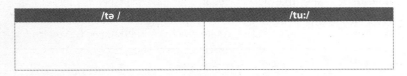

London East London England
Manchester America
New York Oxford San Francisco
Dallas Edinburgh

/tə /	/tu:/

3 06.06 **Listen, check your answers, and practise.**

Conversation 1: Questions about travel

1 06.07 **A tourist is in a tourist information centre in London asking about travelling in the UK. Listen to the conversation and answer the questions.**

a Where does the tourist want to go?

b How far is it?

Tourist	Good morning
Advisor	Good morning. Can I help you?
Tourist	Yes. I want to travel to Scotland, to Edinburgh. What's the best way to get there?
Advisor	Well, you can hire a car and drive, but that takes about eight hours and it is very expensive.
Tourist	How far is it?
Advisor	It's about 400 miles.
Tourist	Mmm …
Advisor	Or you can go by coach. Coach tickets are usually very cheap.
Tourist	How long does it take by coach?

Advisor	It takes about ten hours….
Tourist	Wow … what time does it leave?
Advisor	Very early in the morning … yes, it leaves at six o'clock.
Tourist	Wow, that is early … what about the train?
Advisor	The train usually takes about five hours. If you book tickets in advance, you can get them quite cheaply.
Tourist	Can I fly?
Advisor	Yes, there are flights from Heathrow and Gatwick, so for example, there is a flight at ten o'clock in the morning.
Tourist	OK … and what time does it arrive?
Advisor	That flight arrives an hour and fifteen minutes later at 11.15.
Tourist	Wow, that's quick … and how much is a ticket?
Advisor	Tickets can be quite expensive. But they can be very cheap if you book in advance. Use one of the budget airlines and check-in online.
Tourist	OK, well a cheap flight would be great. Can I go online here to try and book a ticket?
Advisor	Yes, of course. Let me know if you've got any problems.

2 06.07 **Listen to the conversation again and complete the table.**

WAYS OF TRAVELLING	JOURNEY TIME	JOURNEY COST
a hire a car		
b	about ten hours	
c		quite cheap if you book in advance
d	an hour and 15 minutes	

3 **The tourist asks a lot of useful questions. Here are the answers. What are the questions?**

a _____ Just over 400 miles.

b _____ £20.

c _____ Six o'clock in the morning.

d _____ About twelve hours later.

e _____ About three hours.

f _____ Probably by train, it is quick and cheap.

4 06.08 **Listen and repeat. Note the stress, for example,** *How far is it?* **Note where one word links to the next word, for example** *How far is it?*

Practise saying the questions.

5 06.09 **Listen to the answers. Say the correct question – you will hear the answer again.**

Conversation 2: Using *can/can't* for permission

1 06.10 **Listen to the conversation. Answer the questions.**
- **a** Where are the two people?
- **b** Does the passenger want to go to Manchester?

Train manager	Good morning.
Passenger	Good morning.
Train manager	Excuse me sir … you can't smoke on the train.
Passenger	Oh, OK. I'm sorry.
Train manager	And you can't use your phone in this carriage. It's a quiet carriage.
Passenger	Sorry. Can I use my phone in the next carriage?
Train manager	Yes, no problem.
Passenger	OK I think I will go and sit in the next carriage then …
Ten minutes later …	
Train manager	Hello again.
Passenger	Hello.
Train manager	I'm afraid you can't sit here.
Passenger	Oh. Why?
Train manager	This seat is reserved.
Passenger	Oh. OK. Can I sit here?
Train manager	Yes, this seat is free, but you can't put your bags on the floor. People can't walk past.
Passenger	Right. Where can I put them?
Train manager	You can put them in the rack above your seat or on the left there at the end of the carriage. Can I see your ticket, please?
Passenger	Yes, of course … um … it's … um … mmm … I can't find it …

Train manager	You can't travel on the train without a ticket.	
Passenger	Yes, I know that. Can I buy one from you?	
Train manager	Yes, of course. Where are you going?	
Passenger	Reading.	
Train manager	Oh dear … this is the Manchester train … we don't go to Reading …	

2 06.10 **The passenger does five things that it is not OK to do on the train. Listen to and read the conversation. Put the five things in part B of the table (use the pictures to help you).**

A	B	
	smoke	

3 06.10 **Listen again to the conversation. What words does the train manager use to say it is not OK to do something? Put the words in Part A of the table.**

We use *can* and *can't* to say it is OK or it is not OK to do something. It is the same word we used in Unit 4 (*I can cook, I can sing*) but this is a different meaning. Here we are using it for rules and permission.

4 Look at the icons. Choose the correct phrase and make a sentence about what you can't do in a place.

Example: a *You can't park here.*

drink alcohol

take photographs

eat or drink

run

smoke

park

swim

use a mobile

5 How does the passenger ask if it is OK to do something? Fill in the gaps.

a _____ I use my phone in the next carriage?

b _____ I sit here?

c Where _____ I put my suitcase?

d _____ I buy one from you?

6 Use the icons and the words in the table to make questions and ask permission.

Example: *Can I pay by credit card?*

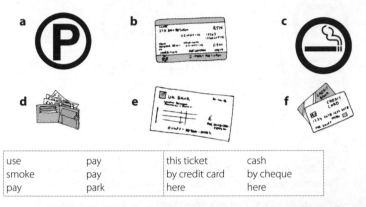

a

b

c

d

e

f

use	pay	this ticket	cash
smoke	pay	by credit card	by cheque
pay	park	here	here

ASKING FOR AND GIVING DIRECTIONS

1 You want to go to the train station but you don't know where it is. Look at the different questions. One is more polite. Is it a or b?

a Where is the train station?

b Could you tell me where the train station is?

2 06.11 Listen to someone asking for directions to the train station. Find the station on the map. Choose the correct letter.

Tourist	Excuse me …
Person in the street	Yes?
Tourist	Could you tell me where the train station is? Is it a long way?
Person in the street	Oh, no, it's not far. If you go along this road and take the first right, it's on the right, in front of the big supermarket.
Tourist	Thank you very much.

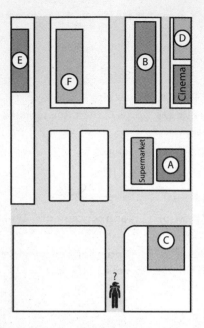

3 06.12 **Listen to three tourists asking for directions. Find the places on the map. Note the places and the correct letters.**

4 **Read the directions. You are the tourist on the map. Note the places.**

Example: a *the taxi rank*

a Take the first left. Then take the second right. Go along the road for about 50 metres. It's on the right.

b Take the first right and it's on your left next to the supermarket.

c Take the second right, then take the first left. It's on your right.

d Go along this street and take the second left. Then take the first right. It's on the left. It's about five minutes from here.

5 06.13 **Listen and repeat. Note the stress, for example, *It's on the left*. Note where one word links to the next word, for example *It's on the left*. Practise saying the question and the directions.**

6 **Look at the map in Exercise 3. Complete the text about how to get to the places.**

a The post office
_____ along the road _____ _____ 50 metres and _____ the
_____ _____, it's on the _____, _____ _____ the cinema.

b The taxi rank

_____ the _____ left , then take _____ _____ _____.

_____ _____ the road _____ about 50–100 metres. _____

on _____ right. It's _____ five _____ _____ _____.

7 Look again at the map in Exercise 3. Describe how to get to …
  a The bus station
  b The Station Hotel

Listening and speaking

LISTENING 1: AIRPORT ANNOUNCEMENTS

1 06.14 **Listen to the airport announcements. Are all the flights leaving on time?**

2 06.14 **Listen again to the airport announcements. Read the sentences and choose T (true) or F (false).**
  a Flight TP409 to Lisbon leaves from gate 49.   T/F
  b Flight TP409 is leaving in a few hours.   T/F
  c Flight BA4369 to New York leaves from gate 34.   T/F
  d Passengers can get on flight BA4369 to New York now.   T/F
  e Flight VA345 to Rio leaves from gate 70.   T/F
  f Passengers with children can get onto Flight VA345.   T/F
  g Flight TE549 is going to Hong Kong.   T/F
  h Passengers can't get on flight TE549 because it is cancelled. T/F

LISTENING 2: PUBLIC TRANSPORT IN LONDON

1 06.15 **Listen to the people talking about travelling around London by public transport. Look at the pictures of transport in Vocabulary 1. Note the ones you hear.**

2 06.15 **Listen again. Use the words in the box to complete the summary about travelling around London by public transport.**

> can can can't can't underground
> travel card ticket bus bus
> bus bus tube tube tube

Most people travel around London by **a** _____ or **b** _____ (called the
c _____). The **d** _____ is quick, but a lot of it is under the ground so
you **e** _____ see London. On a **f** _____ you **g** _____ see a lot of
the famous places in London. You **h** _____ pay for a **i** _____ on a
j _____ with cash so it is a good idea to buy a visitor **k** _____. You
pay once for one day or seven days and you **l** _____ do all the journeys
you want to on the **m** _____ or **n** _____.

SPEAKING: PUBLIC TRANSPORT IN A CITY IN YOUR COUNTRY

**1 Imagine you are telling some tourists about how to travel
around a city in your country. Change the text to describe
your city.**

There are a lot of different ways to travel around London. Two good ways
are by bus or underground train (called 'the tube').

Do you want to go across London? The tube is great because it is quick.
You can travel across London, for example from Knightsbridge (and
Harrods) to Tower Hill (and the Tower of London) and the journey takes 30
minutes.

Or do you want to see the sights in the centre of London? Travelling
by bus is a good way to see famous London sights. You can take a bus
that goes next to the river or in front of the Houses of Parliament or
Buckingham Palace.

**2 Cover your complete text. Look again at the text in Exercise 1.
Can you give the talk, remembering the words you added?**

3 Cover Exercise 1 and your completed text. Can you give the talk?

Reading and writing

READING 1: A WEB PAGE ABOUT HEATHROW AIRPORT

**1 Read the information from a web page about what you can do
at Heathrow Airport. Look at pictures a–j. What does the web
page say you can do? Choose the correct pictures.**

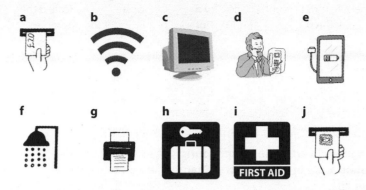

a   b   c   d   e

f   g   h   i   j

Heathrow terminal facilities and services

You can use the pay-as-you-go computer desks with broadband access in every terminal.

You can access Wi-Fi in the terminal to help you stay in touch.

You can buy stamps from coin-operated stamp machines in each terminal.

You can withdraw money from cash dispensers (ATMs) both before and after security in every terminal at Heathrow.

You can leave bags at the left luggage/luggage storage facilities in each terminal at Heathrow Airport.

You can charge your phone at one of the free mobile charging stations before and after security.

You can make telephone calls from the public telephones in each Heathrow terminal with either cash or cards.

2   Have a look online at the website and read about more things you can do at Heathrow.

http://www.heathrowairport.com/heathrow-airport-guide/services-and-facilities

3   What do you know about plane travel? Read the sentences and choose T (true) or F (false).

   a   You can't take a large suitcase as hand luggage.   T/F

   b   You can't take liquids in containers over 100 ml in
      hand luggage.   T/F

   c   You can take a 125 ml bottle of perfume in hold luggage.   T/F

d You can take a 75 ml bottle of perfume in hand luggage.   T/F
e You can't take a bottle of water through security.   T/F
f You can take liquids in containers over 100 ml in
hold luggage.   T/F
g You can take a 125 ml tube of toothpaste in hand luggage.   T/F
h You can take a laptop in your hand luggage.   T/F
i You can take lots of bags as hand luggage.   T/F
j You can travel from London to Scotland without your
passport.   T/F

WRITING: DIRECTIONS IN AN EMAIL

1 Cristina is coming to London to visit her friend Joanna. Joanna writes her an email. What is the email about? Choose the correct answer.

a Things they can do in London.
b How Cristina can find Joanna's flat.
c Advice about packing her suitcase.

B *I* U̲ A̲a̲ ∕ ☰ ☰ ☰◄ ►☰ ☰ ☰ ☰ ∞ ☺

Hi Cristina!
I am so happy you are coming to London ☺ and I am really sorry that I can't meet you at the airport when you arrive because I am working all day but it is easy to get to my house.

At the airport, look for the signs to the train station. It is really easy to find and not far from Arrivals. Take any train to London Victoria. There is one every 15 minutes. It takes about 30 minutes and you can buy a ticket on the train. I think it costs about £20.

When you get to London Victoria, you can walk to my flat. It is very near the train station. Come out of the station and turn left. Go along the road (Victoria Street) for about 100 metres and then take the second right. It is a little street called Brook Place. Go along Brook Place for about 200 metres and then take the first left. My building is on the right. It is called Orchardson House and my flat is number 9.

I usually get home from work at about five o'clock. Your flight arrives at four o'clock and it takes about an hour to get from the airport to my flat, so that is all OK. We can meet at the flat at five o'clock, but don't worry if you are late!

See you next week!!
Love Joanna

---

2 Read the email again and answer the questions.

  a Can Joanna meet Cristina at the airport?
  b What's the best way to get from the airport to London Victoria?
  c How long does it take to get from the airport to London Victoria?
  d Can Cristina get her ticket on the train?
  e How much is a ticket?
  f Is Joanna's flat near London Victoria?
  g What's the best way to get from London Victoria to Joanna's flat?
  h Does Joanna live in Brook Place?
  i Does Joanna live in Orchardson House?
  j What time does Cristina's flight arrive?
  k What time does Joanna get home?
  l How long does it take to get from the airport to Joanna's house?

3 Write a similar email to a friend giving information about how to get from the airport to your house. In your email, fill in the gaps, and give the information for questions a–c. Use Joanna's words as much as possible.

B *I* U Aa ⟋ ⋮☰ ⋮☰ ☰◂ ▸☰ ☰ ☰ ☰ ∞ ☺

Hi _____
I am so happy you are coming to _____ and I am really sorry that I can't meet you at the airport when you arrive because _____ but it is easy to get to my house.

a   Describe how to get from the airport to the city/town/village where you live, say when the transport leaves, how long it takes, where you can buy a ticket and how much is costs.
b   Give directions to your house/flat, say if it is near or far and say where your house is.
c   Say how long the journey from the airport to your house/flat takes.

See you next week!!
Love _____

Test yourself

1 Add the words to the table.

> first class gate a single ticket
> a return ticket check-in delayed
> underground cancelled
> hold luggage security
> boarding card
> airport station
> passport hand luggage platform

PLANES		PLANES AND TRAINS		TRAINS
gate		*first class*		

2 Read the instructions. Draw the picture.

Draw a car. <u>Behind</u> the car, draw a house. <u>In front of</u> the car, draw a man. <u>Next to</u> the man, draw a child. <u>In</u> the car, draw a woman. <u>On</u> the car, draw a suitcase. <u>Under</u> the car, draw a cat. <u>Above</u> the house, draw a plane.

3 Fill in the gaps.

   a Could you _____ _____ _____ the station _____, please?
   b _____ _____ first left.
   c It's _____ _____ left.
   d Go _____ the road _____ about 100 metres.
   e How far _____ _____?
   f It's _____ _____, only about 50 metres.
   g It's about five minutes _____ here.
   h How _____ _____ _____ return ticket?
   i What _____ _____ it leave?
   j How long _____ it _____?
   k What's the best _____ to get to Edinburgh?
   l We arrive _____ London at 10 p.m.
   m We get _____ Paris in the morning.
   n We _____ home tomorrow.

4 Re-write the underlined sentences. Use *can* or *can't*.

   a <u>It isn't OK to smoke here.</u> This is a no-smoking area.

   b <u>It isn't OK to sit here.</u> This is a reserved seat.

   c **A:** <u>Is it OK to pay by credit card?</u>

      B: Yes, of course. We take cash or credit cards.

   d <u>It's OK to take a drink into the theatre.</u>

SELF CHECK

	I CAN ...
⬤	... talk about travel and transport.
⬤	... buy tickets and ask about journey times and distance.
⬤	... understand simple instructions and announcements.
⬤	... ask for and give directions.

7 Hotels and accommodation

In this unit you will learn how to:
▶ *manage simple business in hotels.*
▶ *complain about problems politely.*
▶ *make requests.*

CEFR: (A1) *Can understand very short, simple texts. Can get an idea of the content of simpler informational material and descriptions. Can ask people for things.* **(A2)** *Can find specific, predictable information in simple everyday material. Can understand everyday signs and notices. Can give his or her opinion on practical problems and ask for things.*

Types of accommodation

When you travel what type of accommodation do you stay in?

1 **Read the text about holiday accommodation and label the pictures.**

budget hotel   B+B   youth hostel
full English breakfast   expensive
hotel   continental breakfast

a expensive hotel

b _____

c _____

d _____

e _____

f _____

There are a lot of different types of accommodation in the UK. You can stay in an **expensive hotel** or **a budget hotel**, or in a **B+B** (bed and breakfast). The cheapest accommodation is probably a **youth hostel**. You usually share a large room with other people (either all women or all men) and cook your own meals in a shared kitchen.

Staying in accommodation and paying for your room but no meals is called **room only**. Paying for a room and breakfast is **bed and breakfast**. Paying for a room, breakfast and one other meal (usually dinner) is **half board**. A room, breakfast, lunch and dinner is **full board**. If a B+B has got rooms available, there is a sign saying *Vacancies*. If they are fully booked, there is a sign saying *No vacancies*. Most hotels, guesthouses and B+Bs will offer you either a **full English breakfast** or a **continental breakfast**.

2   **Read the text again. Match the accommodation to the prices. Then match the meals information to the correct phrase.**

£	expensive hotel
££	youth hostel
£££	B+B or budget hotel

no meals	full board
one meal (breakfast)	room only
two meals (breakfast and dinner)	half board
three meals (breakfast, lunch and dinner)	bed and breakfast

Vocabulary builder

VOCABULARY 1: SERVICES AND FACILITIES

Look at the icons a–h and match them with the words 1–8.

Example: a 8

Which are important to you when you choose a hotel?

1 a restaurant
2 a bar
3 a gym
4 a laundry service
5 a pool
6 parking
7 a lift/elevator
8 internet/Wi-Fi

VOCABULARY 2: DESCRIBING ACCOMMODATION

1 Look at the table. There are positive and negative words to describe hotels.

Positive (good 😊)	Negative (bad 😞)
about the hotel and the rooms amazing, good, brilliant, fantastic, excellent, comfy, quiet	**about the hotel and the rooms** awful, expensive, dirty, noisy
about the staff polite, friendly	**about the staff** unfriendly, rude

Add the words in the box to the correct part of the table (use a dictionary if necessary).

> clean comfortable excellent value
> helpful basic central great

2 Look at the table in Exercise 1 again. Find words for the following meanings.
   a a lot of money
   b not clean
   c not quiet
   d not friendly
   e not polite
   f very bad

3 07.01 **Listen and repeat. Note the stressed syllables, for example, _comfortable_. Practise saying the words.**

4 **Look at some hotel reviews online (www.tripadvisor.co.uk). Find some more positive and negative words and add them to the table in Exercise 1.**

VOCABULARY 3: DESCRIBING ROOMS

1 **Look at the pictures a–g and match them with the words 1–7.**

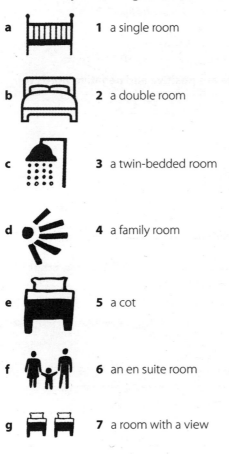

a   **1** a single room

b   **2** a double room

c   **3** a twin-bedded room

d   **4** a family room

e   **5** a cot

f   **6** an en suite room

g   **7** a room with a view

2 07.02 **Listen and repeat. Note the stressed syllables, for example, *a single room*. Practise saying the words.**

VOCABULARY 4: BOOKING ACCOMMODATION

1 Look at the expressions. Put them in the correct part of the table.
  a ~~What time is **check-out**?~~
  b From **Monday 10th July** to **Wednesday 12th July**.
  c For **three** nights.
  d Does the price include **breakfast**?
  e Where is **breakfast** served?
  f It's on the **first** floor.
  g I'd like to book a **twin-bedded** room.
  h For **three** people.
  i I've got a reservation.
  j Have you got any vacancies?
  k We are fully booked.
  l Do I need to pay a deposit?
  m I'd like to make a reservation.

When you make a booking	When you arrive at the hotel
	What time is check-out?

2 You can replace the words in bold in Exercise 1 with other words. Can you think of any examples?

  Example: a *What time is breakfast?*

3 07.03 **Look at some of the phrases from Exercise 1 and listen to the pronunciation.**
▶ Note the stressed words and syllables.
▶ Note where a vowel is pronounced /ə/. Remember, we often use /ə/ for *to* /tə/ and *a* /ə/ and *does* /dəz/. We can also use it for words like *from* /frəm/ and *for* /fə/ and *have* /həv/.
▶ Note where one word links to the next word.

  Example: a Have /həv/ you <u>got</u> any <u>vac</u>ancies?
  a Have you got any vacancies?
  b Do I need to pay a deposit?
  c What time is check-out?
  d Does the price include breakfast?
  e Where is breakfast served?
  f I've got a reservation.

g From Monday 10th of July to Wednesday 12th of July.
h For three nights.
i I'd like to make a reservation.
j I'd like to book a twin-bedded room.

Conversation 1: Complaining about problems

Sometimes things are not working or there are things missing (not there).

1 Look at the words and add them to the correct part of the table. Check any words you are not sure of in your dictionary.

> shower soap clean sheets
> air-conditioning TV
> clean towels toilet paper
> hairdryer lights radio heating
> pillows internet lift/elevator

THINGS NOT WORKING	THINGS MISSING
shower	*soap*

2 07.04 Listen to some guests complaining about problems in their room and read the conversations. Is the receptionist helpful?

Guest 1

Guest 1	Hello? I'm calling from room 245. I'm afraid there isn't any soap and there isn't a hairdryer.
Receptionist	Oh, I'm so sorry. I'll see to it straight away.
Guest 1	Hello? I'm calling from room 245 again. I'm afraid the shower isn't working.
Receptionist	Oh, I'm so sorry. I'll deal with it immediately.

Guest 2

Guest 2	Hello? It's room 96. I'm afraid the lights aren't working.
Receptionist	Oh, I'm so sorry. I'll sort it out straight away.
Guest 2	Hello? It's room 96 again. I'm afraid there aren't any clean towels.
Receptionist	Oh, I'm so sorry. I'll send some up immediately.

3 07.04 **Listen to the conversations again. What are the problems?**
   a What things aren't working?
   b What things are missing?

4 07.04 **How do the guests describe the problems? Fill in the gaps.**
   a The shower _____ working. (*isn't* for singular or uncountable noun)
   b The lights _____ working. (*aren't* for plural _____)
   c _____ _____ _____ hairdryer. (*there isn't a/an* + singular noun)
   d _____ _____ _____ soap. (*there isn't any* + _____ noun)
   e _____ _____ _____ clean towels. (*there aren't any* + _____ noun)

5 Look at the conversations again.
   a What small phrase do the guests use to be more polite?
   b What words tell you that the receptionist wants to do something about the problem quickly?

6 Use the words in Exercise 1 and practise describing the problems.

Conversation 2: Making requests

A hotel receptionist often helps guests.

1 What can a receptionist help you with? Use the words in the box to complete the sentences.

> directions taxi tickets
> reservation theatre
> airport tour luggage car

He or she can . . .
   a . . . make a *reservation* in a restaurant.
   b . . . book _____ or concert _____.
   c . . . arrange a sightseeing _____.
   d . . . arrange _____ hire.
   e . . . give you _____.

f … help you get to the _____.

g … look after your _____ until you leave.

h … call you a _____.

 2 07.05 **Some guests ask a receptionist to help them. Listen to and read the conversations. Are the guests in a hotel, a B+B or a youth hostel?**

Guest 1

Guest	Hello. Could you help me, please?
Receptionist	Yes, of course, sir. What can I do for you?
Guest	Well, my family and I would like to rent a car. Could you arrange car hire for us?
Receptionist	Yes of course, sir.

Guest 2

Receptionist	Good morning. How can I help you?
Guest	Well, my flight leaves this evening and I am checking-out now. Could you look after my luggage until I leave?
Receptionist	Yes, of course, sir.

Guest 3

Guest	Good morning.
Receptionist	Good morning.
Guest	Could you help me, please?
Receptionist	Yes, of course, madam. What can I do for you?
Guest	Could you call me a taxi?
Receptionist	Yes, of course, madam.

 3 07.05 **Listen to the conversation again. Which things from Exercise 1 does the receptionist help with? Note the correct letters from Exercise 1.**

4 **Look at the conversation. What words do the guests use to ask the receptionist to help them?**

a _____ help me?

b _____ arrange car hire?

c _____ look after my luggage?

d _____ call me a taxi?

5 07.06 **Listen to the requests. Note the stress, for example,** *Could you* <u>*help*</u> *me?* **Note the intonation and practise saying the requests in the same way. It sounds polite.**

6 **Practise making more requests by saying** *Could you* **in front of the things in Exercise 1.**

Listening and speaking

LISTENING 1: MAKING A BOOKING AND ARRIVING WITH A BOOKING

1 07.07 **You will hear a conversation at the reception desk of a hotel. Listen and decide. How many different people does the receptionist talk to?**

2 07.07 **Listen again and read sentences a–f. Choose T (true) or F (false).**

a	The first person wants to book a double room.	T/F
b	He wants the room for three nights from Monday 28th April.	T/F
c	The hotel is fully booked.	T/F
d	The second person has got a family room for seven nights.	T/F
e	He is in room 508.	T/F
f	He would like a newspaper in the morning.	T/F

3 07.08 **Listen to the person making a booking on the phone. Choose the correct answers.**

a	What kind of room does he want?	single/double/family
b	For how many people?	2/4/5
c	Which day are they arriving?	Tuesday/Wednesday/Thursday
d	What date are they arriving?	1st September/3rd September/13th September
e	How many nights are they staying?	2/10/12

SPEAKING 1: MAKING A BOOKING

 1 07.08 **Listen again to the person making a hotel booking. Listen carefully to the intonation. Pause the audio and repeat.**

2 07.09 **Use the prompts to make a booking. Practise what you are going to say then play the audio and respond to what the receptionist says. Use the same audio for each booking.**

a Family room/four people/Thursday 3rd September/ten nights/your name

b Double room/two people/Tuesday 4th August/four nights/your name

c Twin-bedded room/two people/Friday 28th April/one week/your name

d Double room with a cot/two adults and a baby/Thursday 7th November/five nights/your name

Receptionist	Good evening.
You	Good evening. I'd like to …

3 07.09 **Now try to do it without looking.**

LISTENING 2: COMPLAINING ABOUT THE ROOM

1 07.10 **Listen to a telephone conversation between a guest and the receptionist. The guest is complaining about his room. How many different things does he complain about?**

2 07.10 **Listen again. Note the two things that are missing and the two things that are not working.**

3 07.10 **Listen again and answer the questions.**

a What does Mr Lopes ask the receptionist to do about the things that are missing?

b What does Mr Lopes want someone to do about the things that are not working?

c What does the hotel do to say sorry for all the problems in the room?

SPEAKING 2: COMPLAINING ABOUT THE ROOM

1 Say the words of Mr Lopes. Try to remember what goes in the gaps.

a

Mr Lopes	_____? I'm _____ _____ _____ 408. I'm _____ the television _____ _____. _____ someone sort it out?
Receptionist	Oh, I'm so sorry. I'll deal with it straight away.

b

Mr Lopes	_____? It's _____ 408 _____. I'm _____ _____ _____ _____ clean towels. _____ _____ send some up?
Receptionist	Oh, I'm so sorry. I'll send some up immediately.

c

Mr Lopes	_____? I'm _____ _____ _____ _____ _____. _____ _____ the lights _____ _____. _____ _____ _____ it out?
Receptionist	Oh, I'm so sorry. I'll see to it immediately.

d

Mr Lopes	_____? It's _____ _____. _____ _____ _____ _____ _____ toilet paper. _____ _____ _____ some up?
Receptionist	Oh I'm so sorry. I'll sort it out straight away.

e

Receptionist	Hello? Is that Mr Lopes in room 408?
Mr Lopes	_____.
Receptionist	Is everything OK now Mr Lopes?
Mr Lopes	Yes, _____ _____. Everything _____ _____.
Receptionist	Mr Lopes, I am so sorry about all the problems with your room. The hotel would like to offer your family a free lunch or dinner. Would you like to have dinner this evening?
Mr Lopes	That _____ _____ lovely, thank _____ _____ _____. What _____ _____ dinner?
Receptionist	From six o'clock. We look forward to seeing you in the dining room later.

2 07.10 **Listen again and check your answers to Exercise 1.**

3 **You are in room 34. Phone the receptionist and use the picture prompts to make complaints about your room.**

a  b  c

d   e

4 07.11 **Listen to the example answers. Did you say the same thing?**

Reading and writing

1 Look at the pictures, then the information, then the reviews. Which hotel would you choose?

Iris Hotel Manchester City (Piccadilly)  A comfortable place to stay, based in the centre of Manchester, near Manchester International airport **Facilities** paid internet, restaurant, bar, paid parking, gym, laundry service **Price** per night inc. taxes and fees £52	'This is a nice hotel. The location is perfect. Our room was spotless but very small. The bed was super comfy. You have to pay extra for the breakfast and the food wasn't great.' 'This is a lovely hotel with a brilliant central location but it is sometimes a bit noisy. The staff are very nice. You will love it here.' 'Good hotel, most of the staff were friendly. The hotel is clean and the staff are helpful. Recommended.'
The Victoria Hotel  A privately-owned hotel and bistro in a peaceful setting only minutes away by metrolink from city centre Manchester **Facilities** bar, free parking, restaurant, free Wi-Fi, laundry service **Price** per night inc. taxes and fees £99	'I really liked my stay here and I would definitely recommend this hotel. The room was lovely and big and the breakfast was very good. It took a long time to get to the centre because the metrolink wasn't working but it was lovely and peaceful in the hotel.' 'The staff were really friendly and the room was very clean but there was no soap in the bathroom. It was nice to have free Wi-Fi. Recommended.' 'The hotel had a lovely garden and it was easy to park the car. We had a really nice meal in the evening but it was quite expensive.'

2 Read the text and again and complete the table with Yes or No.

	HOTEL IRIS	THE VICTORIA HOTEL
central location	*Yes*	*No*
free internet		
free parking		
laundry service		
restaurant		
expensive		
recommended		

3 Read the reviews again. Are the sentences true (T) or false (F)?

a The breakfast at the Iris is good. T/F

b The breakfast at the Victoria Hotel is good. T/F

c The rooms at the Iris are clean. T/F

d The rooms at the Victoria Hotel are clean. T/F

e The rooms at the Iris are big. T/F

f The rooms at the Victoria Hotel are big. T/F

g The rooms at the Iris are quiet. T/F

h The rooms at the Victoria Hotel are quiet. T/F

i The staff at the Iris are friendly. T/F

j The staff at the Victoria Hotel are friendly. T/F

WRITING 1: AN EMAIL BOOKING

1 Read the email from Mr Lopes to the Sandy Bay Hotel. He wants to book a room. Answer the questions.

a What kind of room does he want?

b Does he want half board?

c How many people is the room for?

d How many nights are they staying for?

e When do they arrive?

B / U Aa ∠ ☰ ☷ ☰◄ ►☰ ☰ ☰ ☰ ∞ ☺

Dear Sir/Madam

I would like to book bed and breakfast in a family room with a sea view at The Sandy
Bay Hotel. The booking is for seven nights, from Monday 10th July to Monday 17th
July for four people, two adults and two children (aged eight and eleven).
Could you tell me if I need to send a deposit?
I look forward to hearing from you.

Best regards
Mr Jose Lopes

**2   Read Mr Lopes' email again. Now write a booking for you.
Complete the email.**

B / U Aa ∠ ☰ ☷ ☰◄ ►☰ ☰ ☰ ☰ ∞ ☺

Dear Sir/Madam

I would like to book _____ in a _____ room at the Victoria Hotel.
The booking is for_____ nights, from_____ to_____ for
_____ people.
Could you tell me if I need to send_____?
_____

Best regards
_____

Look at the hotel registration form for Mr Lopes. Complete the form with the missing information.

Hotel   Hotel

REGISTRATION CARD			
Name		Nationality	*Spanish*
Address	*Rua de la Frontera 29, Vila Real, 4306-435 9 Valegio, Spain*		
City or town	*Vila Real*	Car registration Number	*H0 23 42 81 P*
Date of arrival		Date of departure	
Method of payment	Credit card ☒	Cheque ☐	Cash ☐
Room rate	Full board ☐	Bed and breakfast ☐	Room only ☐
Signature		Room number	

Test yourself

1 Complete the table of positive and negative words to describe accommodation and staff.

😊	😠
quiet	**c**
a	dirty
b	expensive
fantastic	**d**
polite	**e**
friendly	**f**

2 Match the two halves of the sentences.

a The rooms	**1**	are unfriendly and rude.
b The staff	**2**	are clean and comfy.
c The hotel	**3**	isn't working.
d There are	**4**	no clean towels in the room.
e The lift	**5**	is excellent value.

3 Match the questions and responses.

a Have you got any vacancies?	**1**	On the ground floor.
b I'd like to book a family room.	**2**	At ten o'clock.
c How much is the deposit?	**3**	Yes, it is half board.
d Does the price include breakfast and dinner?	**4**	For how many people?
e I've got a reservation.	**5**	I am sorry, we are fully booked.
f Where is breakfast served?	**6**	£50.
g What time is check-out?	**7**	In which name?

4 Fill in the gaps.

A man arrives at a hotel. He talks to the receptionist.

a I'_____ _____ a reservation. My name's Johnson.

b _____ you _____ a room with a sea view?

c _____ the price _____ breakfast?

d What time _____ dinner?

There are a few problems with his room so he calls reception ...

   e There _____ _____ soap.
   f _____ _____ _____ towels.
   g The lights _____ _____.
   h The Wi-Fi _____ _____.

He is still not happy and says to the receptionist ...

   i _____ _____ call me a taxi?

SELF CHECK	
I CAN ...	
○	... manage simple business in hotels.
○	... complain about problems politely.
○	... make requests.

8 Sightseeing and the weather

In this unit you will learn how to:
▶ *make recommendations.*
▶ *talk about the weather.*
▶ *talk about the past.*
▶ *compare things.*

CEFR: (A2) *Can describe past experiences and personal experiences. Can make suggestions. Can exchange information and give an opinion. Can use simple descriptive language to compare objects.*

Coming to the UK on holiday

1 Read the text. Find the highlighted places on a map of the UK and a map of London.

When you arrive in the UK, you should visit a tourist information centre where you can get information and maps. Joining a guided tour (with a group and a guide) is a good idea.

London is the capital and there are a lot of famous sights such as **Buckingham Palace** and the **Tower of London**. You should take a trip on the **River Thames** and see landmarks such as **Big Ben** and the **Houses of Parliament**, the **London Eye** and **St Paul's Cathedral**. London's got a lot of museums and art galleries such as the **British Museum** and **Madame Tussaud's**. London is a great place to go shopping or see a show.

There are a lot of interesting places outside London and it's well worth going on an excursion (a short trip) to places such as **Windsor Castle**, the oldest and largest inhabited castle in the world. Or do you prefer the countryside? I'd recommend visiting **Stonehenge**, the villages of the **Cotswolds** or the mountains of **Scotland** or **Wales**. For the seaside, one of the loveliest regions is the **south-west of England**.

2 Find the tourist attractions in the text. Put them into the correct part of the table.

MUSEUM OR ART GALLERY	CHURCH OR CATHEDRAL	MONUMENT, CASTLE OR PALACE	CITY, COUNTRY OR REGION	OTHER ATTRACTION

3 Put these famous tourist destinations in the USA into the table. Add some tourist destinations in your country.

New York City · · · · · · · · · · The Grand Canyon · · · · · · · · Niagara Falls

The Statue of Liberty · · · · · · Yellowstone National Park · · The White House

The Empire State Building · · Museum of Modern Art, New York

4 Find five phrases in the text for making recommendations. Complete the sentences. Then replace the underlined words with information about your own country.

a Joining a guided tour _____ _____ _____ _____.

b You _____ take a trip <u>on the River Thames</u>.

c <u>London</u> is _____ _____ _____ _____ go shopping.

d It's _____ _____ going on an excursion to places such as <u>Windsor Castle</u>.

e I'd _____ _____ <u>Stonehenge</u>.

Vocabulary builder

VOCABULARY 1: THE WEATHER

1 Put these weather phrases in order from cold to hot.

It's chilly.

It's warm.

It's cold.

It's boiling.

It's freezing.

It's hot.

_____ _____ _____ _____

 _____ _____ _____

2 What's the weather like? Match the pictures a–g with the descriptions.

It's raining.	It's showery.	It's cloudy.	It's stormy.
It's snowing.	It's sunny.	It's windy.	

3 Match the weather phrases with the clothing. Put them in the correct part of the table.

It's really sunny.

It's quite windy.

~~It's very cold~~.

It's a really nice day.

It's absolutely freezing!

~~It's really wet~~.

It's pouring with rain.

What terrible weather!

What miserable weather!

~~What a lovely day!~~

It's a beautiful day.

What a lovely day!	*It's really wet.*	*It's very cold.*

4 Add the words from Exercises 1 and 2 to the table.

5 08.01 Listen and repeat: Note the stressed syllable. Practise saying the words.

> **LANGUAGE TIP**
>
> Talking about the weather is a good way to start a conversation.
>
> *It's a nice (lovely, beautiful) day, isn't it?*
>
> *It's terrible (miserable, awful) weather, isn't it?*

VOCABULARY 2: COMPARING

1 Which of these are true about the weather in the UK?

▶ There is a lot of rain throughout the year.

▶ It is wetter in the north and west than in the south and east.

▶ The coldest months are December and January.

▶ It is generally warmer in England than in Scotland.

▶ London is one the warmest places in the UK.

▶ The average summer temperature in the UK is 22°C.

▶ In the summer tourists can get a week of rain or a week of wonderful sunshine.

▶ The weather is often more miserable in the autumn than in the summer.

▶ The weather is the most miserable in winter – cold and wet!

▶ The weather in the summer is usually better than the weather in the winter.

▶ In the spring the weather is sometimes nicer than in the summer.

In fact, they are all true!

2 Look at the temperatures. Use *hotter* or *the hottest* to complete each sentence.

Edinburgh 20°C   Manchester 22°C   London 25°C

a It is _____ in Manchester than in Edinburgh.

b London is the _____ place.

To compare two things we use the **comparative** form of the adjective.

To say something is *more* x than all other things, we use the **superlative** form.

 3 **Make a list of the comparative adjectives and the superlative adjectives in the sentences in Exercise 1. What do you notice? Complete the rules.**

   a You usually add _____ to make the comparative form of the adjective.

   b You usually add *the* and _____ to make the superlative form.

4 **Complete the comparative or superlative forms in the gaps in the table. Look at the instructions to help you with the spelling.**

ADJECTIVE	COMPARATIVE	SUPERLATIVE
cold	*colder*	*the coldest*
warm	_____	_____
nic**e** (ends in *e*)	(+ *r*) _____	(+ *st*) _____
h**ot** (ends in vowel and consonant)	(double the consonant and + *er*) _____	(double the consonant and + *est*) _____
wet	_____	_____
sunn**y** (ends in *y*)	(change the *y* to *i* and + *er*) _____	(change the *y* to *i* and + *est*) *the sunniest*
dry	_____	_____

Two adjectives are irregular:

good	**better**	**the best**
bad	**worse**	**the worst**

If the adjective has more than two syllables, we use *more* or *the most*.

beautiful	*more beautiful*	*the most beautiful*
miserable		

5 **Find the English mistakes in these sentences. Correct the sentences.**

   a It is usually more hot in July than in January.

   b The weather in summer is usually beautifuller than the weather in winter.

182

c It is more wetter in spring than in summer.

d January is the most cold month.

e August is the most hot month.

f The better month for dry weather is July.

Which of these sentences are true about the weather in your country?

Compare the weather in your country with the weather in the UK. Use comparative words from Exercise 4.

Conversation 1: Past simple

1 08.02 **Read and listen to this conversation. Nina is telling her colleague about her holiday. Was it a good holiday?**

Susana	Hi there, Nina! You look very well!
Nina	I am very well, thanks, Susana. We came back from holiday yesterday!
Susana	Oh, I see! Where did you go?
Nina	We got a cheap flight and we went to Portugal. We had a brilliant time.
Susana	I'd love to go to Portugal. What was it like? What did you do?
Nina	We flew to Lisbon and we stayed in a lovely hotel in the centre of the city. We didn't know Lisbon so we went to the Tourist Information Centre. They gave us some good ideas about different things to do. We did so much in just one week and we were never bored! We met some really nice people, we went to the beach, we saw some amazing buildings and monuments and we visited a couple of museums. It was really interesting and I took a lot of photos.
Susana	That sounds lovely! What about the food? Was the food nice?
Nina	The food was really good. We found some nice little restaurants in the old part of the city. They were lovely but they weren't expensive. We ate out nearly every night.
Susana	Did you hire a car?
Nina	No, we didn't, we used the local transport and it was fine.

Susana	Did you spend a lot of money?
Nina	I didn't spend too much, but we bought a lot of souvenirs. I wanted to buy more but we didn't have room in our suitcase!
Susana	Was the weather good?
Nina	The weather was really good for the whole week apart from one day when it rained a bit. When we left it was a lovely day and I felt so sad saying goodbye to Lisbon. I was really tired but I didn't want to go home!
Susana	It sounds like the holiday was amazing!
Nina	It was. I even tried to learn some Portuguese and yesterday I enrolled on a Portuguese course! We are going back next year!

2 08.02 **Read and listen to the conversation again. Choose the true sentences.**

a	They had a good holiday.	They had a miserable holiday.
b	They travelled by plane.	They travelled by train.
c	They didn't do much.	They did a lot of things.
d	They were bored.	They weren't bored.
e	The food was quite cheap.	The food wasn't cheap.
f	They ate in restaurants.	They ate in the hotel.
g	They hired a car.	They didn't hire a car.
h	It poured with rain all week.	It rained once.

3 **Find the past tense of these verbs in the Conversation.**

a	come *came*	**i**	do	**q**	use
b	get	**j**	be (you, we, they)	**r**	buy
c	go	**k**	meet	**s**	want
d	have	**l**	see	**t**	rain
e	be (I, she, he, it)	**m**	visit	**u**	leave
f	fly	**n**	take	**v**	feel
g	stay	**o**	find	**w**	try
h	give	**p**	eat	**x**	enrol

Some verbs are regular – which ones?

How do we make the past tense of regular verbs?

4 Write the past tense of these other regular verbs.

a ask

b work

c arrive

d look

e enjoy

f start

5   Look at the underlined words in the sentences. They are irregular verbs in the past tense. Complete the table with the simple form of the verbs.

I didn't have a good holiday last year. I went to France but I <u>forgot</u> my driving licence, I <u>lost</u> my passport and I <u>spent</u> a lot of money. I <u>knew</u> how to speak French and they <u>told</u> me it was easy to understand people but I <u>made</u> a lot of mistakes and I was very embarrassed!

a	*forget*	forgot
b		lost
c		spent
d		knew
e		told
f		made

Look at the questions and the negative sentences from the conversation.
How do we make questions and negative sentences in the past?

QUESTIONS					NEGATIVE SENTENCES			
What	did	you	do?				know	Lisbon.
Where			go?		We	didn't	spend	too much.
	Did	you	hire	a car?			have	room.

When we make questions or negatives, we use the simple form of the verb (not the past form).

Did you went to New York? ✖ *Did you go to New York?* ✔

I didn't enjoyed it. ✖ *I didn't enjoy it.* ✔

(*what/where*) + *did* + [figure] + verb?   [figure] + + *didn't* + verb

6 How do we make questions and negatives with the verb *to be* in the past? Fill in the gaps in these sentences from the conversation.

a _____ the people friendly?

b They _____ expensive.

c _____ the weather good?

> **LANGUAGE TIP**
> To make a question with *to be*, swop the order of the subject and the verb.
> *He was here.*   *Was he here?*
> To make a negative with *to be*, add *not* or *n't* after the verb.
> *He was here.*   *He wasn't here.*

7 Look at the example sentences. Complete the questions.

EXAMPLE SENTENCES	QUESTIONS
a We came home yesterday.	When _____ home?
b We went to New York.	Where _____ go?
c We did a lot of things.	What _____ do?
d We met some nice people.	Who _____?
e We saw some monuments.	What _____?
f I took a lot of photos.	How many photos _____?
g We ate in little restaurants.	Where _____?
h We bought a lot of clothes.	What _____?
i We left yesterday.	When _____?
j I spent a lot of money.	How much _____?

8 **Cover the example sentences In Exercise 7. Write the answers to the questions.**

9 **Put the verbs in brackets into the past simple.**

We _____ (**come**) back yesterday. We _____ (**get**) a cheap flight and we _____ (**go**) to Portugal. We _____ (**have**) a brilliant time. We _____ (**fly**) to Lisbon and we _____ (**stay**) in a lovely hotel in the centre of the city. We _____ (**not know**) Lisbon so we _____ (**go**) to the Tourist Information Centre. They _____ (**give**) us some good ideas about different things to do. We _____ (**do**) so much in just one week. We _____ (**meet**) some really nice people, we _____ (**go**) to the seaside, we _____ (**see**) some amazing buildings and monuments and we _____ (**visit**) a couple of museums. I _____ (**took**) a lot of photos. We _____ (**find**) some lovely little restaurants in the old part of the city and we _____ (**eat**) out nearly every night. We _____ (**not hire**) a car. We _____ (**use**) the local transport and it _____ (**be**) fine. I _____ (**not spend**) too much money but we _____ (**buy**) a lot of souvenirs. I _____ (**want**) to buy more but we _____ (**not have**) room in our suitcase! The weather _____ (**be**) really good for the whole week apart from one day when it _____ (**rain**) a bit. When we _____ (**leave**) it was a lovely day and I _____ (**feel**) so sad saying goodbye to Lisbon. I _____ (**not want**) to go home! I _____ (**try**) to learn some Portuguese and yesterday I _____ (**enrol**) on a Portuguese course!

10 Can you remember the questions Susana asked?

 a What _____ _____ like?
 b What _____ _____ do?
 c Where _____ _____ go?
 d _____ the food nice?
 e _____ _____ _____ a car?
 f _____ _____ _____ a lot of money?
 g _____ the weather good?

11 Look at the verbs in the table. Find the regular verbs. There are five.

come	stay	visit	want	buy	see	enjoy
get	meet	have	rain	eat	fly	forget
go	do	find	leave	be	lose	spend

12 Answer Susana's questions about your last holiday. Try to use all the verbs in the table in the past.

-ED AND -ING ADJECTIVE ENDINGS

1 Look at these sentences from the conversation between Nina and Susana.

We were never bored. It was really interesting. I was really tired. The holiday was amazing.

Some adjectives have two endings, -ed or -ing. For example, *interesting* and *interested*. Complete the table with the correct spelling of the words.

-ED	-ING
	amazing
bored	
tired	
	interesting
	disappointing
	worrying
excited	
	frightening

2 Why do we say *the holiday was amazing* and not *the holiday was amazed*?

Why do we say *I was really tired* and not *I was really tiring*? Complete the words.

a We use the -ed ending to describe how a person feels. *I was bor_____.*

b We use the -ing ending to describe what a person or a thing is like. *It's really excit_____!*

3 08.03 Listen and repeat: Note the stressed syllable. Practise saying the words.

4 Which of the following sentences are correct English?
a I am very interested in sport.
b The film was very frightening.
c I was very frightened.
d My holiday was amazed.

e The weather was very disappointing.

  f There was nothing to do so I felt very boring.

5 Fill in the gaps.

   a The journey was very tir_____ so I felt very tir_____.

   b The film was amaz_____.

   c She talked about the same thing all day. She was very bor_____!

6 When was the last time you were tired? Bored? Frightened? Disappointed?

Can you think of someone or something that is interesting? Boring? Exciting?

> ### LANGUAGE TIP
> **Be careful!**
> *I am very tired* means I am very tired **now** (because of the word *am*).
> The *-ed* ending doesn't mean the past (it **isn't** the past simple).
> If you want to talk about the past, you say I **was** *very tired*.

PRONUNCIATION 1: -*ED* VERB ENDINGS

1 08.04 **Look at the three groups of regular past tense verbs. Listen to their pronunciation. Can you hear the different ways we pronounce the 'ed' ending?**

/t/	/d/	/id/
worked	tried	visited
stopped	stayed	wanted
looked	arrived	started

> ### LANGUAGE TIP
> When do we pronounce the **-*ed*** ending as /t/, when as /d/ and when as /id/?
>
> ► /t/ if you say the last sound in the verb without using your voice (for example, /k/ as**k**)
>
> ► /d/ if you say the last sound in the verb using your voice (for example /ei/ *st***ay** or /v/ *lo***ve**)
>
> ► /id/ if the last sound in the verb is /t/ or /d/ (for example /t/ *wan***t** or /d/ *deci***de**)

2 08.05 **How do you pronounce these regular verbs in the past tense? Put the verbs into the correct part of the table in Exercise 1. Listen and check your answers. Practise saying the words.**

talked	loved	needed	liked	waited	played	enjoyed
used	asked	watched	helped	studied	rained	started

PRONUNCIATION 2: IRREGULAR PAST SIMPLE VERBS

1 08.06 **Look at the verbs. Can you remember the past form? Listen and check. Practise saying the words.**

come, get, go, have, fly, give, do, meet, see, take, find, eat, buy, leave, feel, forget, lose, spend, know, tell, make

Listening and speaking

LISTENING 1: A CONVERSATION ABOUT THE WEATHER

1 08.07 **Listen to Nina and her friend from work, Peter, talking about the weather. Put 😊 for good weather or 😞 for not good weather.**

a Today

b When Anna was in Portugal

c When Anna's friends were in Portugal

d When Anna was in Dubai

e Last week

f Next week

2 08.07 **Listen to the conversation again. Cross out any words that are not true and add any extra information you hear.**

TODAY	WHEN NINA WAS IN PORTUGAL	WHEN NINA'S FRIENDS WERE IN PORTUGAL	WHEN NINA WAS IN DUBAI	LAST WEEK	NEXT WEEK
chilly windy	fantastic boiling	it rained every day cloudy	really sunny 36 degrees too hot to go out	miserable poured with rain windy chilly cloudy	good lovely sunny

LISTENING 2: A CONVERSATION ABOUT A HOLIDAY

1 08.08 **Mark is going to New York next week, and Julie went to New York last year. Listen to their conversation. Did Julie have a good holiday in New York?**

2 **Listen again to the conversation and choose the correct answers.**
   a How long is Mark in New York for?   one week/two weeks
   b Which attractions does Julie recommend?

The Statue of Liberty	Rockefeller Centre
The Chrysler Building	Times Square
The Brooklyn Bridge	The Empire State Building
The Metropolitan Museum of Art	Chinatown Coney Island
	Central Park
Museum of Modern Art	Grand Central Station

   c How long does a guided tour of the city take? three hours/four hours
   d Does Julie recommend eating in the hotel?   Yes/No
   e Did Julie recommend hiring a car?   Yes/No

SPEAKING: TALKING ABOUT A HOLIDAY

1 **Mark asked Julie a lot of questions. Complete questions a–f.**

Mark	We don't really know where to go or what to do. **a** _____ _____ _____ _____ _____?
Julie	I'd recommend going on a cruise to see the Statue of Liberty.
Mark	**b** _____ _____ _____ _____ _____ _____ _____?
Julie	Yes. Going on a guided tour is a great way to see the main sights.
Mark	**c** _____ _____ _____ _____ _____ _____ _____ _____ _____?
Julie	Most nights we went out. I think that's the best idea.
Mark	What about getting around? **d** _____ _____ _____ _____ _____ _____?
Julie	No. I didn't like the idea of driving in New York! We travelled by subway.

Mark	e _____ _____ _____ _____?
Julie	Good. It was a lot better than I expected and sunnier and warmer than London.
Mark	f _____ _____ _____ _____ _____ _____?
Julie	If you are not sure of anything, just ask! Everyone was friendly and helpful.

2 08.09 **Listen to the questions, note the stress and practise saying them.**

3 08.10 **Imagine you are Mark. Ask questions a–f and wait for the answer.**

4 08.11 **Listen to how Julie uses phrases for making recommendations. Note the stress and practise saying the phrases.**

5 08.12 **Now imagine someone is asking YOU similar questions about where YOU are from. Plan your answers to the same questions. Try to use the phrases for making recommendations. Then play the audio, listen to the question and give your answer.**

Reading and writing

READING: A TOURIST INFORMATION LEAFLET

1 **Look at the tourist information. Find two interesting places for each person.**
   a A child
   b Someone who likes art, old clothes and furniture
   c Someone who likes shopping
   d Someone who loves eating

2 **Look at the information again. Read the sentences and choose T (true) or F (false).**
   a The National Gallery closes at 7 p.m.
   b Children are usually bored at the National Gallery.
   c Saturday is the best day to visit Portobello Market.
   d You cannot go to Hyde Park at night.
   e There is late night shopping on Oxford Street on a Wednesday night.

Great free things to do in London

National Gallery (nearest tube Charing Cross)

The National Gallery is an art museum on Trafalgar Square in London.
There are over 2,300 paintings dating from 1250 to 1900. You can see paintings by Leonardo da Vinci, Michelangelo, Rembrandt, Turner, Van Gogh, Claude Monet and lots of other famous artists. It also has lots of exciting activities for children!
Open daily 10 a.m.–6 p.m. (closed 1 January and 24–6 December)

Portobello Market (nearest tube Ladbroke Grove or Notting Hill Gate)

Portobello Road market is one of the most famous markets in the world.
You can find interesting antiques, vintage clothes, food, lots of craft stalls and independent shops as well as souvenirs.
It is open every day from 8 a.m. but the busiest and most interesting day is Saturday.

Hyde Park (nearest tube Marble Arch)

Hyde Park is one of the largest parks in London and many people think it is one of the most beautiful. There is a children's play area, a lake where you can go swimming or hire a boat, and lots of cafés and places to have a snack.
Hyde Park is open from 5 a.m. until midnight all year round.

Oxford Street (nearest tube Oxford Street)

Oxford Street is the busiest shopping street in Europe. There are over 300 shops of all kinds, from very cheap to very expensive. If you are interested in fashion, this is the place to visit. Shops are generally open until 8 p.m. Monday to Saturday and later on a Thursday when they close at 9 or 10 p.m. but the best time to go is just after 9 a.m. when it is usually quiet. Later on it gets very busy.

WRITING: DESCRIBING A HOLIDAY

1 **Look quickly at this social media post from someone describing her holiday in Edinburgh. Is she having a good time?**

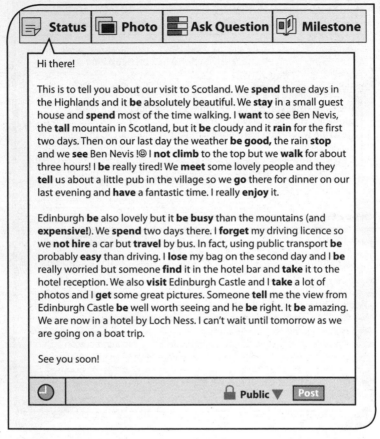

Hi there!

This is to tell you about our visit to Scotland. We **spend** three days in the Highlands and it **be** absolutely beautiful. We **stay** in a small guest house and **spend** most of the time walking. I **want** to see Ben Nevis, the **tall** mountain in Scotland, but it **be** cloudy and it **rain** for the first two days. Then on our last day the weather **be good,** the rain **stop** and we **see** Ben Nevis !☺ I **not climb** to the top but we **walk** for about three hours! I **be** really tired! We **meet** some lovely people and they **tell** us about a little pub in the village so we **go** there for dinner on our last evening and **have** a fantastic time. I really **enjoy** it.

Edinburgh **be** also lovely but it **be busy** than the mountains (and **expensive!**). We **spend** two days there. I **forget** my driving licence so we **not hire** a car but **travel** by bus. In fact, using public transport **be** probably **easy** than driving. I **lose** my bag on the second day and I **be** really worried but someone **find** it in the hotel bar and **take** it to the hotel reception. We also **visit** Edinburgh Castle and I **take** a lot of photos and I **get** some great pictures. Someone **tell** me the view from Edinburgh Castle **be** well worth seeing and he **be** right. It **be** amazing. We are now in a hotel by Loch Ness. I can't wait until tomorrow as we are going on a boat trip.

See you soon!

2 **Now correct the description, changing the highlighted words. Put the verbs into the past tense and the adjectives into the comparative or superlative form.**

3 **Think about your last holiday and write a similar description. Fill in the gaps in the sentences and answer the questions.**

📝 Status	📷 Photo	📊 Ask Question	📖 Milestone

Hi there!

This is to tell you about our visit to_____. We spent_____days in_____and it was_____.

Describe where you stayed.

Describe what you did (for example, go shopping, buy a lot of souvenirs, visit places, take photos).

Describe where you went (for example, to a museum, to the beach, on a guided tour).

Describe how you felt (for example, bored, tired, disappointed, excited).

Describe what the weather was like (for example, chilly, boiling, pouring with rain).

Describe what places were like (for example, boring, interesting, tiring, amazing, frightening, exciting).

Compare it with another place and use the comparative form of adjectives (for example, busy, noisy, beautiful, expensive, cheap, interesting, nice, small, big, quiet).

Describe a problem (use forget or lose) and describe how you felt (for example, worried, frightened).

Describe how you travelled around (for example, hire a car, use public transport, walk, travel by bus).

Describe something that was well worth doing or something someone recommended doing.

We are now in a hotel_____. I can't wait until tomorrow because we are _____.

See you soon!

🕐 　　　　　　　　　　🔒 Public ▼ 　Post

Test yourself

1 Note in the table all the words you can remember for weather.

GOOD WEATHER	BAD WEATHER

2 What is the past simple tense of these verbs?

  a go
  b have
  c enjoy
  d be (x2)
  e want
  f get
  g do
  h come
  i arrive
  j take

3 Correct the mistakes in these sentences.

  a Did you went to Scotland last year?
  b I not see him yesterday.
  c They wasn't here last week.
  d You were on holiday last week?
  e I were in New York.
  f I taked a lot of photos.
  g Did you lost your passport?
  h I am forgot my money.
  i He not buy any souvenirs.
  j I spending a lot of money.
  k We really enjoied it.
  l I tryed to learn Spanish.

4 Complete the sentences.

a London is hot but Mexico City is hot_____.

b Paris is cold but Oslo is c_____.

c A 3 star hotel is good but a 4 star hotel is _____ and a 5 star hotel is _____.

d A 2 star hotel is bad but a 1 star hotel is _____.

e A 3 star hotel is expensive but a 4 star hotel is _____.

5 Choose the correct form.

a I'd recommend **to visit/visiting** The Empire State Building.

b You should **visit/visiting** Times Square.

c It's well worth **do/doing** a guided tour.

d **Travelling/Travel** by public transport is a good idea.

e I went everywhere on foot and I was really **tiring/tired**.

f Some of the museums are a bit **boring/bored**.

g The weather was very **disappointing/disappointed**.

h I am very **exciting/excited** about visiting London.

SELF CHECK

	I CAN ...
⬤	... make recommendations.
⬤	... talk about the weather.
⬤	... talk about the past.
⬤	... compare things.

Restaurants and food

9

In this unit you will learn how to:

▶ *talk about food and drink.*
▶ *describe food and restaurants.*
▶ *manage conversations in cafés and restaurants.*

CEFR: (A1) *Can get an idea of the content of simpler informational material and short simple descriptions.* **(A2)** *Can find specific, predictable information in simple everyday material. Can understand sentences and frequently used expressions related to areas of most immediate relevance. Can order a meal.*

Food in the UK

1 **Read the text. For each topic a–c choose the correct paragraph 1–3.**

   a Snacks and sandwiches
   b International food
   c Traditional British food

   1 If you come to the UK you can eat food from all over the world. The British love eating Chinese and Thai food (like noodles, sweet and sour chicken and fried rice), Indian food (like curry), Italian food (such as pizza and pasta) and American food (for example, burgers, chips (fries) and fried chicken). We often buy this food in a restaurant but eat it at home (called a 'takeaway').

   2 Traditionally, there is a lot of meat (chicken, beef, lamb and pork) or fish, potatoes, flour, butter and eggs in British cooking. The most famous British dishes, very popular with tourists, are fish and chips, roast beef, cream teas, and a cooked breakfast (bacon, sausages and eggs). The British also love pies (meat pies and fruit pies) and steaks (usually beef), and puddings such as treacle pudding.

   3 Between meals, a lot of people have snacks: 64% of people under 20 eat something between breakfast and lunch or between lunch and dinner. The most popular snack is a packet of crisps, but biscuits and chocolate are also very common as well as fizzy drinks (like coke). A lot of snacks are not very healthy because they contain a lot of sugar or salt or fat. Another very popular food in the UK is the sandwich, particularly for lunch. People in the UK eat 11 billion sandwiches every year! The most popular sandwich is cheese, then ham and then chicken.

2 Read the text again and match the food and the picture.

a   b   c   d   e   f

a cream tea a Chinese meal
roast beef fish and chips a packet of crisps
a cheese sandwich

3 Choose your five favourite things to eat from the foods in the text.

Vocabulary builder

VOCABULARY 1: TYPES OF FOOD

1 Use the letters under the pictures to make the correct spelling of the words.

1

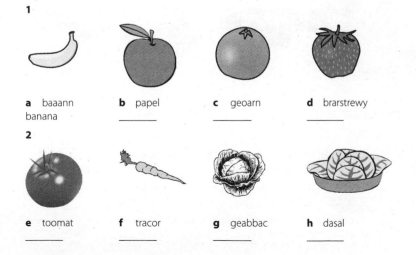

a baaann
banana

b papel
_____

c geoarn
_____

d brarstrewy
_____

2

e toomat
_____

f tracor
_____

g geabbac
_____

h dasal
_____

3

i geg

j ceeesh

k troughy

l trebut

4

m ckichen

n feeb

o blam

p shif

5

q dreab

r crie

s staap

t toopat

6

u gruas

v scuiitb

w keac

x thealococ

2 Choose the correct titles for parts 1–6 of the table.

Sugary foods Fruit Dairy foods Carbohydrates Vegetables Meat and fish

3 09.01 **Listen and repeat. Note the stressed syllable. Practise saying the food items.**

> **LANGUAGE TIP**
> Some of the food nouns are uncountable. Uncountable nouns are nouns which have no plural and we can't count them.

4 List the uncountable nouns in Exercise 1.

> **LANGUAGE TIP**
> The other foods in the table are countable. We usually add an s to make the plural,
> but not always.

 **5 Write the plural forms of the countable nouns in Exercise 1. Then
check your answers. What do you notice? Complete the rules.**

If a word ends in *y*, we change the *y* to _____ and add _____.

If a word ends in *o*, we add _____.

 6 Read the rules and fill in the gaps in the examples.

With countable nouns, we can say:

    a *a* or *an* (+ singular noun)   *I'd like _____ **apple**.*

    b a number (+ _____ noun)   *Can I have **two eggs**?*

    c *some* (+ plural noun)   *I ate _____ **carrots**.*

With uncountable nouns, we use:

    d *some* (+ uncountable noun)   *I'd like _____ **bread**. Can I have
                                            _____ **rice**?*

> **LANGUAGE TIP**
> With some nouns (countable and uncountable), we can also use the following
> phrases:

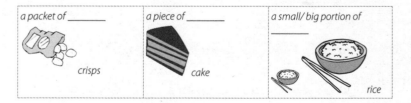

a packet of _____   *a piece of _____*   *a small/ big portion of
_____*

          crisps   cake   rice

**7 Add more food items from Exercise 1 to the correct part of
the table.**

VOCABULARY 2: DRINKS

**1 Look at these drinks and answer questions a–c. Put Yes or No in
the table.**

	a Do we usually drink it hot?	**b** Is it an alcoholic drink?	**c** Is it good for you?	**d** 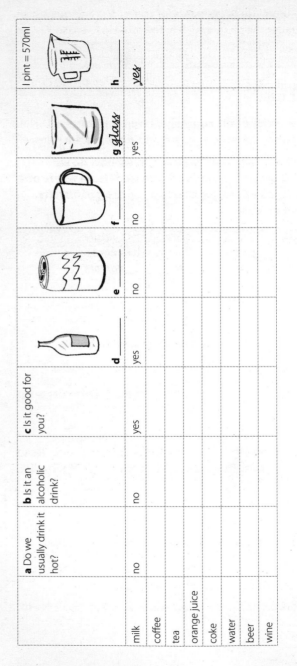	**e**	**f**	**g** glass	**h** 1 pint = 570ml
milk	no	no	yes	yes	no	no	yes	_yes_
coffee								
tea								
orange juice								
coke								
water								
beer								
wine								

202

2 With drinks, we often use these words for containers and quantities. Put the words under the pictures d–h in the table in Exercise 1.

glass bottle cup can pint (UK)/litre

3 Which words from Exercise 2 do we use with which drinks? Put Yes or No in the table.

PRONUNCIATION: CONTAINERS AND QUANTITIES

1 09.02 Listen to the containers and food and drinks and note the stressed syllable. When we say the phrase, how do we pronounce *a* and *of*? Which words are stressed? Note where one word links to the next word, for example, *a packet̮of biscuits*. Listen again and practise.

A/AN	CONTAINER	OF	FOOD OR DRINK
	packet		biscuits
a	glass	of	milk
/ə/	piece	/əv/	cake
	cup		tea

2 09.03 Listen to more phrases and practise saying them.

Conversation 1: Countable and uncountable nouns + *much/many*

1 09.04 Joanna and Peter are in a café. They are talking about food. Joanna likes to keep fit and she prefers healthy food. Read and listen to the conversation. What did Joanna eat? Make a list.

Peter	Hello Joanna! How are you?
Joanna	Hi Peter! I'm hungry!
Peter	Hungry?
Joanna	Yes, I'm trying to eat just good, healthy food and it's really difficult in a café like this with all the cakes and biscuits.
Peter	Oh, because you can't have any sugary foods?
Joanna	Exactly!
Peter	So what can you eat?

Joanna	Well, I eat a little of most things but not too much. I eat a lot of fruit.
Peter	How much fruit?
Joanna	Well, I probably have six pieces of fruit each day.
Peter	Wow! And what about things like potatoes and pasta?
Joanna	Yes, I can eat carbohydrates but not too many potatoes and only a small portion of rice or pasta with each meal.
Peter	And what about meat?
Joanna	Meat is OK but not too much red meat like beef, pork and lamb. That's fine because I like eating chicken. And fish. Fish is one of the best things you can eat. The worst things are fizzy drinks. Do you know how many grams of sugar are in the average fizzy drink?
Peter	Ten? Twenty?
Joanna	No, 35!
Peter	Wow! So no fizzy drinks then! What did you have for breakfast this morning?
Joanna	Well, I had some orange juice, a cup of coffee, some yoghurt, some strawberries, an egg and some toast.
Peter	How much toast did you have?
Joanna	Two small pieces!
Peter	Sounds good. And what about dinner last night? What did you have for dinner?
Joanna	Chicken, rice and salad.
Peter	How much rice?
Joanna	A small portion! And it was brown rice!
Peter	Very good!
Joanna	Yes, that was good but my daughter made some biscuits in the afternoon …
Peter	Oh dear … how many biscuits did you have?
Joanna	Well, only one … in the afternoon … and a couple more in the evening!
Peter	Mmmm … so are there any left?
Joanna	I hope not!

2 Look at the questions from the conversation. Put *much* or *many* in the gaps and then look at the conversation and check your answers.

   a How _____ fruit?
   b How _____ grams of sugar?
   c How _____ toast?
   d How _____ rice?
   e How _____ biscuits?

3 When do we say *how much* and when do we say *how many*? Fill in the gaps in these questions.

   a How _____ pieces of fruit?
   b How _____ apples?
   c How _____ sugar?
   d How _____ pieces of toast?
   e How _____ pasta?
   f How _____ grams of rice?

4 We can also use *much* and *many* in negative sentences and phrases. Put *much* or *many* in the gaps in the table.

WITH UNCOUNTABLE NOUNS			WITH PLURAL, COUNTABLE NOUNS	
There isn't			There aren't	
I can't have			I can't have	
He doesn't want	_____ rice.		He doesn't want	_____ potatoes.
They didn't eat			They didn't eat	
You haven't got			You haven't got	
I ate too			I ate too	
Not too			Not too	

5 There are mistakes in six of the sentences. Find the mistakes and correct them.

   a I'd like some salad but not too many, please.
   b The meal was fantastic but I ate too much pasta.
   c There isn't much wine. Let's get another bottle.
   d I'm on a diet. I can't have too much potatoes.
   e The restaurant was very good but there weren't much people there.
   f I haven't got much money. Is it expensive?
   g We haven't got many time. Is the restaurant near here?
   h I don't want much carrots, thank you. Just some cabbage.

i Can I have a banana? Yes, but only one. There aren't many.

j Would you like some coffee? Yes, thank you but not too much.

k I didn't eat much biscuits, really!

Conversation 2: Phrases to use in a restaurant

1 09.05 **Sam and Anna are having dinner in a restaurant. Put the different parts of their conversations in order and find all the phrases that the waiter says. Then listen and check your answers.**

a

What are you having?

Mmm. I'm not sure. What do you fancy?

I don't know. It all looks very good. How about a burger?

I think I'd prefer to have fish. I fancy the salmon.

Well I'm really hungry. I'm having a burger, and let's get some extra chips!

b

Excuse me ... I'm sorry but I think there is a mistake with the bill. We didn't have any wine.

I'm so sorry. I'll see to it straight away.

c

My burger was lovely. How was your salmon?

It was delicious.

Excuse me. Can I have the bill, please?

d

Here you are. I'm sorry about the mistake.

That's OK. Never mind. Is service included?

No, people can leave a tip if they think the service was good.

e

Here's the menu and the wine list. Someone will be with you shortly to take your order. Can I get you any drinks while you look at the menu?

Yes, please. Can we have a large bottle of sparkling mineral water?

f

Are you ready to order?

Yes.

What would you like?

Can I have a burger?

Certainly.

I'd like the salmon.

Good choice. Would you like any side orders or salads?

Yes, please. Can we have a green salad and some extra chips?

g

Good evening.

Good evening. We'd like a table for two, please.

Certainly. Come this way.

h

Excuse me … I'm sorry but we ordered some extra chips. We haven't got them yet.

And I ordered a green salad.

I'm so sorry. I'll sort it out immediately.

2 **Read and listen to the conversations again and answer the questions.**
   a Did they have a good meal?
   b What did they order?

3 **Read the conversation again.**
   a Find two ways of asking what someone wants.
   b Find two ways of saying what you want.
   c Find one way of making a suggestion. Can you remember another way?

d Find one way of saying what you prefer. Can you remember another way?

e Find three adjectives they use to describe food. Can you remember any other adjectives from Units 1 to 8 that you can use to describe food?

4 Fill in the gaps in the useful restaurant phrases from the conversations.

THE PHRASE	WHEN TO USE IT
a We'_____ _____ _____ _____ _____ _____, please.	when you go in to a restaurant
b What _____ you _____?	to see if someone knows what they want
c _____ I _____ + (the food). _____ _____ + (the food).	to order food
d _____ _____ + (the food)?	to find out if someone's food was good
e _____ me … I'_____ _____ but … + (the problem).	to introduce a complaint
f _____ _____ _____ the bill, _____?	to ask for the bill
g Is _____ included?	to ask about leaving a tip
h I'm sorry but _____ _____ _____ _____ _____ _____ the bill.	to say the bill is not correct
i I'm _____ _____.	to apologize
j That's _____. _____ mind.	to say the mistake is not a problem

> **LANGUAGE TIP**
> We can use too + (adjective) or not + (adjective) + enough to complain in a restaurant.

5 Fill in the gaps in the phrases in the table.

THE PROBLEM	HOW YOU SAY IT
a The table is very near the kitchen / the toilets.	The table is _____ near the kitchen. The table is _____ near the toilets.
b There is a lot of salt / sugar in the food.	This/It is _____ salty. This/It is _____ sweet.
c The food is cold.	This/It is _____ hot _____.

6 09.06 **Listen and repeat. Note the stress, for example,** _**What**_ **do you** _**fancy**_**? Mark /ə/ (remember, we often use /ə/ for** _to_ **/tə/,** _a_ **/ə/,** _can_ **/kən/,** _was_ **/wəz/,** _are_ **/ə/,** _and_ **/ən/ and for /fə/).**

Note where one word links to the next word, for example _steak and chips_**?**

Practise saying the phrases.

Listening and speaking

LISTENING 1: IN A CAFÉ

1 09.07 **Two friends are shopping and they go to a café. Listen to the conversation. Do they want a meal or a snack?**

2 09.07 **Listen to the conversation again. Read the sentences and choose T (true) or F (false).**

a   There are a lot of people in the café.   T/F
b   The café is quiet.   T/F
c   They choose a table near the window.   T/F
d   There are three different kinds of coffee with milk. T/F
e   An Americano is smaller than an espresso.   T/F
f   They think a sandwich is a good idea.   T/F
g   They both fancy something sweet.   T/F
h   They both go to buy their own food and drink.   T/F
i   They both pay for their own food and drink.   T/F

LISTENING 2: IN A RESTAURANT

1 09.08 **It's Steve's birthday. Jenny and Steve go to a restaurant. Listen to the conversation. Do they have a good meal?**

2 09.08 **Listen to the conversation again. Answer the questions.**

a   What do they usually do to celebrate Steve's birthday?
b   What food and drink do they order?
c   There are two problems with the food and one other problem. Note the problems.
d   How much do they pay for their champagne?
e   Where do Jenny and Steve have dinner?

SPEAKING: IN A RESTAURANT

1   **Imagine you are in a restaurant. Look at the menu in Reading 2: A restaurant website. Read the questions and prepare your answers.**

The waiter	Here's the menu and the wine list. Someone will be with you shortly to take your order. Can I get you any drinks while you look at the menu?
Your friend	What are you having?
The waiter	Are you ready to order?
The waiter	What would you like?
The waiter	Would you like any side orders or salads?
Your friend	How was your meal?

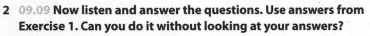

2 **09.09 Now listen and answer the questions. Use answers from Exercise 1. Can you do it without looking at your answers?**

3 **Look at the list of problems. Prepare what you say to the waiter. Use *Excuse me, I'm sorry but ...***

   a The table is very near the toilets and your glass is not clean.

   b There is a lot of salt in the salad and the soup is cold.

   c They brought red wine and you ordered white wine.

   d They didn't bring the bread.

   e The bill is not correct because they charged you for the burger twice (and you only had one).

4 **09.10 Listen to the answers to Exercise 3. Then practise. Can you explain the problems without looking at the answers?**

Reading and writing

READING 1: RESTAURANT DESCRIPTIONS AND REVIEWS

1 **Read the descriptions of places to eat and drink. Match the names to the type of place.**

   a A café/snack bar   *Coffee Time*

   b A riverside pub with a garden

   c A busy city centre pub

   d A restaurant

2 **Read the descriptions again. Match the reviews to the four places.**

   a 'A lovely place to have a fantastic lunch if you've got a lot of time and money.'

   b 'This is a great place to have a cheap cup of coffee but it's popular with students and families and can be very busy and noisy. Not very central.'

c 'It was a long walk but I really enjoyed my pint of beer and cheese sandwich in this typically British pub.'

d 'We had an excellent, traditional British dinner of roast lamb with a lovely bottle of Portuguese wine.'

The Red Lion (closed Mondays)
Peter Street
This is a fantastic city centre pub serving traditional, good quality British meals with a wide selection of wines and beers from around the world. It can get very busy at lunchtime with local office workers and it isn't cheap but the service is excellent and quick and the people are very friendly. The dining room is open at lunchtime and in the evening until 10 p.m.

The King's Head (open every day)
Greenall Road
This is a small, traditional country-style pub. There is a good selection of British beers and lagers as well as some excellent whiskeys from Ireland. You can buy some delicious and very reasonably-priced sandwiches and other bar snacks at lunchtime but there is no food available in the evenings. It is usually quiet as it is about ten minutes on foot from the city centre but it's well worth the walk! It's a lovely place to have a drink and sit by the river on a warm, summer evening.

Coffee Time (Mon–Sat until 7 p.m.)
Black Lane
Popular with mums and kids after school, and a favourite with college students, this friendly snack bar and cafe is usually very busy, especially in the afternoon. The coffee is great, you can buy a wide selection of good home-made cakes, biscuits and sandwiches as well as hot snacks and everything is very cheap. Coffee Time is a great place for a coffee or a quick snack but it is a ten-minute bus ride from the city centre, near the college.

City Deli (Mon–Sat 11 a.m. till late)
Arnott Square
This restaurant serves great European food, either eat-in or takeaway. You can buy snacks and sandwiches or a meal or just have a quiet coffee and enjoy the wonderful atmosphere of this fantastic modern space. The food is expensive and you sometimes have to wait a long time but it is very good. It's quiet. The staff are OK but not always very friendly. The City Deli is located in the city centre in the main shopping area.

3 Read the reviews again and fill in the gaps in the table.

	THE RED LION	KING'S HEAD	COFFEE TIME	THE CITY DELI
Where is it?		ten-minute walk from the city centre, by the river		in the city centre in the main shopping area
What kind of food is there?		sandwiches, bar snacks	cakes, biscuits sandwiches, hot snacks	
What's the food like?			good, home-made	

When is it open?				Monday–Saturday 11 a.m.–late
What's it like?	fantastic, busy, excellent and quick service, very friendly staff			
Is it cheap or expensive?	not cheap			

4 **Look at the situations and choose the best place. You want:**

a A traditional British meal such as a pie or fish and chips

b To try a pint of British beer

c A special celebration lunch with friends

d A takeaway lunch while shopping

e Somewhere peaceful to have a drink on a sunny afternoon

f A quiet cup of coffee after shopping

g A cheap cup of coffee and something to eat

h Dinner with friends at 9 p.m. on a Sunday

WRITING: A REVIEW

1 **Write a review of a pub, restaurant or café you know. Use the questions in the table in Reading 1: Exercise 3. Here are some sentence starters you can use. Look for more ideas in the reviews in Reading 1: Exercise 1.**

This is a …

It is a short walk from …

It serves …

The food is …

It is open …

2 **Look on TripAdvisor for more ideas and then add your review to www.tripadvisor.co.uk!**

READING 2: A RESTAURANT WEBSITE

1 **Look at the information about The National Café from a tourist information website. Can you find the café on a map of London?**

Where to eat in London …

The National Café in the National Gallery, Trafalgar Square

(Monday–Friday 8 a.m.–11 p.m., Saturday 9 a.m.–11 p.m., Sunday 9 a.m.–6 p.m.)

The National Café is a great place for breakfast, lunch, afternoon tea or dinner and well worth a visit. Its location makes it an excellent choice for anyone in central London, people who work near Trafalgar Square, shoppers and tourists visiting the Houses of Parliament or Westminster Abbey.

Why not drop in for breakfast? We are open early every weekday morning. We also make a great lunch destination and our glorious afternoon teas are hard to beat. The café menu features a selection of regional dishes and includes a children's menu. You can choose from a selection of cakes, pastries and baguettes or soups, salads and puddings as well as a range of hot and cold drinks.

'Grab and Go' is our self-service takeaway café, open from 10 a.m.–6 p.m., offering coffee, tea and a superb selection of freshly made sandwiches, salads and cakes.

If you are going to the theatre, The National Café is the perfect place for a pre-theatre dinner. We are located a short walk from many of London's theatres and offer a pre-theatre dinner menu for a special reduced price. The offer is available 5.30–7.30 p.m.

Sample pre-theatre dinner menu

Pre-Theatre Dinner Menu

Starters
Spring vegetable soup
Roast chicken, lettuce, bacon & tomato salad

Mains
Wild mushroom omelette
Beef burger with cheese and fries
Fish of the day, broccoli and buttered carrots

Side Orders
Green salad
Garlic bread

Desserts
Apple crumble, custard
Vanilla ice cream, gingerbread biscuit
Fresh melon
A selection of teas and coffees

2 Read the information again. Read the sentences and choose true (T) or false (F).

  a The National Café is in the centre of London.   T/F

  b It is open at 8.30 a.m. on a Tuesday morning.   T/F

  c There are a lot of different things to choose
     from for lunch.   T/F

  d You can buy a takeaway coffee at 9 a.m.   T/F

  e You can buy fish and chips to take away.   T/F

  f The pre-theatre menu is cheaper than the normal
     dinner menu.   T/F

  g You can have the special pre-theatre menu if you
     arrive at 5 p.m.   T/F

  h You can have breakfast on Sunday at 8.30.   T/F

3 Look at the sample menu.

  a What can a vegetarian eat?

  b What would you choose from the menu?

Test yourself

1 Put the words into the correct part of the table.

> salad   beer   pasta   a hamburger
> a cheese sandwich   chocolate
> tomatoes   potatoes   bread   an apple
> milk   a banana   roast beef   a biscuit
> a packet of crisps   fried chicken   tea
> water   rice   fish and chips

FRUIT AND VEGETABLES	SNACKS	DRINKS	CARBOHYDRATES	MEALS

2 Look at the phrases. Note the phrases we **don't** usually say.
- **a** A can of milk
- **b** A piece of egg
- **c** A cup of tea
- **d** A glass of water
- **e** A piece of fish
- **f** A piece of salad
- **g** A litre of coffee
- **h** A packet of yoghurt
- **i** A bottle of orange juice
- **j** A pint of tea
- **k** A portion of rice
- **l** A can of water

3 Write sentences for things to say in a restaurant. You want …
- **a** … a table for five people.
- **b** … to order a steak and chips.
- **c** … to know if your friend's fish is good.
- **d** … to complain because your meal is not very hot.
- **e** … the bill.
- **f** … to know if it is a good idea to leave a tip.
- **g** … to say the bill is not correct.

h … to say the mistake is not a problem.

i … to know the number of millilitres there are in a pint.

j … to know the price of an Americano coffee.

4 Complete the matching sentence. Use **too** or **enough**.

a My soup is too cold.	My soup is not _____.
b This portion _____.	This portion is not big enough.
c The service is too slow.	_____.
d _____.	The restaurant isn't cheap enough.

5 Complete the opposite sentence.

a I want a lot of potatoes.	I don't want _____.
b They can have a lot of rice.	They can't _____.
c There was a lot of wine.	There _____.
d He's got a lot of biscuits.	_____.
e I didn't eat enough pasta.	_____.

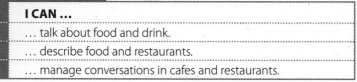

SELF CHECK

I CAN …
… talk about food and drink.
… describe food and restaurants.
… manage conversations in cafes and restaurants.

10 Shopping and money

In this unit you will learn how to:
- ▶ *manage simple business in shops.*
- ▶ *shop online.*
- ▶ *return products to shops.*

CEFR: (A1) *Can handle numbers, quantities, cost.* **(A2)** *Can locate specific information in lists and isolate the information required. Can ask about things and make simple transactions. Can give and receive information about quantities, numbers, prices. Can make simple purchases.*

Shops and shopping in the UK

1 Read the text. Choose the correct word for each picture.

chemist

newsagent

shopping centre

supermarket

department store

market

a

b

c

d

e

f

Shopping is one of the most popular free-time activities in the UK and there are a lot of different places to go shopping. Some people like going to **shopping centres** where there are a lot of different shops in one building. In a shopping centre there are probably shops you know from your country.

Some people like shopping in a **market**. You can find a lot of things in markets. Markets are usually cheaper than shops and they are usually outside. Markets often sell fruit and vegetables, but a lot of markets sell other things, such as clothes, and they are usually interesting to walk around.

There are also some very famous **department stores** in the UK, such as Selfridges or Harrods. A department store sells a lot of different things but it is just one (very big) shop.

Most people in the UK do their food shopping in supermarkets because they are sometimes quite cheap. All supermarkets sell food and drink, but most supermarkets also sell other things, including clothes, health and beauty products and books and CDs.

People also buy things from newsagent's and chemist's shops. **A newsagent** sells newspapers and magazines, cigarettes, drinks, sweets and crisps. At a **chemist's** you can get medicines but also health and beauty products, for example, shampoo, soap or suncream.

Complete the table. Put Yes, No or Sometimes for each question.

	IS IT CHEAP?	CAN YOU BUY FOOD AND DRINK?	CAN YOU BUY CLOTHES?	CAN YOU BUY HEALTH AND BEAUTY PRODUCTS?
shopping centre				
department store				
market				
supermarket				
chemist				
newsagent				

2 **What about you? Where do you buy clothes? Where do you buy food and drink?**

Vocabulary builder

VOCABULARY 1: CLOTHES AND COLOURS

1 Choose the correct phrase for each picture.

> a pair of red shoes
>
> some gold rings
>
> a pair of white trousers
>
> a silver bag
>
> ~~a pair of black jeans~~
>
> a grey coat
>
> a green dress
>
> a pink jacket
>
> a blue T-shirt
>
> a purple shirt
>
> a brown skirt
>
> a blue and yellow jumper

a

a pair of black jeans

b

_____

c

_____

d

_____

e

_____

f

_____

g

h

_____

i

j

_____

k

l

_____

 2 10.01 **Say your answers to Exercise 1. Then listen and repeat. Note the stressed syllables.**

3 **Where do we put the colour adjective? Before the noun or after the noun? Look at Exercise 1 and decide.**

VOCABULARY 2: SHOPPING ONLINE

1 **Look at the different sections of a website. You want to buy the items in pictures a–j. Which website section do you click on?**

entertainment and books

health and beauty

technology

clothing

jewellery and watches

home and garden

sport and leisure

food and wine

baby and child

flowers and gifts

2 **Describe the pictures in Exercise 1. Use *a, some,* or *a pair of.* Say the colour of the item.**

Example: a *some green soap*

VOCABULARY 3: IN THE SUPERMARKET

1 **Complete the text about shopping in a supermarket. Look at the pictures and use the words in the box.**

barcode	receipt	trolley	~~basket~~	aisle	shelf
carrier bag	change	pay for	checkout		

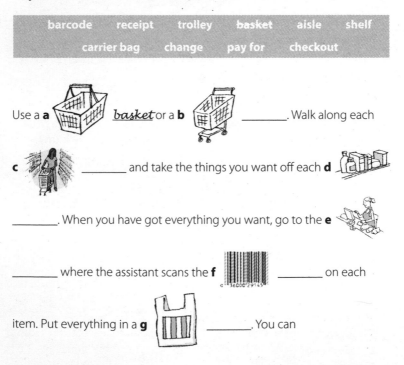

Use a **a** *basket* or a **b** _____. Walk along each

c _____ and take the things you want off each **d** _____. When you have got everything you want, go to the **e** _____ where the assistant scans the **f** _____ on each

item. Put everything in a **g** _____. You can

222

h £ _____ your shopping by credit card, by debit card or in cash. If you use cash, you sometimes get **i** _____ . The assistant then gives you a **j** _____ . If you bought something

and there is a problem, go to Customer Services.

VOCABULARY 4: MONEY

1 Choose the correct word or phrase for each picture.

cash	coins	credit card	debit card	gift card
purse	wallet	get some money out/use a cashpoint		

a | **b** | **c** | **d**

e £30 | **f** | **g** | **h** DEBIT 2432 5384 7814 4437 A.B.BYER

2 10.02 Listen and repeat. Note the stressed syllable. Practise saying the words.

3 Answer the questions for you.

    a How do you usually pay for your food shopping?
    b How do you usually pay for things in a market?
    c How do you usually pay for a holiday?
    d Have you got a purse or a wallet?
    e Have you got a lot of coins in your purse or wallet?
    f Do you like getting gift cards as presents? Why/Why not?
    g How often do you use a cashpoint to get some money out?
    h When you shop online, do you pay by debit card or credit card?

4 Cover the words and look at the pictures. Can you remember the words?

VOCABULARY 5: SPECIAL OFFERS

1 T-shirts are £12 each and you want to buy three. Look at the special offers. How much do you pay for three T-shirts? Complete the table.

SPECIAL OFFERS	HOW MUCH ARE THREE T-SHIRTS?
a Buy two get one free!	
b Buy two for £15!	
c Three for two on T-shirts!	
d Buy three save 20%!	
e 50% off when you buy two or more!	
f Save 1/3 on T-shirts!	
g Save £3 on all T-shirts!	
h Half price T-shirts (maximum two per customer)!	

2 Look at the completed table in Exercise 1. Which is the best offer?

Listening

LISTENING 1: BUYING SOUVENIRS

1 10.03 Listen to someone talking about five places to buy souvenirs in the UK. Put the places in the order she talks about them.

department stores

clothes shops

souvenir shops

supermarkets

museum shops

2 10.03 **Listen again and look at pictures a–e. Where does she recommend buying these things?**

a b c

d e

LISTENING 2: ENGLISH MONEY

1 10.04 **Listen to a student asking his teacher about English money. Read sentences a–f and decide if they are correct or incorrect. Correct the incorrect sentences.**

a There are £1, £2, £5, £10, £20 and £50 notes (paper money).
b There are 1p, 2p, 10p, 20p, 50p and £1 coins.
c £1 coins are gold and silver in colour.
d A fiver is the same as £50.
e A tenner is the same as £100.
f Five quid is the same as £5.

2 10.05 **Listen and note the prices a–l. Choose from the prices in the box.**

£4.28	£428	28p	£28	42p	£4	£10
£10.28	10p	£4.10	£41	41p		

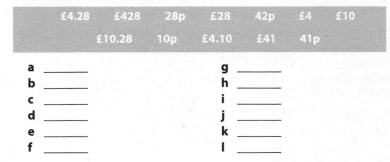

a _____ g _____
b _____ h _____
c _____ i _____
d _____ j _____
e _____ k _____
f _____ l _____

3 10.06 **Listen to the prices a–h. Are the prices more or less than £6.50? Listen and put *less* or *more*.**

a _____   e _____
b _____   f _____
c _____   g _____
d _____   h _____

4 10.06 **Listen again and note the prices.**

a _____   e _____
b _____   f _____
c _____   g _____
d _____   h _____

Conversation 1: Buying clothes

1 10.07 **Listen to eight customers in a clothes shop. Match the situations a–h with the customers 1–8.**

a She wants to pay by card.
b She wants a bigger size.
c She wants the trousers but she doesn't want the dress.
d She wants a different colour.
e She wants to try something on.
f She wants to know the price.
g She can't find trousers.
h She wants an umbrella.

2 **Now read the conversations and look at the highlighted phrases. Put the phrases in the correct part of the table.**

Customer 1
Customer   Excuse me. I'm looking for some red trousers.
Shop assistant   All our jeans and trousers are over there by the window.
Customer   Thank you.

Customer 2
Customer   Hello. Can you help me? Have you got this in a bigger size?
Shop assistant   Let me see … No, I'm sorry.
Customer   Oh. OK.

Customer 3
Customer   Excuse me. Can you help me? Have you got this in a different colour?

| Shop assistant | Yes, it comes in black, white or blue. Here you are. |
| Customer | Oh great, thanks. |

Customer 4

Customer	Excuse me. Can I try this on?
Shop assistant	Yes, of course.
Customer	Where are the fitting rooms?
Shop assistant	Just over there.
Customer	Oh, thank you

Customer 5

| Shop assistant | How were they? Any good? |
| Customer | Well, the trousers are really nice but the dress is no good. It doesn't fit. It's too big. |

Customer 6

| Customer | Sorry … How much is this T-shirt? |
| Shop assistant | It's £20. |

Customer 7

Customer	Excuse me. Have you got any umbrellas?
Shop assistant	No. I'm afraid we haven't, sorry. You could try a supermarket.
Customer	Is there a supermarket near here?
Shop assistant	Yes, it's about a five-minute walk along this street. It's on the left.

Customer 8

Shop assistant	That's £36.98.
Customer	Can I pay by gift card?
Shop assistant	Yes, that's fine. Shall I put the receipt in the bag?
Customer	Thank you.

WHEN YOU ARE …	… YOU USE THESE PHRASES
… looking for things	a _____ b _____ c _____ d _____ e _____
… trying things on	f _____ g _____ h _____
… paying for things	i _____ j _____

1 **10.08 Listen and repeat. Note the stress, for example,** *Have you got any T-shirts?* **Mark /ə/. Remember, we often use /ə/ for** *there* **/θə/,** *a* **/ə/,** *can* **/kən/,** *have* **/həv/,** *are* **/ə/ and** *for* **/fə/.**

Note where one word links to the next word, for example *try this on?* **Practise saying the phrases.**

2 **Correct the mistakes. You can listen again to the audio for Exercise 1 (10.08) to help you. Then practise saying the sentences.**
  a I looking a dress.
  b Is a bank near here?
  c Have you some trousers?
  d Is there smaller?
  e Have you got this on different colour?
  f I can try this?
  g Where the fitting rooms?
  h The shirt not fit.
  i How much this?
  j I can pay dollars?
  k Can I pay with card?

3 **What do you say?**
  a You can't find the men's clothes.
  b You want to pay in cash but you need to get some money from the bank first.
  c You found a nice jacket but it is very small.
  d You found a lovely coat but it is too big.
  e You found a blue jumper but you want it in black.
  f You want to see if the T-shirt fits.
  g You want to know the price of the shoes.
  h You want to pay in euros.
  i You want to pay with a credit card.

VOCABULARY 6: CUSTOMER SERVICES

> **LANGUAGE TIP**
> You bought something but there is a problem. You take it back to the shop and talk to Customer Services. What can you get? You can usually get a *replacement*, a *refund*, a *credit note*, or an *exchange*.

1 Match the phrases to the descriptions.

get a replacement

get a credit note

get a refund

get an exchange

a The shop gives you the money you paid.

b The shop gives you a new item, the same as the one you bought, but the new one has no problems.

c The shop gives you the same item but, for example, in a smaller size.

d The shop doesn't give you the money you paid, but you can have something else in the shop, for the same price.

Conversation 2: Taking things back to the shop

1 10.09 **Listen to four short conversations. Four customers are taking things back to a shop. The shop assistant asks them all for something. What is it?**

Customer 1

Customer Good morning. I bought this hairdryer yesterday but it isn't working.

Shop assistant Oh, I am sorry about that. Have you got the receipt?

Customer Yes, here you are.

Shop assistant Would you like a refund or a replacement?

Customer I'd like a replacement, please.

Shop assistant Have you got the card you paid with?

Customer Yes, here you are.

Customer 2

Customer Good morning. I bought this but it doesn't fit. Can I exchange it for a smaller one?

Shop assistant Have you got the receipt?

Customer Yes.

Shop assistant And the card you paid with?

Customer	Yes, here you are.
Shop assistant	Thank you. That's fine.

Customer 3

Customer	Good morning. I bought this dress but it's damaged. I'd like a refund, please.
Shop assistant	Oh yes, I see. That's no good. Have you got the receipt?
Customer	Yes, here you are.
Shop assistant	That's fine. I'm sorry about that.
Customer	That's OK. Thank you.

Customer 4

Customer	Good morning. I bought this last week but I don't want it now. Can I get a refund?
Shop assistant	Is there anything wrong with it?
Customer	No, I just changed my mind.
Shop assistant	I'm afraid we only give refunds if the item is faulty or damaged. We can do an exchange or give you a credit note.
Customer	Oh. OK. A credit note is fine. Thank you.
Shop assistant	But I'll need the receipt.
Customer	No problem – here it is.

 2 10.09 **Listen again, and read the conversations. For each customer, choose the correct words from the options below and write the correct sentence.**

There **is/isn't** a problem and she gets **a refund/a credit note/a replacement/an exchange**.

Example: Customer 1: *There is a problem and she gets a replacement.*

 3 10.09 **Why did the customers take their items back? Listen again and write a sentence for each customer.**

Example: Customer 1: *It isn't working.*

4 Fill in the gaps in part B of the table. The sentences in part A and part B have the same meaning.

A	B
a I want a new one because this one is damaged.	I'd _____ a _____, please Can I get a replacement, please?
b I want you to return the money I paid.	I'd like a refund, please. Can I _____ a _____, please?
c I'd prefer a different size/colour.	I'd _____ to exchange it for a bigger/smaller/red one, please. _____ I _____ it for a bigger/smaller/red one, please?
d I wanted it before, but now I don't want it.	I just _____ my _____.

 5 Look at the table in Exercise 4. Which phrases are polite? The ones in Part A, or the ones in Part B?

SPEAKING AND PRONUNCIATION 2

1 10.10 Listen and repeat. Note the stress, for example, *I bought this but it isn't working*. Mark /ə/. Remember, we often use /ə/ for *but* /bət/, *doesn't* /dəznt/, *a* /ə/, *can* /kən/ and *for* /fə/. Note where one word links to the next word, for example *but it isn't working*.

2 Look at the pictures. Describe the problem and say what you want.

Example: a I bought this yesterday but it's not working. I'd like a replacement, please.

a bought yesterday/not working/new one

b bought last week/damaged/money back

c bought on Monday/not fit/different one

d bought last weekend/not want/money back

e bought them yesterday/not fit/different pair

3 **Look at the questions. Choose the correct answers from the box. Use one of the answers twice.**

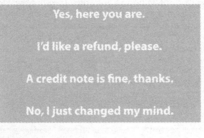

Yes, here you are.

I'd like a refund, please.

A credit note is fine, thanks.

No, I just changed my mind.

a Is there anything wrong with it?
b Have you got the receipt?
c Have you got the card you paid with?
d Would you like a refund or a replacement?
e We can do an exchange or give you a credit note. Which would you prefer?

4 **10.11 Practise the answers to Exercise 3 until you can say them without looking. Now imagine you are talking to a shop assistant. Listen and respond.**

Reading and writing

READING 1: A SOCIAL MEDIA POST

1 **Paulina is on holiday in London. Read her social media post. Is Paulina's holiday good?**

Paulina Bartosz
16 June at 21:25
Well here I am in London. The weather is fantastic and I love it here. We arrived on Thursday and I spent all day Friday, all day Saturday and all day yesterday shopping!!

On Friday I went to Portobello Market. It is a wonderful place, with lots of stalls outside on Portobello Road. There are a lot of second-hand market stalls and antiques and so many people walking about. Some things are very expensive but some things are really cheap. I bought a bag with a picture of a London bus and a couple of really nice T-shirts.

On Saturday we went to Oxford Street. The street is very long and really busy but it is great fun and there are so many things to look at and buy. There is every clothes shop you can think of on Oxford Street. I looked at a lot of different things but I didn't spend too much money. There are also a lot of souvenir shops. I love all those things with pictures of the British flag and all the famous landmarks and I bought a few things to give to my family. I also went to a couple of the large department stores on Oxford Street. Selfridges is amazing. It is so big it is possible to spend a whole day there. It's got a lot of clothes and health and beauty things, the most expensive watches and jewellery, anything you can think of really. I spent a long time in the technology department looking at all the photography equipment. I didn't have enough money to buy a new camera but I bought a really nice new case for my phone. It's my souvenir from London!

I bought quite a few things to bring back as presents. I bought a lovely tin of biscuits for my mum and some make-up for my sister – it was cheaper in the supermarket than in Selfridges. And I bought my dad a book so he can practise his English!

write a comment

You and 4 others like this

Like   🔒 Public ▼   Post

2 Read the post again. Are the sentences a–m true or false? Choose T or F.

a She spent two days shopping.   T/F

b Everything at Portobello Market is very cheap.   T/F

c She bought a bag and two T-shirts at Portobello Market.   T/F

d It takes a long time to walk along Oxford Street.   T/F

e Oxford Street isn't very interesting.   T/F

f There are a lot of fashion shops on Oxford Street.   T/F

g There aren't many souvenir shops on Oxford Street.   T/F

h She spent a lot of money on Oxford Street.	T/F
i Selfridges is on Oxford Street.	T/F
j Selfridges sells a lot of different things.	T/F
k She didn't buy anything in Selfridges.	T/F
l She bought things for her family in the supermarket.	T/F
m She bought four presents in the supermarket.	T/F

READING 2: TAKING THINGS BACK TO SHOPS

1 Read the information. What does it give advice about? Choose the two correct answers.

a Returning something if you decide you don't want it.

b Returning something you bought online.

c Returning something because it isn't working.

Guide to returning purchases in the UK
I bought something and there is a problem with it. Can I get my money back?
I bought something but now I don't want it. Can I get my money back?

A lot of shops say you can return a purchase if you change your mind or if you buy the wrong size or if you want a different colour. You can look on the shop's website or on the back of your receipt and see if they accept returns and offer an exchange, refund or credit note. Some shops say you can have a refund. Some shops say you can only exchange things for something else or have a credit note, so you can't have a refund. All shops usually ask for the receipt. There is usually a time limit and it is often 30 days.

If you buy something and it is damaged or not working, or there is something missing, you can usually return it to the shop with your receipt and get a refund or a replacement. If you haven't got a receipt, many shops give customers a credit note.

---

2 Read the advice again and fill in the gaps. Choose the correct phrase from the box.

> can usually   can sometimes
> can't usually

a If you buy something and change your mind you _____ get a refund.

b If you change your mind and you haven't got a receipt, you _____ get a refund.

c If you change your mind but you used the item you _____ get a refund.

d If you change your mind after two months you _____ get a refund.

e If you buy something and want a different colour you _____ get an exchange.

f If you buy something and it doesn't work, you _____ get a refund.

g If you buy something and it is damaged, you _____ get a refund.

3 **Read this information from a shop called Better Buys. Answer Yes or No to questions a–c.**

a You bought a handbag and it was damaged. You haven't got your receipt. Can you get a refund?

b You bought some earrings yesterday but now you don't like them. You have got your receipt. Can you get a refund?

c You bought a mobile phone case but it is too small for your phone! You have got the receipt. Can you get a replacement?

At Better Buys we want you to be happy with everything you buy

- Are you unhappy with your purchase?
- Did you change your mind?
- Is the item in its original condition?
- Have you got your receipt?

If you are not 100% satisfied you can have a replacement or your money back.

- Is there a problem with your purchase?
- Have you got your receipt?

If you buy something and it is faulty you can have a replacement or your money back.

WRITING: COMPLAINING TO A SHOP

1 Tom bought a camera from a shop but it was faulty. Read the email he sent to the shop. Did he get a replacement?

From: tom.mitcham@canadamail.com
Subject: Faulty Neonsurepix XL6870 compact digital camera
Date: 16 March
To: thegeneralmanager@camerasforyou.co.uk

Dear Sir/Madam

On **15 March** I bought a **Neonsurepix XL6870 compact digital camera and a Sundak memory card** from your shop, **Cameras For You**, at **23 High Street, Dunwich**. I enclose a copy of the receipt.
When I tried to use **the camera, it didn't work. The camera did not recognize the memory card**. I took **the camera** back to your shop the same day and asked for a **replacement**. The shop assistant told me he didn't have any more of the same **cameras** and so I asked for a refund. The assistant told me you don't give refunds, only a replacement or a credit note. I'm not happy about this! The **camera** was **faulty** when I bought it and I'd like a replacement or a refund.
Please let me know by email when I can collect a replacement or get a refund.
I look forward to hearing from you.

Best regards
Tom Mitcham

---

2 Using Tom's email in Exercise 1 to help you, write an email about problem A. Change the words in bold text. Then write an email about problem B. Can you do it without looking at Tom's email?

the item	**A**	**B**
the date	3 September	4 August
the shop	Phone Centre	BG's Homestore
the address	2, Main Street, Littleton	91, High Street, Newtown
the problem	it didn't work	it was damaged

Test yourself

1 Look at the sentences about buying things from a website. Are the sentences true or false?

   a You can buy a basketball in the Health & Beauty section.

   b You can buy a birthday card in the Flowers & Gifts section.

   c You can buy DVDs in the Entertainment & Books section.

   d You can buy a radio in the Technology section.

   e You can buy a packet of biscuits in the Clothing section.

   f You can buy a ring in the Jewellery & Watches section.

   g You can buy a towel in the Home & Garden section.

   h You can buy painkillers in the Sport & Leisure section.

   i You can buy a box of chocolates in the Food & Wine section.

   j You can buy a coat in the Baby & Child section.

2 Do we use the words when we shop online, when we shop in the supermarket or both? Put the words in the correct place in the table.

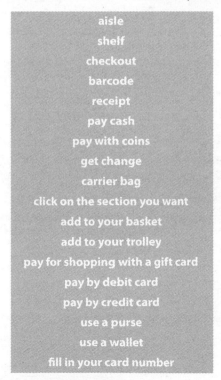

aisle

shelf

checkout

barcode

receipt

pay cash

pay with coins

get change

carrier bag

click on the section you want

add to your basket

add to your trolley

pay for shopping with a gift card

pay by debit card

pay by credit card

use a purse

use a wallet

fill in your card number

IN THE SUPERMARKET	ONLINE	BOTH

3 Choose the correct response to each question or sentence a–j.

a I'm looking for a swimming costume.　**1** OK, a credit note is fine.

b Can I try this on?　**2** Try a bigger size.

c This doesn't fit.　**3** Yes, of course you can.

d Have you got this in a size 12?　**4** It's £40.

e How much is this T-shirt?　**5** Have you got a receipt?

f Can I pay by card?　**6** Yes, the fitting rooms are over there.

g I bought this radio but it isn't working.　**7** No, I just changed my mind.

h Is there anything wrong with it?　**8** Would you like a refund or a replacement?

i I can't give you a refund without a receipt.　**9** Our sports department is on the fifth floor.

j Can I exchange this for a different colour?　**10** I'm afraid that's the smallest size we've got.

4 Books usually cost £5 each. Look at the special offers. Are the amounts correct? Correct the wrong amounts.

Example: **a** *Not correct. The correct amount is £10.*

SPECIAL OFFERS	HOW MUCH ARE THREE BOOKS?
a Buy two get one free	£15
b Three for two on books	ten quid
c 50% off when you buy two or more	£10
d Save 1/3 on books	£12
e Half price books (maximum two per customer)	a tenner

I CAN ...
... manage simple business in shops.
... manage shopping online.
... manage returning products to shops.

This Review tests the main vocabulary and language from Units 6–10. Each task has a number of points. Do all the tasks. When you finish, check your answers. How many points can you get? There is a table at the end of the test. It tells you your score.

1 Read the examples. Write five more phrases to describe good weather and five more phrases to describe bad weather.

Good weather: It's a lovely day!

Bad weather: What terrible weather!

Points: _____ /10

2 Add three more words to each group.

Example: newsagent, shopping centre, clothes shop, chemist, supermarket, souvenir shop

a red, blue, green, _____ _____ _____

b bus, train, ferry, _____ _____ _____

c a single room, _____ _____ _____

d full board, _____ _____ _____

e a jacket, a shirt, _____ _____ _____

Points: _____ /15

3 There is a mistake with the prepositions in each sentence. Correct the mistakes.

Example: I am flying for Italy.   I am flying **to** Italy.

a The train arrives to London this evening.

b We are travelling to Italy in train.

c I am going by foot.

d She is visiting to London next year.

e What time do you usually get to home?

f Where's my passport? I left it in the table.

g The taxi rank is at the left in front of the cinema.

h The bus stop isn't far. It's about two minutes of here.

i Can I pay for the tickets by cash?

j I paid with credit card.

Points: _____/10

4 Read the sentences. Fill in the gaps with the correct form of the adjective.

Example: It is usually *colder* (cold) in the north than in the south.

a A B+B is usually _____ (cheap) than a hotel but a youth hostel is usually the _____ (cheap).

b A café is usually _____ (expensive) than a takeaway but a restaurant is usually the _____ (expensive).

c In the UK, it is usually _____ (hot) in the summer than in the winter. The weather in the winter is usually _____ (bad) than the weather in the summer.

d One of the _____ (good) places to go sightseeing is London but a lot of cities are _____ (beautiful) than London.

e The _____ (quick) way to travel is by plane but it is sometimes _____ (easy) to travel by train than by plane.

Points: _____/10

5 Look at the sentences. Choose the correct word.

Example: The film was very ~~interested~~/**interesting**.

a The journey took twelve hours. It was really **tired/tiring**.

b There was nothing to do on the journey. I was very **bored/boring**.

c The hotel was old and the rooms were dirty. We were really **disappointed/disappointing**.

d I'm going on holiday tomorrow! I'm really **excited/exciting**.

e We stayed in a fantastic hotel. It was **amazed/amazing**.

Points: _____/5

6 Complete the words. Then choose the correct word, travelling or hotels.

Example: return ticket travelling/~~hotels~~

a v _ _ _ n _ _ _ s travelling/hotels

b pas _ _ _ _ t travelling/hotels

c co _ _ _ _ t _ _ le travelling/hotels

d rec _ _ _ _ _ n travelling/hotels

e b _ _ _ _ ing c_ _ d travelling/hotels

f ha_ _ lu _ _ _ ge travelling/hotels

g del _ _ _ d travelling/hotels

h cen _ _ _ l travelling/hotels

i _ n _ _ i _ _ travelling/hotels

j sec _ _ _ _ y travelling/hotels

Points: _____/10

7 Make the sentences negative.

Example: I speak Spanish. I don't speak Spanish.

a You can smoke here. You _____

b We were in London. We _____

c She went to France. She _____

d I was tired. I _____

e It's very interesting. It _____

Points: _____/5

8 Read about Isabella and Mike's weekend. Then write about it. Use the past simple form of the verbs and change the highlighted words. Start:

Her weekend was brilliant. She went to the beach with Paul and they had a great time …

My weekend _____ (be) brilliant. I _____ (go) to the seaside with Paul and **we** _____ (have) a great time.

We _____ (stay) in a small hotel with a view of the sea and when **we** _____ (arrive) the weather _____ (be) lovely. On Saturday morning, **we** _____ (spend) a little time shopping at a local market. I _____ (buy) some souvenirs and then **we** _____ (walk) down to the sea and _____ (find) a lovely little café. **We** _____ (eat) lunch outside and _____ (go) for a walk on the beach. It _____ (be) beautiful. I _____ (take) a lot of photos and **we** _____ (visit) a castle just outside the town. The tourist office _____ (say) it was the oldest castle in the area. On Sunday **we** _____ (get) up late. After a fantastic breakfast, **we** _____ (hire) two bikes and _____ (go) cycling. It was lovely but after about an hour it _____ (start) raining so **we** _____ (not go) very far. The views _____ (be) amazing!

Points: _____/30

9 Write the verbs in the past simple.

Example: like liked

a	feel	k	ask
b	fly	l	enjoy
c	forget	m	try
d	get	n	travel
e	give	o	use
f	know	p	enrol
g	leave	q	want
h	lose	r	work
i	make	s	look
j	see	t	do

Points: _____/20

10 Look at the problems. How do you complain? Use the word in brackets and write sentences.

Example: You are in a hotel room. The lights don't turn on (working).

Excuse me. I'm afraid the lights aren't working.

a   You are in a hotel room. You can't connect to the hotel Wi-Fi. (working)

b   You are in a hotel room. You've got sheets but no pillows. (there)

c   You are in a restaurant. The rice is very salty and you can't eat it. (too)

d   You are in a restaurant. The soup is cold and you want it to be hot. (enough)

e   You are in a restaurant. They put wine on your bill. You didn't have any wine. (mistake)

Points: _____/5

11 Read the answers. Use the words in brackets and write the questions.

Example: Perhaps the steak. (like) What would you like?

a   It's about 250 kilometres. (far)

b   It's £23 return. (ticket)

c   At half past ten. (train, leave)

d   Three and a half hours. (take)

e   Probably by train. (best, there)

f   Take the first left and it's on the right. (train station)

g   Sorry. We are fully booked. (vacancies)

h   Yes, the price is for full board. (dinner)

i   Ten o'clock. (check-out)

j   It's hot and sunny. (weather)

k He was at home. (where, yesterday)

l I bought a T-shirt and a couple of books. (what)

m £4.99. (much, this T-shirt)

n We only accept cash I'm afraid. (credit card)

o No, I'm afraid that's the smallest size we've got. (size)

Points: _____ /15

12 Choose the correct container. Use each word once.

> **can   piece   glass   portion**
> **packet   cup**

Example: a glass of water/wine

a a _____ of crisps/biscuits

b a _____ of toast/bread

c a _____ of coke/beer

d a _____ of rice/vegetables

e a _____ of coffee/tea

Points: _____ /5

13 Make the sentences more polite.

Example: I want to exchange it for a bigger one.
I'd like to exchange it for a bigger one.

a Where is The Rex Hotel?

b I want to make a reservation.

c The TV isn't working.

d Please book theatre tickets for me.

e We want a table for two.

f I want a steak.

g I want a refund.

h Give me the bill.

i The bill is not correct.

j Help me, please.

Points: _____ /10

14 Are the foods countable or uncountable? Choose C (countable) or U (uncountable) and complete the phrase with *some* ...

Example: orange C/U̶ some oranges

a biscuit C/U some _____

b cheese C/U some _____

c egg C/U some _____

d tomato C/U some _____

e burger C/U some _____

f butter C/U some _____

g meat C/U some _____

h broccoli C/U some _____

i bread C/U some _____

j fruit C/U some _____

Points: _____/20

15 Look at the sentences from conversations in a tourist office, a restaurant and a clothes shop. Find the mistakes. Write the sentences correctly.

Example: You should to visit the Art Gallery.
You should visit the Art Gallery.

a It's well worth to go on a guided tour.

b I'd recommend to hire a car.

c How many pasta would you like?

d I don't want much vegetables.

e Can I have a rice?

f Can I to try this on?

g I'm looking for some pair of jeans.

h Have you got this in different colour?

i It not fit.

j I can have replacement?

Points: _____/10

Check your answers in the Answer key. How many points did you get?

Look at the table. Is your score excellent, very good, quite good or not too bad? Is it a good idea to do some more practice?

140–180	Excellent – congratulations! You are ready to move on to a higher level.
100–139	Very good. You understand a lot of English and can use a lot of vocabulary and language points from Units 6–10. Note the things that are difficult and practise them again.
60–99	Quite good. You understand some English and can remember some of the vocabulary and language points from Units 6–10. It is a good idea to look at the difficult points and practise them again.
59 or less	Not too bad! English can be difficult to learn. It is a good idea to read Units 6–10 again and repeat some of the exercises for more practice. When you feel more confident, do the test again.

Answer key

KEY POINTS ABOUT ENGLISH PRONUNCIATION

1 a yes **b** yes **c** yes **d** no **e** no **f** no
3 a what **b** name **c** give **d** friendly **e** hospital
4 a 2 **b** 1 **c** 3
5 a <u>London</u> **b** Aust<u>ra</u>lia
6 a Good <u>morn</u>ing. **b** How are <u>you</u>? **c** My name's <u>Cin</u>dy.
7 a I <u>live</u> in <u>Rome</u>. **b** I <u>come</u> from <u>Spain</u>. **c** I <u>don't know</u>.
8 a no **b** yes **c** no **d** no **e** yes **f** no
9

Does she <u>speak English</u>?	<u>Yes</u>, she <u>does</u>.
Can you <u>swim</u>?	I can <u>speak French</u>.
<u>Yes</u> I <u>can</u>.	She can <u>speak Arabic</u>.
I'd <u>love to</u>.	I'm <u>going</u> to <u>France</u>.
There are <u>two chairs</u>.	<u>How</u> are <u>you</u>?
Are there any <u>more</u>?	<u>Yes</u>, there <u>are</u>.

10 The words 'name' and 'is' sound like one word. The last sound in 'name' (/m/) links to the first sound in 'is' (/ɪz/)
11 a I live͜ in China. **b** Get Started͜ in͜ English!
12 Person A
13

	FRIENDLY, POLITE, INTERESTED 😃 ⌇⌇⌇	NOT FRIENDLY, RUDE, NOT INTERESTED 😠 ___
a Hello	X	
b Good morning		X
c How are you?	X	
d Thank you		X
e Sorry	X	

| **f** Excuse me | X | |
| **g** OK | | X |

UNIT 1 HELLO! WHERE ARE YOU FROM?

US and UK cities
1 and 2 a London, **b** Manchester, **c** Glasgow, **d** Belfast, **e** Birmingham,
f Washington D.C., **g** New York, **h** Los Angeles, **i** New Orleans, **j** San Francisco

Vocabulary 1: Greetings
1 and 2 'Hello': (informal) Hi, Hi there, Hello; (formal) Good morning, Good afternoon, Good evening.
'Goodbye': (informal) Bye, Bye bye, Goodbye, See you later, See you tomorrow; (formal) Good night

Vocabulary 2: Countries
1 a Japan, **b** Canada, **c** Russia, **d** Brazil, **e** France, **f** Indonesia, **g** Australia, **h** The United States, **i** Korea, **j** Germany, **k** Egypt, **l** Spain, **m** India, **n** South Africa, **o** The UK, **p** China
2 a United Kingdom **b** Scotland **c** England **d** Wales **e** Northern Ireland
3 Japan, France, Korea, Spain, Canada, Indonesia, Germany, India, Russia, Australia, Portugal, South Africa, Brazil, The United States, Egypt, China, England, Scotland, Wales, Northern Ireland, The United Kingdom

Conversation 1: *What's your name? Where are you from?*
1 Tom
2 and 3 My name's Tom. I'm from England. My name's Anita. I'm from India.
5 and 6 What's your name? Where are you from?

Vocabulary 3: Nationalities
1

COUNTRY	NATIONALITY
India	Indian
Germany	German
France	French
The United States	American
Spain	Spanish
Brazil	Brazilian
Egypt	Egyptian

Indonesia	Indonesian
England/the UK	English
Wales/the UK	Welsh
Russia	Russian
South Africa	South African
Canada	Canadian
Japan	Japanese
Korea	Korean
Australia	Australian
China	Chinese
Portugal	Portuguese
Ireland/the UK	Irish
Scotland/the UK	Scottish
The UK	British

2 Indian, German, French, American, Spanish, Brazilian, Egyptian, Indonesian, English, Welsh, Russian, South African, Canadian, Japanese, Korean, Australian, Chinese, Portuguese, Irish, Scottish, British

Conversation 2: *I'm* + nationality
Tom I'm English; **Anita** I'm Indian.
2
My name's Tom. I'm from England. I'm English.
My name's Anita. I'm from India. I'm Indian.
3

Sarah	South Africa	South African
Yuki	Japan	Japanese
Natasha	Russia	Russian.

b My name's Nelson. I'm from Brazil. I'm Brazilian.
c My name's Sarah. I'm from South Africa. I'm South African.
d My name's Yuki. I'm from Japan. I'm Japanese.
e My name's Natasha. I'm from Russia. I'm Russian.
5

Ali	Hello!
Anita	Hi.
Ali	My name's Ali. What's your name?
Anita	My name's Anita. Where are you from?
Ali	I'm from France. I'm French. And you?

Anita	I'm from India. I'm Indian.
Nelson	Hello!
Sarah	Hi.
Nelson	My name's Nelson. What's your name?
Sarah	My name's Sarah. Where are you from?
Nelson	I'm from Brazil I'm Brazilian. And you?
Sarah	I'm from South Africa. I'm South African.

6

Yuki	Hello!
Natasha	Hi.
Yuki	My name's Yuki. What's your name?
Natasha	My name's Natasha. Where are you from?
Yuki	I'm from Japan. I'm Japanese. And you?
Natasha	I'm from Russia. I'm Russian.

Vocabulary 4: Languages
1 and 2

COUNTRY	LANGUAGE	NATIONALITY
Spain	Spanish	Spanish
Germany	German	German
Brazil	Portuguese	Brazilian
England	English	English
The United States	English	American
China	Chinese	Chinese
France	French	French
Egypt	Arabic	Egyptian
Russia	Russian	Russian
Japan	Japanese	Japanese
Korea	Korean	Korean
India	Hindi, Bengali	Indian

3 ese, (i)an

4 Top 10 languages: 1 Mandarin Chinese; 2 English; 3 Spanish; 4 Arabic; 5 Hindi; 6 Portuguese; 7 Bengali; 8 Russian; 9 Japanese; 10 German.

5 Top 10 internet languages: 1 English, 2 Chinese, 3 Spanish, 4 Japanese, 5 Portuguese, 6 German, 7 Arabic, 8 French, 9 Russian, 10 Korean.

Conversation 3: *Where do you live? Do you speak English?*

1 a Canada, **b** France, **c** English, **d** a little French, **e** French

2 Sally: I live in Canada. I speak English. I don't speak French.
Mike: I live in France. I speak a little French.

3 and 4 a I <u>live</u> in <u>Canada</u>. **b** I <u>speak English</u>. **c** I <u>speak</u> a little <u>French</u>. **d** I <u>don't</u> speak <u>Chinese.</u>

5 a I live in India. I speak Bengali. **b** I live in Egypt. I speak Arabic. **c** I live in Hong Kong. I speak Chinese.

6 a I speak Spanish. I speak a little Arabic. I don't speak English. **b** I speak Russian. I speak a little Portuguese. I don't speak Bengali. **c** I speak German. I speak a little English. I don't speak Korean.

7 and 8 <u>Where</u> do you <u>live</u>? Do you <u>speak French?</u>

Conversation 4: Polite phrases

1 First picture, Conversation 2. Second picture, Conversation 1.

2 a excuse me **b** sorry **c** sorry **d** excuse me

3 d, a, b, c, e

4 please

5 a please **b** please **c** please **d** thank you **e** thank you

6 <u>Exc</u>use me, <u>Sorry</u>, Please, <u>Thank</u> you, I don't unde<u>rstand</u>, Can you speak more <u>slowly</u>, please?

Listening: Meeting people

1a

2

Claudia	German	England	English
Rama	Indonesian	Canada	English French Indonesian

3

	FATIMA	SOFIA
I'm from Russia.		√
I'm from Pakistan.	√	
I live in Dubai.	√	
I live in London.		√

I speak Russian.	√	√
I speak English.		√
I speak Arabic.	√	

Pronunciation 1: Greeting people and sounding friendly

1 a ☺, **b** ☹, **c** ☹, **d** ☺, **e** ☺

Pronunciation 2: Letters of the alphabet, spelling

2

/ei/	/iː/	/e/	/ai/	/eu/	/uː/	/aː/
A, H	B, C	F, L	I, Y	O	Q, U	R
J, K	D, E	M, N			W	
	G, P	S, X, Z				
	T, V					

3 a America, **b** New York, **c** United Kingdom, **d** Quebec, **e** European, **f** Italian, **g** Australia, **h** New Zealand, **i** Jamaica, **j** Spanish

Pronunciation 3: Saying email and web addresses

2 a www **b** . **c** @ **d** .com **e** / **f** .org **g** .co.uk **h** -
4 www.tripadvisor.co.uk
www.visitbritain.com
www.washington.org
enquiries@visitlondon.com

Reading and writing: Personal forms

1 a children, **b** date of birth, **c** married, **d** address, **e** single
2 Female: Mrs, Miss, Ms; Male: Mr
3 All correct (✓)

Reading: A visa application form

1d

Test yourself

1

	INFORMAL	FORMAL
Hello	Hi Hi there Hello	Good morning Good afternoon Good evening
Good bye	Bye bye Bye See you later See you tomorrow	Good night Goodbye

2

Live in ...	Speak ...	Nationality
England	English	English
France	French	French
The United States	English	American
Saudi Arabia	Arabic	Saudi (Arabian)
Germany	German	German
China	Chinese	Chinese
Spain	Spanish	Spanish

3

a What's your name?	My name's (your name).
b Where are you from?	I'm from (your country). I'm (your nationality).
c Where do you live?	I live in (your city/country).
d Do you speak English?	No, I don't. Yes, I do./a little. I speak (your first language). I speak a little (language). I don't speak (language).

UNIT 2: FAMILY AND FRIENDS, JOBS AND HOME

Family life and homes in the UK
1 b **2** a **3** c **4** a **5** a

Vocabulary 1: Family, plural nouns

1

grandfather	grandmother	grandparents
father	mother	parents
son	daughter	children
brother	sister	
husband	wife	

2

	Prudence (grandmother) + Hamish (grandfather)	
	Jean (mother) + Bryan (father)	
Ruby (sister)	**ME!** + Michael (husband)	Julian (brother)
	Ellie (daughter) Paul (son)	

3 a Hamish is my grandfather and Prudence is my grandmother; **b** Jean is my mother and Bryan is my father; **c** Michael is my husband, Ruby is my sister and Julian is my brother. **d** Ellie and Paul are my children.

4 b father **c** children **d** grandmother **e** grandfather

5 and 6

1 +s	2 y → i +es	3 fe → v + es	IRREGULAR PLURALS
girl – **girls** son – sons daughter – daughters brother – brothers sister – sisters boy – boys	family – **families** baby – **babies**	wife – **wives** life – lives	child – **children** man – **men** woman – **women** person – **people**

7 <u>grand</u>mother, <u>grand</u>father, <u>grand</u>parents, <u>mo</u>ther, <u>fa</u>ther, <u>pa</u>rents, <u>sis</u>ter, <u>bro</u>ther, <u>hus</u>band, wife, son, <u>daugh</u>ter, <u>chil</u>dren, men, <u>wo</u>men, <u>peo</u>ple, girls, boys, <u>fa</u>milies, <u>ba</u>bies, <u>li</u>ves

Vocabulary 2: Jobs and workplaces

1 a4 **b**2 **c**6 **d**5 **e**1 and 7 **f**3

2 a1 **b**2 **c**4 **d**6 **e**7 **f**3 **g**5

3 I'm a <u>nurse</u>. I work in a <u>hosp</u>ital. I'm a <u>busi</u>nesswoman. I work in an <u>off</u>ice. I'm a <u>fac</u>tory worker. I work in a factory. I'm a <u>teach</u>er. I work in a <u>school</u>. I'm a <u>doctor</u>. I work in a <u>hos</u>pital. I'm a comp<u>uter</u> <u>prog</u>rammer. I work at <u>home</u>. I'm a <u>shop</u> assistant. I work in a <u>shop</u>.

Conversation 1: *Have got; a, an* and *any*

1 Bob b, David c

2 We've got three children. I've got a sister and a brother. My sister hasn't got any children. They've got two children. David's got a very good job.

3

+	–	?
I/you/we/they have got	I/you/we/they haven't got	Have I/you/we/they got?
He/she/it has got	He/she/it hasn't got	Has he/she/it got?

4 and 5

A	AN	ANY
with singular nouns	with singular nouns that begin with a, e, i, o, u	with plural or uncountable nouns in a question or a negative sentence
house job car garden house job	iPod umbrella iPhone	brothers or sisters children free time questions friends grandparents

6

Mary	Tell me about your family.
Joanna	Well, I am married and we've got three children, two girls and a boy. I've got two sisters and a brother. My brother is married but he hasn't got any children.
Mary	What about your sisters?
Joanna	My older sister hasn't got any children. She isn't married. She's got a very good job. She's an engineer. My other sister is married and they've got two children, a boy and a girl.

My, his, her, etc.

1 b His **c** Her **d** Their **e** Our

Conversation 2: Questions and answers about *he* or *she*

1 a, b

2

		Nationality	Lives in	Speaks
Amélie	wife	French	Canada	English (+ French)
Louise	sister	American	Brazil	Spanish (+ English)

3

QUESTIONS	ANSWERS
What's her name?	Her name's Amélie.
Where is she from?	She's from France. She's French.
Where does she live?	She lives in Brazil.
Does she speak English?	No, she doesn't. Yes, she does.
What about Spanish and Portuguese?	She speaks Spanish but she doesn't speak Portuguese.

4 She works in an office. She is/'s a businesswoman.

Vocabulary 3: Describing your home

1 a3 **b**6 **c**1 **d**2 **e**7 **f**4 **g**5

2 a detached house, a terraced house, a semi-detached house, a flat, a village, a town, a city

3 I live in France. I live in the north of England. I live in the south of France. I live in the east of Japan. I live in the west of Germany. I live in a town near London. I live in a village ten miles from Manchester.

Conversation 3: *Where do you live? What's it like?*

1 a

Vocabulary 4: Describing people and places

1 Places: modern; Places and people: beautiful, important, noisy, interesting; People: hard-working, funny, young

2

small	big
new (places) young (people)	old
quiet	noisy
funny	serious
boring	interesting

3 boring

5 b quite small **c** quite big **d** very big/really big

6 typical, big, small, new, modern, lovely, nice, friendly, boring, old, quiet, great, important, noisy, beautiful, young, serious, kind, funny, hard-working, very small, quite small, quite big, very big, really big

Adjectives with *to be*

1 is/'s, are

2

	+	–	?
I	I am (I'm)	I'm not	Am I?
you we they	you are (you're) we are (we're) they are (they're)	you aren't we aren't they aren't	Are you? Are we? Are they?
he she it	he is (he's) she is (she's) it is (it's)	he isn't she isn't it isn't	Is he? Is she? Is it?

3 b Is it very big? **c** Is she funny? **d** They're / They are nice and friendly. **e** I'm / I am hard-working.

4 Where do you live? What's it like?

Using *there is, there are*; articles

1 Yes

2 There are a lot of places to visit. There is a really good market in the town. There aren't any nightclubs. There isn't any Wi-Fi or mobile reception at the house.

3 a a gym, a nightclub, a post office **b** mobile reception **c** internet cafés, banks, people

4 b There is mobile reception. **c** There is a pub./There are some pubs. **d** There isn't a cinema. **e** There isn't any 3G coverage. **f** There are some banks.

g There are some hotels./There is a hotel. **h** There are a lot of supermarkets.
i There is mobile reception. **j** There isn't a post office. **k** There aren't any shops.
5 a T **b** F **c** T
6 In the town, there is a hotel and there are some pubs. There isn't a
cinema but there are a lot of internet cafés. There's a market and there are
some supermarkets.
7 In the city there are a lot of hotels and a lot of pubs. There are some
cinemas, a lot of internet cafès and a lot of banks.

Listening: Describing family and where you live
1 Michael c, Christina b
2 b M **c** L **d** C

Pronunciation: Weak forms and linking – prepositions and articles
1 There's a <u>ca</u>fé. There <u>isn't</u> a <u>shop</u>. There <u>isn't</u> any <u>Wi</u>-Fi. There <u>aren't</u> any
<u>tour</u>ists. <u>Is</u> there a ho<u>tel</u>? <u>Are</u> there any <u>shops</u>? <u>I've</u> got a <u>cat</u>. <u>He's</u> got a <u>car</u>.
She <u>has</u>n't got an <u>um</u>brella. We <u>haven't</u> got a <u>gar</u>den. Have you <u>got</u> an
<u>iPho</u>ne?

Speaking: Describing family and where you live
1

Christina	Is this your family, Michael?
Michael	Yes. It's not a very good photo but this is my wife, Helen, and our son, Harry. We've got three children. This is a good photo, my wife with Harry and next to Harry is his brother, Paul and his sister, Anna.
Christina	Is this where you live?
Michael	Yes. It's a small detached house in a very beautiful village in the south of England. It's about 50 miles from London. It's very quiet and there isn't a lot to do, but we like it. There is a shop and a pub but there aren't any restaurants or cafés and there isn't a bank or a post office. What about you, Christina? Where do you live?

Reading 1: Personal details
1 a He's from The United States. **b** (Her name's) Amélie Lafayette. **c** She's
from France. /She's French. **d** Yes, they've/they have got a daughter. Her
name is Marie. **e** He lives (in Montreal) in Canada.

Reading 2: Describing your home
1 b
2 a, b, c, d, e, g, k, m

Writing 1: A description of where you live
There is a big living room with a sofa and a TV. There are two bedrooms, one with a single bed and one with a double bed. There's a bathroom with a shower but there isn't a bath. In the kitchen, there is an oven and a fridge but there isn't a microwave. There is Wi-Fi in the flat but there isn't a phone. There isn't a garden.

Test yourself
1 b husband **c** son **d** sister
2 b women **c** children **d** brothers **e** lives **f** babies **g** people **h** families
3 a I am a nurse. I work in a hospital. **b** I am a teacher. I work in a school. **c** I am a computer programmer. I work at home. **d** My sister is a businesswoman. She works in an office. **e** My grandmother hasn't got a job. She doesn't work.
4 b Her name is Susana. **c** She lives in Spain. **d** She speaks Spanish. **e** She doesn't speak French. **f** She's from Australia. **g** She's Australian. **h** She works in a hospital. **i** She's a nurse. **j** She's very kind. **k** She's got two children. **l** She hasn't got a car.
5 b Where is he from? **c** What's his name? **d** Does he speak English? **e** Does he live in a city? **f** What's it like? **g** Has he got any children? **h** Are there any hotels in his town?
6 b It's quite small. **c** It's very boring. **d** The people are really friendly. **e** There are some beautiful old houses. **f** There's a lovely pub. **g** There aren't any shops. **h** There isn't a café. **i** There isn't any Wi-Fi in the pub.
7

PLACES	PEOPLE AND PLACES	PEOPLE
noisy, modern, new, big, typical, small	Any three of: beautiful, lovely, nice, boring, great, old, interesting, friendly, noisy, quiet, important	Any three of: serious, kind, funny, young, hard-working

UNIT 3: NUMBERS, TIMES AND DATES

Festivals, celebrations and important dates
1 and 2

A	B	C
Festival	**2016**	**2017**
Chinese New Year	8 February	28 January
Easter	25–8 March	14–17 April
Passover	22–30 April	10–18 April
Ramadan	6 June–5 July	27 May–25 June
Eid al-Adha	11 September	1 September
Jewish New Year (Rosh Hashana)	2–4 October	20–2 September
Diwali	30 October–3 November	19–23 October
Christmas	25 December	25 December

3 a 1876, **b** 1973, **c** 1943, **d** 1927, **e** 1901, **f** 1903, **g** 1885, **h** 1817

Vocabulary 1: Numbers

1 1 one, 3 three, 4 four, 5 five, 6 six, 7 seven, 9 nine, 11 eleven, 12 twelve, 13 thirteen, 15 fifteen, 16 sixteen, 17 seventeen, 18 eighteen, 19 nineteen
2 b 32, **c** 48, **d** 56, **e** 64, **f** 75, **g** 89, **h** 97, **i** 100
3 b 200, **c** 2200, **d** 220, **e** 2000, **f** 202 **g** 2,022
4 One thousand and twenty and two; One thousand and two hundred. The word *and* is pronounced /ənd/.
6 5, 11, 16, 60, 20, 33, 71, 95, 100, 206, 350, 2000, 2010, 3053, 4900

Vocabulary 2: Days, months, seasons

1 Sunday, Monday, Tuesday, Wednesday, Thursday, Friday, Saturday
2 January, February, March, April, May, June, July, August, September, October, November, December
3 a spring, **b** summer, **c** autumn (US fall), **d** winter
4 a winter, **b** summer, **c** autumn
5 Monday, Tuesday, Wednesday, Thursday, Friday, Saturday, Sunday, January, February, March, April, May, June, July, August, September, October, November, December, spring, summer, autumn, winter

Vocabulary 3: Dates

1 3/1 the third of January, 25/11 the twenty-fifth of November, 4/4 the fourth of April, 8/10 the eighth of October

2 1st first, 3rd third, 4th fourth, 5th fifth, 7th seventh, 8th eighth, 12th twelfth, 20th twentieth, 22nd twenty-second, 25th twenty-fifth, 31st thirty-first. Different ending: ones with **first**, **second**, **third**

3 first, second, third, fourth, fifth, sixth, seventh, eighth, ninth, tenth, eleventh, twelfth, thirteenth, fourteenth, fifteenth, sixteenth, seventeenth, eighteenth, nineteenth, twentieth, twenty-first, twenty-second, twenty-third, twenty-fourth, twenty-fifth, twenty-sixth, twenty-seventh, twenty-eighth, twenty-ninth, thirtieth, thirty-first

5 7/11, 12/4, 3/9, 5/6, 25/12, 1/1, 3/5, 31/7, 4/8, 21/4, 30/3, 22/9, 8/12, 2/10, 20/3

6 a the first of January, **b** the twenty-third of November, **c** the fourth of October, **d** the fifteenth of April, **e** the twenty-second of March **f** the thirty-first of July

7 23rd November b, 1st January a, 31st July f, 4th October c, 22nd March e

8 b 1789 **c** 2015 **d** 1830 **e** 1066 **f** 1642 **g** 2013 **h** 1974

9 b 1900 **c** 1702 **d** 2000 **e** 2001 **f** 2009

Conversation 1: Using numbers in questions and answers

1 b

2 b 05/04/1993 **c** 19, **d** WB14 7JR, **e** 01723 453123, **f** 07396 213431

3 b When were you born? **c** What's your address? **d** What's your postcode? **e** What's your phone number? **f** What's your mobile number?

4 a When were you born? **b** When was your daughter born? **c** I was born in 1989. **d** He was born in 1972. **e** She was born in the first year of the 21st century, in 2000!

5 a 3 (1935), **b 1** (1881), **c 3** (1869), **d 2** (19th C), **e 2** (16th C), **f 2** (15th C)

Phone numbers

1 For 0 we usually say *oh* not *zero*. For 55 we say *double five*.

3

453123	four five three one two three
01925	oh one nine two five
213431	two one three four three one
07322	oh seven three double two
664011	double six four oh double one

The time

1 Excuse me. Could you tell me what time it is, please?

2 a It's midday, **b** It's one o'clock, **c** It's eleven o'clock, **d** It's midnight. **e** It's four o'clock, **f** It's six o'clock

3 a It's ten past six, **b** It's twenty past six, **c** It's twenty-five past six, **d** It's twenty to seven, **e** It's five to seven

4 a It's six fifteen. **b** It's half past six. **c** It's quarter to seven.

5 it's <u>one</u> o'<u>clock</u>, it's <u>six</u> o'<u>clock</u>, it's <u>mid</u>night, it's el<u>even</u> o'<u>clock</u>, it's mid<u>day</u>, it's <u>quarter</u> to <u>six</u>, it's <u>six</u> fif<u>teen</u>, it's <u>half</u> past <u>six</u>, it's <u>six thir</u>ty, it's <u>quarter</u> to <u>seven</u>, it's <u>six</u> forty-<u>five</u>, it's <u>ten</u> past <u>six</u>, it's <u>twenty</u> past <u>six</u>, it's <u>six twenty</u>, it's <u>twenty</u>-five to <u>seven</u>, it's <u>six</u> thirty-<u>five</u>, it's <u>ten</u> to <u>seven</u>, it's <u>six fifty</u>

6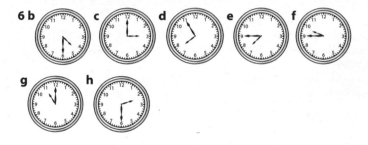

7

6 a.m.	9 a.m.	2 p.m.	4.30 p.m.	7.45 p.m.	9 p.m.	11 p.m.	2 a.m.
06.00	09.00	14.00	16.30	19.45	21.00	23.00	02.00

Conversation 2: *What time …?*

1 a, c, d

2 a It opens at 9.30, **b** It closes at 6 p.m., **c** It starts at 11 o'clock, **d** It finishes at 12.15, **e** 2.

3 and 4

the museum, the bank, the park, the post office, the art gallery, the shop	What time does it open?	**a** What time does it close?
the tour of the city, the football match, the tour of London, the film, the TV programme, the English class, the concert	**b** What time does it start?	What time does it finish?

5 b How long does it last? It lasts one hour. **c** How long does it last? It lasts three hours. **d** How long does it last? It lasts five hours.

Prepositions of time

1 a False. He was born in 1978. **b** False. He was born in the twentieth century. **e** False. His daughter was born in April. **f** False. His daughter was born in spring.

2 a F **b** T **c** T **d** F **e** F **f** F **g** F

3 and 4

IN	ON	AT
the morning, the afternoon, months, the evening, seasons, years, centuries January, autumn, 2012, 1999, March, spring, the 20th century	dates, days Monday, 21 July, Friday, 10/11/14	festivals, night, the weekend, time dinnertime, Christmas, 8 o'clock, Easter, 7.30, lunchtime

5 b in, **c** in, **d** in, **e** on, **f** in, **g** at, **h** on, **i** at, **j** at, **k** at, **l** in, **m** at

Pronunciation: Weak forms of *does, was, were, of, at, and*

1 The underlined words are all stressed and we say them with a strong voice. The highlighted words are not stressed and we say them with a weak voice. They all have the sound /ə/ does /dəz/, were /wə/, was /wəz/, of /əv/, at /ət/, and /ənd/

Listening 1: A phone conversation about meeting

1 no

2 a 07795 340431 **b** 07452 456 799 **c** 020 8563 4536. Date next Tuesday is 3(rd) April or 03/04.

Listening 2: UK and US festivals and celebrations

1 a Hallowe'en **b** Thanksgiving **c** Mother's Day **d** Christmas **e** US Independence Day **f** Easter

2 Thanksgiving, US Independence Day.

Speaking 1: Enrolling for a course

Receptionist Hello, can I help you?

Student Good morning. Can I enrol for the English conversation class?

Receptionist Yes, of course. You just need to complete the enrolment form. We can do that now if you like. What's your name?

Student	**a** Maria Costa.
Receptionist	And your date of birth? What's your date of birth?
Student	**b** The seventh of November 1992.
Receptionist	And where do you live?
Student	**c** 4, Cross Street, Millchester.
Receptionist	And what's your postcode?
Student	**d** SK38 5RR.
Receptionist	Fine. And what's your phone number?
Student	**e** 0161 458 6950.
Receptionist	And have you got a mobile number?
Student	**f** 07943 345 675.
Receptionist	Just two more questions … have you got an email address?
Student	**g** mariacosta567@gmail.sp.
Receptionist	And where are you from, what's your nationality?
Student	**h** Spanish.
Receptionist	Great. So if I could just take payment, that is all done and you can start on Monday.
Student	Lovely. Thank you very much.
Receptionist	See you Monday.

Speaking 2: In a tourist office
1

Advisor	Good morning. Can I help you?
Tourist	Yes please. I'd like some information about the City Art Gallery. **a** What time does it open?
Advisor	Ten o'clock in the morning.
Tourist	**b** And what time does it close?
Advisor	Seven thirty in the evening.
Tourist	Thank you. And there is a concert today in the Royal Albert Hall. **c** What time does it start?
Advisor	Six o'clock.
Tourist	**d** Great, and how long does it last?
Advisor	About two hours.
Tourist	**e** What time does it finish?
Advisor	About eight thirty. There's an interval of about 30 minutes.
Tourist	Thank you.

Reading: Tourist posters

1 b yes, **c** yes, **d** no **e** yes

2 b yes, **c** yes, **d** yes

3 b 12.20 p.m. **c** Saturday **d** 11.30 p.m. **e** 08712 231 231 **f** 1st January or 1/1 or New Year's Day **g** 7:30 p.m. **h** 01852 566430 **i** 7 p.m. **j** 3 p.m. **k** No. **l** 1 p.m. **m** No **n** Yes **o** 3 p.m. **p** 10 a.m. **q** 4 p.m.

Writing 2: Greeting cards

1 a Happy Birthday! **b** Happy Anniversary! **c** Merry Christmas! **d** Happy Diwali! **e** Happy Mother's Day! **f** Happy Thanksgiving! **g** Happy New Year! **h** Congratulations!

Test yourself

1

Days of the week	Months of the year	Seasons	Parts of the day
Tuesday, Monday, Wednesday, Thursday, Friday, Sunday	January, March, December, April, August, October	summer, autumn, spring, winter	morning, afternoon, night, evening

2 Five hundred, Five hundred and five, Five hundred and fifty, Five hundred and fifty-five, Five thousand, Five thousand and five, Five thousand and fifty, Five thousand and fifty-five, Five thousand five hundred, Five thousand five hundred and fifty

3 b in **c** in **d** in **e** at **f** on **g** at **h** at

4

4 a.m.	four in the morning
five o'clock in the afternoon	5 p.m.
half past four	four thirty
five twenty	twenty past five
four o'clock in the afternoon	16.00
ten to five	four fifty
4.15	quarter past four

5 4/1, 19/4, 12/6, 31/10, 2/12

6 a does **b** last **c** were **d** 's

UNIT 4: EVERYDAY LIFE, SPORTS AND FREE TIME

Popular sports in the UK and the US

1

THE UK	THE US
swimming	American football
running	baseball
cycling	basketball
football	ice hockey

3 Answers and Audioscript 04.01 b Over 50% of young people (16–25 years old) play sport once a week. **c** About 50% of people don't play any sport. **d** 46% of English people watch football on television. **e** 25% of people in the UK watch the Wimbledon final. **f** 90% of the UK population watched some of the 2012 Olympics on television.

Vocabulary 1: Sports

1 football, cricket, jogging, basketball, hockey, swimming, tennis, volleyball, baseball, rugby, golf, cycling
2 b American football
3

play	football, cricket, basketball, hockey, tennis, volleyball, baseball, rugby, golf
go	cycling, jogging, swimming

Vocabulary 2: Other leisure activities

1 a watch TV/television **b** listen to music **c** read **d** go to the cinema **e** go to a museum/an art gallery **f** go out with friends **g** go shopping **h** go on the internet **i** play computer games **j** go on social media
2 watch TV, watch television, go out with friends, listen to music, go shopping, go on the internet, go on social media, read, play computer games , go to the cinema, go to a museum, go to an art gallery

Conversation 1: *like/love/hate* + verb +*ing*

1 Sandra

2

Tom	♡	♡		✕		♡	♡	✕	✕
Sandra		♡			♡	♡	✕	♡	♡

3

♡♡♡	**e** I love going on Facebook™.
♡♡	**d** I like going on the internet.
♡	**a** I quite like reading.
✗	**c** I don't like using social media.
✗✗	**b** I hate playing computer games.

4 b I love watching TV. **c** I like going out with friends. **d** I like going on the internet. **e** I quite like listening to music. **f** I don't like going to museums or art galleries. **g** I hate playing computer games. **h** I love going out with friends and family. **i** I like watching television. **j** I quite like going to museums and art galleries. **k** I don't like reading. **l** I don't like listening to music.

Vocabulary 3: Everyday verbs and nouns
2

get up early	06.30	go to bed early	20.30
get up late	10:00	go to bed late	01.30

3 and 4

do	**have**	**get**	**go**
the <u>house</u>work	a <u>shower</u>	<u>up</u>	to <u>work</u>
the <u>clean</u>ing	<u>break</u>fast	<u>dressed</u>	<u>out</u>
the <u>shop</u>ping	<u>lunch</u>	<u>home</u>	to <u>bed</u>
the <u>wash</u>ing	<u>dinner</u>	up <u>early</u>	to bed <u>early</u>
the washing <u>up</u>		up <u>late</u>	to bed <u>late</u>

Vocabulary 4: *How often?*
1 c I go out for lunch twice a month
2 once (one time); twice (two times)
3

<u>al</u>ways	✓	✓	✓	✓
<u>usu</u>ally	✓	✓	✓	✗
<u>some</u>times	✓	✓	✗	✗
<u>ne</u>ver	✗	✗	✗	✗

4 We say 'once /ə/ month'.

5 a and **c** are correct.

6 b twice a month **c** always **d** usually **e** never **f** sometimes

Conversation 2: Present simple third person (*he* or *she*)

1 Yes

2 a F **b** T **c** T **d** F **e** F **f** F

3 and 4

I You We They	**He She verb + s**	I You We They	**He She verb + es (if the verb ends in ss, x, ch, sh or o)**	I You We They	**He She + irregular verb**
play	**a** plays	watch	**f** watches	have	**j** has
listen	**b** listens	finish	**g** finishes		
live	**c** lives	do	**h** does		
cook	**d** cooks	go	**i** goes		
get	**e** gets				

5

I/You/We/They	He/She	I/You/We/They	He/She
use	uses	say	says
live	lives	choose	chooses
speak	speaks	know	knows
read	reads	decide	decides
write	writes	see	sees
look	looks	start	starts
practise	practises	give	gives
put	puts	help	helps

6 a Do I …? / Do you …? **b** I don't … / You don't … **c** Does he …? / Does she …? **d** He doesn't … / She doesn't … **e** Does he go on Facebook™? He doesn't go on Facebook™.

7 a He doesn't watch television. **b** He doesn't listen to music. **c** Does he use the computer? **d** Does he go to work early?

8 She **gets up** early and **goes** to the gym at seven o'clock. She **has** a shower and breakfast and then she **goes** to work. She **starts** work at nine o'clock and **finishes** at five thirty. She usually **has** lunch in a café near work. She **doesn't like** staying in the office for lunch. She **does** the shopping before she **goes** home. She **gets** home at about seven o'clock and **cooks** dinner. In the evening, she usually **watches** television or **uses** the computer. She **likes** going on the internet. She **doesn't go** to bed late but she often **reads** before she **goes** to sleep.

Can/Can't
1 b drive **c** speak French **d** use a computer **e** ride a bike **f** cook **g** sing **h** swim **i** use Microsoft Excel
2 a
3 a F **b** T **c** T
4 a I can do it. **b** I can't do it.
5 a He can cook. **b** He can speak French. **c** I can't speak French. **d** He can't ride a bike. **e** Can you play the piano?
6

		?
I You He/She/It **can + verb** We They	I You He/She/It **can't + verb** We They	I you **Can** he/she/it **+ verb?** we they
I can swim. He can cook. He can speak French.	I can't speak French. He can't ride a bike.	Can you play the piano?

Listening: A journalist asks people about their everyday life
1 Person 1
2 Person 1 a F **b** F **c** F **d** T **e** F **f** T **Person 2 g** T **h** T **i** F **j** F **k** F **l** T
3 a five o'clock **b** eleven thirty **c** Friday, Saturday **d** doesn't like **e** loves using

Pronunciation 1: Third person singular verb endings

There are three ways of pronouncing the final 's', /s/, /z/ and /iz/.

2

/S/	/Z/	/IZ/
visits	plays	watches
takes	goes	finishes
gets	reads	uses
starts	stays	
	listens	

Pronunciation 2: *Can* and *can't*

1 I can speak <u>French</u> but I <u>can't</u> speak <u>Spanish</u>. Can <u>you</u>? <u>Yes</u>, I <u>can</u>, and I can speak <u>Japanese</u>. Can <u>you</u> speak <u>Japanese</u>? <u>No</u>, I <u>can't</u>.

2

affirmative	I can speak French	**/kən/**
question	Can you?	**/kən/**
negative	I can't speak Spanish	**/ka:nt/**
short answer negative	No, I can't	**/ka:nt/**
short answer affirmative	Yes, I can	**/kæn/**

Pronunciation 3: Questions in the present simple

1 <u>Where</u> does he <u>work</u>? What <u>time</u> does he <u>start</u>? <u>When</u> do you <u>go</u>? <u>What</u> do you <u>cook</u>?

2

QUESTION WORD	DO/DOES	SUBJECT	MAIN VERB
When What	do /də/	you	go? cook?
Where What time	does /dəz/	he/she	work? start?

Reading 1: A free time questionnaire

1 yes

2 a T **b** F **c** T **d** F **e** T **f** F

Reading 2: A personal profile

1 a Tracy **b** Susan **c** Margaret

2

	MARGARET	SUSAN	TRACY
♡	going out with friends, visiting family, going to museums and art galleries, going to the cinema, watching sports, listening to music, going on the internet	going to the theatre and the cinema, watching television, going out with friends to restaurants, listening to jazz music	animals, going on the internet, playing computer games, playing the guitar and listening to music
✗	playing sports, using Facebook™	cooking, using the computer, going on the internet	watching television
(figure)	use a computer speak English	speak German, English and Japanese play tennis swim	speak English
(figure)	play the piano	speak French	play the guitar very well speak French

3 Tracy

Test yourself
1 a football **b** cricket **c** jogging **d** basketball **e** hockey **f** swimming **g** tennis
h volleyball **i** baseball **j** rugby **k** golf **l** cycling
2

DO	HAVE	GET	GO
the washing	breakfast	home	jogging
the washing up	a shower	up	to work
the housework	lunch	dressed	out
the cleaning	dinner	up early	to bed
the shopping		up late	to bed early
			to bed late

3 a I have breakfast at eight o'clock. **b** I go to English classes once a week.
c I am never late. **d** I love learning English. **e** I don't like doing homework.
f I can't speak English very well. **g** My teacher helps me a lot. **h** My
girlfriend speaks English very well.

4 a She goes to the gym every day. **b** He has breakfast at eight o'clock. **c** He doesn't work in the evening. **d** I play tennis twice a week. **e** I like going to the cinema. **f** He doesn't like cooking dinner. **g** He loves watching TV. **h** She doesn't like going on Facebook™. **i** I can play the piano. **j** He can't play the guitar.

UNIT 5: GOING OUT

Popular places for going out
1 b, c, a
2 a F **b** F **c** F **d** T **e** F **f** F

Vocabulary 1: Asking how people are and responding
1 c, e, b, d, a
2 b ☺ **c** ☺ ☺ ☺ **d** ☺ **e** ☺ ☺ ☺
f ☺ ☺

3 <u>How</u> are <u>you</u>? I'm <u>very</u> <u>well</u>. I'm <u>fine</u>. I'm <u>good</u>, <u>thanks</u>. I'm <u>OK</u>. I'm <u>not bad</u>. <u>So</u>-<u>so</u>.

Vocabulary 2: Social activities
1 a go to a concert **b** go to an art gallery **c** go to someone's house for a meal **d** go to a restaurant or a café **e** go to the cinema **f** go to the theatre **g** go to the pub
2 a go to a restaurant or a café **b** go to someone's house for a meal **c** go to the cinema **d** go to the pub
3 <u>go</u> to a <u>concert</u>, <u>go</u> to an <u>art</u> gallery, <u>go</u> to someone's <u>house</u> for a <u>meal</u>, go <u>round</u> for <u>dinner</u> or <u>lunch</u>, <u>go</u> to a <u>restaurant</u>, <u>go</u> to a <u>café</u>, go <u>out</u> for a <u>meal</u>, go <u>out</u> for <u>dinner</u>, go <u>out</u> for <u>lunch</u>, go <u>out</u> for something to <u>eat</u>, <u>go</u> to the <u>cinema</u>, <u>go</u> and see a <u>film</u>, <u>go</u> to the <u>theatre</u>, <u>go</u> to the <u>pub</u>, go <u>out</u> for a <u>drink</u>
4 b He likes going out for dinner. **c** She likes going to the theatre. **d** I like going to the pub. **e** I like going to a restaurant. **f** They like going out for a meal.

Vocabulary 3: Time phrases
1 b tomorrow **c** Wednesday **d** Thursday **e** the day before yesterday **f** Saturday **g** Sunday
2 a next **b** last **c** this
3 a 1st September **b** 8th September **c** 5th September **d** 29th August **e** 10th September **f** 4th September
4 <u>today</u>, <u>yesterday</u>, the <u>day</u> before <u>yes</u>terday, to<u>morrow</u>, the <u>day</u> after to<u>morrow</u>, <u>last week</u>, <u>this week</u>, <u>next week</u>, last <u>Tues</u>day, this <u>Thurs</u>day, next <u>Wedne</u>sday

Conversation 1: Making, accepting and declining an invitation

1 a Saturday **b** go to the pub **c** go for a coffee, now

2 b to **c** go **d** Do **e** fancy **f** going **g** Do **h** to **i** go

3 a to do **b** doing **c** to do

4 *Would you like to do something?* is the most polite; the other two are quite informal.

5 Would you <u>like</u> to go to the <u>cinema</u>? Do you <u>fancy</u> going to the <u>cinema</u>? Do you <u>want</u> to go to the <u>cinema</u>?

6 a Do you fancy going *or* Do you want to go **b** Do you fancy going out *or* Do you want to go out **c** Do you want to go

7 a Would you like to go **b** Would you like to go out **c** Would you like to go

8 Saying *yes*: Yes, that would be great. Yes, I'd love to. Saying *no*: I'm really sorry, I can't. I'm afraid I can't. I can't do (Friday etc.). (Thursday etc.) is no good.

9 <u>Yes</u>, <u>that</u> would be <u>great</u>. <u>Yes</u>, I'd <u>love</u> to. I'm <u>really</u> <u>sorry</u>, I <u>can't</u>. I'm af<u>raid</u> I <u>can't</u>. I <u>can't</u> do <u>Friday</u>. I <u>can't</u> do <u>next week</u>. I <u>can't</u> do <u>eight thirty</u>. <u>Thursday</u> is no <u>good</u>. 23 <u>July</u> is no <u>good</u>. The <u>eve</u>ning is no <u>good</u>.

Vocabulary 4: Using *It's too* + adjective

1 a nice **b** quiet **c** lovely **d** beautiful **e** great **f** new **g** typical **h** noisy **i** big

2 a expensive **b** good **c** cheap **d** bad

3 It's too big.

4 b too expensive **c** too noisy **d** too small

5 bad, good, cheap, ex<u>pen</u>sive, It's <u>too big</u>. It's <u>too noisy</u>. It's <u>too</u> ex<u>pen</u>sive. It's <u>too small</u>.

Conversation 2: Making suggestions and arrangements

1 a No **b** Yes

2 b How about **c** Let's **d** Why don't we + verb? **e** How about + verb + ing or noun? **f** Let's + verb

3 That's a great/nice/lovely idea. That sounds great/nice/lovely.

4 <u>How</u> about going <u>out</u> for a <u>meal</u>? <u>How</u> about a <u>drink</u>? <u>Why</u> don't we go to the <u>cinema</u>? <u>Let's</u> watch TV. <u>No</u>, it's too <u>noisy</u>. <u>No</u>, it's too ex<u>pen</u>sive. <u>No</u>, I'm not <u>hungry</u>. <u>That's</u> a good <u>idea</u>. <u>That</u> sounds <u>lovely</u>.

5 a Let's go out for lunch. **b** Why don't we meet at the train station? **c** That sounds great. Let's meet at two o'clock. **d** Why don't we go out for a drink? **e** How about meeting in The King's Head at seven tomorrow?

6 a How about going out for lunch? **b** Let's meet at the Manchester Deli at one o'clock. **c** Why don't we go and see a film? **d** How about meeting in front of the cinema at six o'clock?

Conversation 3: Talking about preferences

1 a café

2 a T **b** F **c** F **d** T

3 a I'd prefer to, I'd rather **b** I'd prefer to **c** I'd rather

4 prefer to have, rather have

5 c They'd prefer to go in the evening.

6 I'd pre<u>fer</u> to have a <u>sand</u>wich. She'd pre<u>fer</u> to go to the <u>cin</u>ema. We'd pre<u>fer</u> to meet to<u>mor</u>row. I'd <u>rath</u>er go to a <u>café</u>. He'd <u>rath</u>er stay at <u>home</u>. They'd <u>rath</u>er go to the <u>cin</u>ema.

7 a A sandwich is OK but I'd prefer to have a meal. **b** A glass of water is OK but I'd rather have/I'd prefer to have a glass of wine. **c** A restaurant is OK but I'd rather go/I'd prefer to go to the pub. **d** A cup of coffee is OK but I'd rather have/I'd prefer to have a cup of tea. **e** The TV is OK but I'd rather go/I'd prefer to go to the cinema.

Conversation 4: Using the present continuous for plans

1 going out to the cinema

2 a Friday **b** Saturday **c** Sunday **d** because

3 a is coming, are going **b** 'm going

4 a is **b** coming **c** are **d** going **e** am/'m **f** going **g** he **h** she **i** you **j** they

5 all true

6 My <u>mum</u> is <u>com</u>ing to <u>Lon</u>don on <u>Fri</u>day. We are /ə/ <u>go</u>ing out for <u>lunch</u> on <u>Fri</u>day. I am /əm/ <u>go</u>ing to a <u>con</u>cert on <u>Thurs</u>day. She is <u>work</u>ing at <u>home</u> on <u>Tues</u>day. We are /ə/<u>go</u>ing to the <u>cin</u>ema at the <u>week</u>end. I'm <u>see</u>ing him this <u>eve</u>ning.

7 Wed – coffee with Sarah, Thurs – lunch with Suzy, Sun – cinema with Sam, because they are not planned/arranged, it is just an idea or a suggestion.

8 a On Monday I am going to the dentist. **b** On Tuesday I am working at home. **c** On Tuesday I am having lunch with mum. **d** On Friday Mum and I are going to London for the day. **e** On Saturday I am meeting Paula at the Manchester Deli. **f** On Saturday evening we are going to the cinema. **g** On Sunday I am having lunch with mum and dad at one o'clock. **h** On Sunday afternoon Paul is playing football at two o'clock.

9 a On Monday, she is going to the dentist at ten o'clock and she is having lunch with Jackie at two o'clock. **b** On Wednesday, Jackie and Linda are going to the cinema. **c** On Thursday she is going to the doctor at eleven o'clock. **d** On Saturday morning she is playing tennis at eleven o'clock. **e** On Sunday she is having lunch with her mum and dad at one o'clock.

10 a Are you doing anything on Friday? **b** Is Friday/Saturday/Sunday any

good? **c** Are you free on Friday/Saturday/Sunday? **d** How about Friday/Saturday/Sunday?
11 Are you <u>do</u>ing anything on <u>Fri</u>day? Is <u>Sa</u>turday any <u>good</u>? <u>How</u> about <u>Sun</u>day? Are you <u>free</u> on <u>Sun</u>day?

Listening 1: Planning to meet
1 a Go to a café and go to the cinema. **b** At the café at six.
2 a F **b** T **c** F **d** F **e** T **f** F **g** T **h** F **i** F **j** F

Listening 2: Plans and arrangements
1 a Go to a café and go to an art gallery **b** At the gallery at twelve
2 a good **b** Tuesday **c** Tuesday **d** on Wednesday **e** is **f** Simon **g** Simon **h** Simon

Reading: A party invitation
1a wedding **b** New Year **c** birthday
2 a T **b** T **c** F **d** F **e** T **f** T **g** F

Writing: Email invitations: Making and changing plans
1 a first email – Linda, second email – Paula **b** go for a coffee **c** 11 a.m. on Friday
2 Linda's email: I'm good, Thursday is no good, I'd rather go to, It's really nice./It's great./It's really good. Let's meet at 11 on Friday./ How about meeting at 11 on Friday? How about 11 on Friday? **Paula's email:** Would you like/Do you want/How about, Are you doing anything on Thursday or Friday?/How about Thursday or Friday?/ Is Thursday or Friday any good? How about/Let's meet at/Why don't we meet at, I'd prefer to go, How about 11?/Are you free at 11?/Are you doing anything at 11?

Test yourself
1 I'm very well, I'm fine, I'm good, thanks, I'm OK, I'm not bad, So-so.
2 b go to a pub, go out for a drink **c** go to a concert **d** go to the theatre **e** go to an art gallery **f** go to someone's house for a meal, go round for a meal/dinner/lunch/coffee **g** go to a restaurant/café, go for coffee/out for a meal/dinner/lunch/something to eat
3 a Would you like to go out for a meal? Yes, I'd love to. **b** Do you fancy going for a coffee? I'm really sorry, I can't. **c** Do you want to go to the cinema? Yes, that would be great. **d** Do you fancy a meal? I'm afraid I can't. **e** Would you like a cup of tea? I'd rather have a cup of coffee. **f** Do you fancy a sandwich? I'd prefer to have a meal. **g** How about meeting on Friday? I can't do Friday.

h Let's meet at six o'clock. Six o'clock is no good. **i** Why don't we meet at the train station? That's a great/good idea. **j** How about a café? That sounds great. **k** Let's meet in The Queen's Head. No, it's too noisy. **l** How about The Red Lion? No, it's too expensive. **m** Are you free on Tuesday? I'm sorry, I can't do Tuesday. I'm meeting my dad. **n** Are you doing anything at the weekend? My brother is visiting us. **o** How about Monday? We are going out for dinner.

4 a tomorrow **b** Sat 16th **c** Wed 13th **d** the day before yesterday **e** last Monday **f** Sat 16th **g** next Saturday **h** Tues 12th **i** Fri 15th **j** next Friday

REVIEW 1

1 So-so, good, not bad, very well, OK

2 a Tuesday, Thursday **b** yesterday, the day after tomorrow **c** July

3 b I live in England. **c** I live in a detached house. **d** It's too noisy. **e** I am really tired. **f** He works in a factory.

4 a The first of February nineteen fifty-six **b** The twenty-second of December two thousand and two **c** The fifth of January nineteen ninety-nine **d** The thirtieth of October two thousand and ten **e** The fourteenth of August two thousand and sixteen

5 (a) in **(b)** at **(c)** in **(d)** in **(e)** on **(f)** on **(g)** at **(h)** in **(i)** at **(j)** on

6 a   **b**   **c**   **d**   **e**

7 a babies **b** boys, girls **c** children **d** families **e** cities **f** people **g** countries **h** men, women

8 a www.londonlife/shopping.org.uk **b** info@visitamerica.com **c** www.englishhelp/grammar/presenttenses.co.uk

9 a W W W dot U-K-T-O-U-R-I-S-T dot org slash A-D-V-I-C-E **b** M-A-R-E-K-O dot Y-U-M-I three five seven at yahoo (Y-A-H-O-O) dot com

10 a What time does it start? **b** How long does it last? **c** When were you born? **d** How old are you? **e** When's your birthday? **f** What's your telephone number? **g** What's your postcode? **h** What's your address? **i** What's your name? **j** Where are you from? **k** Where do you live? **l** What's his name? **m** Where does he live? **n** Does he speak English? **o** Has he got any children?

11 a They don't live in New York. **b** I don't like listening to music. **c** He doesn't get up early. **d** She doesn't speak Japanese. **e** There aren't a lot of people. **f** He isn't from New Zealand. **g** It isn't very beautiful. **h** He can't speak French. **I** He hasn't got a car. **j** I haven't got a lot of free time.

12 a quite **b** really **c** too **d** There is **e** there are **f** there isn't a **g** there aren't any **h** there are a lot of **i** there isn't a **j** there isn't any

13 a fancy going **b** to go **c** a good idea **d** about **e** is no **f** I am **g** How about meeting/Are you free **h** prefer to **i** to go **j** rather **k** meet **l** is/sounds **m** too **n** don't we meet **o** perfect/great/good/OK

14 a He is **b** He works **c** He loves **d** He's got **e** he can **f** He loves his **g** he hasn't got **h** he can't **i** He goes **j** plays **k** goes **l** He cooks **m** he doesn't like **n** he goes **o** he goes **p** he has **q** he goes **r** He stays **s** he doesn't **t** he's

15 a He can speak English. **b** I can't speak Japanese. **c** He is friendly. **d** They are hard-working. **e** This is my family. I have got three children. **f** This is Anna's family. She has got two sisters. **g** She doesn't like going to the cinema. **h** She loves watching TV. **i** On Sunday I am having lunch with mum and dad. **j** On Sunday Paul is playing football at 2 o'clock.

UNIT 6: TRANSPORT AND DIRECTIONS

Travelling around the UK by public transport
1 a (plane), **g** (coach), **h** (train)
2 a Y **b** Y **c** N **d** Y **e** Y

Vocabulary 1: Travel and places
1 a plane, **b** ferry, **c** taxi, **d** car **e** bicycle **f** bus **g** coach **h** train **i** underground (tube) **j** foot
2 a airport – plane, **b** station – train, **c** taxi rank – taxi, **d** bus stop – bus, **e** coach station – coach
3 on foot
4 train, underground (in London), tube, bus, plane, coach, taxi, mini cab, car, ferry, bicycle, bike, by train, by car, on foot, airport, station, taxi rank, bus stop, coach station, ferry port

Vocabulary 2: Public transport
1 a book, single, return **b** hand luggage, hold luggage **c** check-in, security, gate **d** boarding card, **e** passport **f** delayed **g** cancelled **h** platform
2 delayed, cancelled, platform, check-in, security, gate, book a ticket, hold luggage, hand luggage, suitcase, single ticket, return ticket, passport, boarding card, arrive

Vocabulary 3: Prepositions of place and movement
2 a under **b** next to **c** behind **d** in **e** in front of **f** on **g** above
3 in, on, next to, in front of, behind, above, under
4 a in **b** next to **c** behind **d** in front of **e** on, above **f** under

5 a No (arrives in Liverpool) **b** Yes, yes **c** No (leave Manchester) **d** Yes **e** No (going home) **f** Yes **g** Yes **h** No (visiting London)
6 a in **b** to **c** – **d** to **e** to **f** to **g** –

Pronunciation 1: Sentence stress, /ə/ for *a* and *an* and linking

1 a Can I have a /ə/ return ticket, please? **b** I'd like to book a /ə/ flight. **c** The flight is cancelled. **d** The train is delayed. **e** Which platform is it? **f** How much is a /ə/ first class ticket? **g** It's above the seat. **h** I've got a /ə/ single ticket. **i** Quick! The flight is boarding! **j** The train arrives in London at ten o'clock.

Pronunciation 2: The word *to*

1 a /tə/ **b** /tu:/
2 /tə/ to London, to Manchester, to New York, to San Francisco, to Dallas; / tu:/ to East London, to England, to America, to Oxford, to Edinburgh

Conversation 1: Questions about travel

1 a Edinburgh (Scotland) **b** (about) 400 miles
2 a eight hours, very expensive **b** by coach, very cheap **c** by train, about five hours **d** by plane, can be very cheap if you book in advance
3 a How far is it? **b** How much is a ticket? **c** What time does it leave?
d What time does it arrive? **e** How long does it take? **f** What's the best way to get there?
4 How far is it? How much is a ticket? What time does it leave? What time does it arrive? How long does it take? What's the best way to get there?
5 a How much is a ticket? **b** How long does it take? **c** What's the best way to get there? **d** How far is it? **e** How long does it take? **f** What time does it leave? **g** What time does it arrive? **h** How much is a ticket?

Conversation 2: Using *can/can't* for permission

1 a in a train **b** No
2 and 3

A	B
You can't	smoke
You can't	use a phone
You can't	sit in a reserved seat
You can't	put bags on the floor
You can't	travel without a ticket

4 a You can't park here. **b** You can't drink alcohol here. **c** You can't take photographs here. **d** You can't smoke here. **e** You can't use a mobile (phone) here. **f** You can't run here. **g** You can't eat or drink here. **h** You can't swim here.
5 a Can **b** Can **c** can **d** Can

6 a Can I park here? **b** Can I use this ticket? **c** Can I smoke here? **d** Can I
pay cash? **e** Can I pay by cheque? **f** Can I pay by credit card?

Asking for and giving directions
1 b
2 C
3 Tourist 1 the post office D, the shopping centre B; **Tourist 2** the taxi
rank F, the bus station E; **Tourist 3** the Station Hotel A
4 b the Station Hotel **c** the post office **d** the bus station
5 Could you <u>tell</u> me where the <u>taxi</u> rank <u>is</u>? Take the <u>first</u> <u>left</u>, take the <u>second</u>
<u>right</u>. Go <u>along</u> the <u>road</u> for about <u>100 metres</u>. It'<u>s on</u> your <u>right</u>. It'<u>s</u> about
<u>five</u> <u>minutes</u> from <u>here</u>. Could you <u>tell</u> me where the <u>bus</u> station <u>is</u>? It'<u>s not</u>
<u>far</u>. It'<u>s on</u> the <u>left</u> <u>in</u> <u>front</u> of the <u>taxi</u> rank.
6 a Go, for about, take, second right, right, next to **b** Take, first, the second
right, Go along, for, It's, the, about, minutes from here

Listening 1: Airport announcements
1 No
2 a F **b** F **c** T **d** T **e** F **f** T **g** T **h** F

Listening 2: Public transport in London
1 bus and underground (tube)
2 a bus **b** underground **c** tube **d** tube **e** can't **f** bus **g** can **h** can't **i** ticket
j bus **k** travel card **l** can **m** bus **n** tube

Reading 1: A web page about Heathrow Airport
1 a, b, d, e, g, h, j
3 a T **b** T **c** T **d** T **e** T **f** F **g** F **h** T **i** F **j** T

Writing: Directions in an email
1 b
2 a no **b** train **c** 30 minutes **d** yes **e** about £20 **f** yes **g** on foot **h** no **i** yes
j four o'clock **k** five o'clock **l** about an hour

Test yourself
1 Planes: check-in, hold luggage, security, boarding card, airport,
passport, hand luggage; **Planes and trains**: a single ticket, a return ticket,
delayed, cancelled; **Trains**: underground, station, platform

2

3 a tell me where, is **b** Take the **c** on the **d** along, for **e** is it **f** not far **g** from **h** much is a **i** time does **j** does, take **k** way **l** in **m** to **n** go
4 a You can't smoke here. **b** You can't sit here. **c** Can I pay by credit card? **d** You can take a drink into the theatre.

UNIT 7: HOTELS AND ACCOMMODATION

Types of accommodation
1 b youth hostel **c** budget hotel **d** full English breakfast **e** B+B **f** continental breakfast
2 £ youth hostel, ££ B+B or budget hotel, £££ expensive hotel; no meals = room only, one meal = bed and breakfast, two meals = half board, three meals = full board.

Vocabulary 1: Services and facilities
b 5 **c** 3 **d** 4 **e** 6 **f** 1 **g** 7 **h** 2

Vocabulary 2: Describing accommodation
1 Positive: hotel and rooms: clean, comfortable, excellent value, central, great; staff: helpful, great; **Negative**: hotel and rooms: basic
2 a expensive **b** dirty **c** noisy **d** unfriendly **e** rude **f** awful
3 clean, comfortable, excellent value, helpful, central, great, amazing, good, brilliant, fantastic, excellent, comfy, quiet, awful, expensive, dirty, basic, noisy, rude, polite, friendly, unfriendly

Vocabulary 3: Describing rooms
1 a a cot **b** a double room **c** an en suite room **d** a room with a view **e** a single room **f** a family room **g** a twin-bedded room
2 a single room, a double room, a twin-bedded room, a family room, a cot, an en suite room, a room with a view

Vocabulary 4: Booking accommodation
1 When you make a booking: b, c, d, g, h, j, k, l, m; **When you arrive at the hotel:** e, f, i,

3 b Do I need to /tə/ pay a /ə/ de<u>pos</u>it? **c** What <u>time</u> is <u>check</u>-out?
d Does /dəz/ the <u>price</u> include <u>break</u>fast? **e** <u>Where</u> is <u>break</u>fast served?
f I've got a /ə/ reservation. **g** From /frəm/ <u>Mon</u>day <u>10th</u> of /əv/ July to /tə/
<u>Wednes</u>day <u>12th</u> of /əv/ Ju<u>ly</u>. **h** For /fə/ <u>three</u> <u>nights</u>. **i** I'd like to /tə/ make a
/ə/ reser<u>va</u>tion. **j** I'd like to /tə/ book a /ə/ <u>twin</u>-bedded <u>room</u>.

Conversation 1: Complaining about problems
1 Things not working: air-conditioning, TV, hairdryer, lights, radio,
heating, internet, lift/elevator; **things missing:** clean sheets, clean towels,
toilet paper, hairdryer, pillows
2 yes
3 Things not working: shower, lights; **things missing:** soap, hairdryer,
clean towels
4 a isn't **b** aren't, noun **c** there isn't a **d** there isn't any, uncountable **e** there
aren't any, plural
5 a I'm afraid **b** straight away, immediately

Conversation 2: Making requests
1 b theatre, tickets **c** tour **d** car **e** directions **f** airport **g** luggage **h** taxi
2 a hotel
3 d, g, h
4 a–d Could you
5 Could you <u>help</u> me? Could you arrange <u>car</u> hire? Could you look after my
<u>luggage</u>? Could you call me a <u>taxi</u>?

Listening 1: Making a booking and arriving with a booking
1 2
2 a F **b** T **c** F **d** T **e** F **f** F
3 a family **b** 4 **c** Thursday **d** 3rd September **e** 10

Listening 2: Complaining about the room
1 4
2 Missing: clean towels and toilet paper; Not working: television, lights
3 a send some up **b** sort it out **c** The hotel offers Mr Lopes and his family a
free meal.

Speaking 2: Complaining about the room
1 and 2 a Mr Lopes **Hello**? I'm **calling from room** 408. I'm **afraid** the
television **isn't working**. **Could** someone sort it out?

b Mr Lopes **Hello**? It's **room** 408 **again**. I'm **afraid there aren't any** clean towels. **Could you** send some up?

c Mr Lopes **Hello**? I'm **calling from room 408 again**. **I'm afraid** the lights **aren't working**. **Could someone sort** it out?

d Mr Lopes **Hello**? It's **408 again**. **I'm afraid there isn't any** toilet paper. **Could you send** some up?

e Mr Lopes **Yes;** Yes, **thank you**. Everything **is fine**; That **would be** lovely, thank **you very much**. What **time is** dinner?

3 and 4 a Hello? I'm calling from room 34. I'm afraid the air-conditioning isn't working. Could someone sort it out? **b** Hello? It's room 34. I'm afraid there aren't any pillows. Could you send some up? **c** Hello? I'm calling from room 34. I'm afraid the internet isn't working. Could someone sort it out? **d** Hello? It's room 34 again. I'm afraid there isn't any shampoo. Could you send some up? **e** Hello? I'm calling from room 34. I'm afraid the television isn't working. Could someone sort it out?

Reading: Descriptions and reviews
2

	HOTEL IRIS	THE VICTORIA HOTEL
free internet	no	yes
free parking	no	yes
laundry service	yes	yes
restaurant	yes	yes
expensive	no	yes
recommended	yes	yes

3 a F **b** T **c** T **d** T **e** F **f** T **g** F **h** T **i** T **j** T

Writing 1: An email booking
1 a a family room **b** No (bed and breakfast) **c** 4 **d** 7 **e** Monday 10 July

2 (sample answer)

Dear Sir/Madam

I would like to book **full board** in a **double** room at the Victoria Hotel. The booking is for **five** nights, from **Saturday 3 September** to **Wednesday 7 September** for **two** people.

Could you tell me if I need to send **a deposit**?

I look forward to hearing from you.

Best regards

[your name]

Writing 2: A hotel registration form

Name	*Jose Lopes*	Nationality	Spanish
Address	Rua de la Frontera 29, Vila Real, 4306-435 9 Valegio, Spain		
City or town	Vila Real	Car registration number	HO 23 42 81 P
Date of arrival	*Monday 10 July*	Date of departure	*Monday 17 July*
Method of payment	Credit card ☒	Cheque ☐	Cash ☐
Room rate	Full board ☐	Bed and breakfast ☒	Room only ☐
Signature	*Jose Lopes*	Room number	*408*

Test yourself

1 a clean **b** cheap / excellent value **c** noisy **d** awful **e** rude **f** unfriendly

2 a 2 **b** 1 **c** 5 **d** 4 **e** 3

3 a 5 **b** 4 **c** 6 **d** 3 **e** 7 **f** 1 **g** 2

4 a I've **got** a reservation. **b Have** you **got** a room with a sea view? **c Does** the price **include** breakfast? **d** What time **is** dinner? **e** There **isn't any** soap. **f There aren't any** towels. **g** The lights **aren't working**. **h** The Wi-Fi **isn't working**. **i Could you** call me a taxi?

UNIT 8: SIGHTSEEING AND THE WEATHER

Coming to the UK on holiday

2 and 3

MUSEUM OR ART GALLERY	CHURCH OR CATHEDRAL	MONUMENT, CASTLE OR PALACE	CITY, COUNTRY OR REGION	OTHER ATTRACTION
British Museum Madame Tussaud's Museum of Modern Art, New York	St Paul's Cathedral	Buckingham Palace the Tower of London the Houses of Parliament Windsor Castle Stonehenge The Statue of Liberty	London the Cotswolds Scotland Wales the south-west of England New York City	River Thames Big Ben the London Eye The Empire State Building The Grand Canyon Yellowstone National Park The White House Niagara Falls

4 a is a good idea **b** should **c** a great place to **d** well worth **e** recommend visiting

Vocabulary 1: The weather

1 It's freezing, it's cold, it's chilly, it's warm, it's hot, it's boiling

2 a It's sunny. **b** It's cloudy. **c** It's windy. **d** It's showery. **e** It's snowing. **f** It's stormy. **g** It's raining.

3 and 4

What a lovely day! It's really sunny. It's a really nice day. It's a beautiful day. It's warm. It's hot. It's boiling. It's sunny.	It's really wet. It's quite windy. It's pouring with rain. What terrible weather! What miserable weather! It's cloudy. It's windy. It's showery. It's stormy. It's raining.	It's very cold. It's absolutely freezing! It's freezing. It's cold. It's chilly. It's snowing.

5

What a <u>lovely day</u>! It's a <u>beau</u>tiful <u>day</u>, it's <u>really sunny</u>, it's <u>hot</u>, it's <u>boil</u>ing, it's <u>warm</u>, it's <u>really wet</u>, it's <u>quite win</u>dy, it's <u>pour</u>ing with <u>rain</u>, what <u>terrible weat</u>her! What <u>mis</u>erable <u>weat</u>her! It's <u>rain</u>ing, it's <u>show</u>ery, it's <u>cloudy</u>, it's <u>stormy</u>, it's <u>very cold</u>, it's <u>ab</u>solutely <u>freez</u>ing, it's <u>snow</u>ing, it's <u>chilly</u>

Vocabulary 2: Comparing

2 a hotter **b** hottest

3 a er **b** est

4

ADJECTIVE	COMPARATIVE	SUPERLATIVE
cold	colder	the coldest
warm	warmer	warmest
nice	nicer	nicest
hot	hotter	hottest
wet	wetter	wettest
sunny	sunnier	sunniest
dry	drier	driest
beautiful	more beautiful	the most beautiful
miserable	more miserable	the most miserable

5 a It is usually hotter in July than in January. **b** The weather in summer is usually more beautiful than the weather in winter. **c** It is wetter in spring than in summer. **d** January is the coldest month. **e** August is the hottest month. **f** The best month for dry weather is July.

Conversation 1: Past simple

1 Yes

2 a They had a good holiday. **b** They travelled by plane. **c** The did a lot of things. **d** They weren't bored. **e** The food was quite cheap. **f** They ate in restaurants. **g** They didn't hire a car. **h** It rained once.

3 b got **c** went **d** had **e** was **f** flew **g** stayed **h** gave **i** did **j** were **k** met **l** saw **m** visited **n** took **o** found **p** ate **q** used **r** bought **s** wanted **t** rained **u** left **v** felt **w** tried **x** enrolled

Regular verbs: stayed, visited, wanted, rained, tried, enrolled.

We make the past tense of regular verbs by adding -ed. If there is a single vowel and a single consonant, we double the consonant. If the verb ends in -e we just add -d.

4 a asked **b** worked **c** arrived **d** looked **e** enjoyed **f** started

5 b lose **c** spend **d** know **e** tell **f** make

6 a Were **b** weren't **c** Was

7 a When did you come home? **b** Where did you go? **c** What did you do? **d** Who did you meet? **e** What did you see? **f** How many photos did you take? **g** Where did you eat? **h** What did you buy? **i** When did you leave? **j** How much did you spend?

8 a We came home yesterday. **b** We went to New York. **c** We did a lot of things. **d** We met some nice people. **e** We saw some monuments. **f** I took a lot of photos. **g** We ate in little restaurants. **h** We bought a lot of clothes. **i** We left yesterday. **j** I spent a lot of money.

9 We **came** back yesterday. We **got** a cheap flight and we **went** to Portugal. We **had** a brilliant time. We **flew** to Lisbon and we **stayed** in a lovely hotel in the centre of the city. We **didn't know** Lisbon so we **went** to the Tourist Information Centre. They **gave** us some good ideas about different things to do. We **did** so much in just one week. We **met** some really nice people, we **went** to the seaside, we **saw** some amazing buildings and monuments and we **visited** a couple of museums. I **took** a lot of photos. We **found** some lovely little restaurants in the old part of the city and we **ate** out nearly every night. We **didn't hire** a car. We **used** the local transport and it **was** fine. I **didn't spend** too much money but we **bought** a lot of souvenirs. I **wanted** to buy more but we **didn't have** room in our suitcase! The weather **was** really good for the whole week apart from one day when it **rained** a bit. When we

left it was a lovely day and I **felt** so sad saying goodbye to Lisbon. I **didn't want** to go home! I **tried** to learn some Portuguese and yesterday I **enrolled** on a Portuguese course!

10 a What was it like? **b** What did you do? **c** Where did you go? **d** Was the food nice? **e** Did you hire a car? **f** Did you spend a lot of money? **g** Was the weather good?

11 stay, visit, want, enjoy, rain

-ed and -ing adjective endings

1

-ED	-ING
amazed	amazing
bored	boring
tired	tiring
interested	interesting
disappointed	disappointing
worried	worrying
excited	exciting
frightened	frightening

2 a bored **b** exciting

3 I'm amazed, I'm bored, I'm tired, I'm interested, I'm disappointed, I'm excited, I'm frightened, it's amazing, it's boring, it's tiring, it's interesting, it's disappointing, it's exciting, it's frightening

4 a, b, c, e are correct

5 a tiring, tired **b** amazing **c** boring

Pronunciation 1: -ed verb endings

2

/t/	/d/	/id/
talked	loved	needed
liked	played	waited
asked	enjoyed	
watched	used	
helped	studied	
	rained	

Pronunciation 2: Irregular past simple verbs
1 came, got, went, had, flew, gave, did, met, saw, took, found, ate, bought, left, felt, forgot, lost, spent, knew, told, made

Listening 1: A conversation about the weather
1 a 🙂 **b** 🙂 **c** ☹️ **d** ☹️ **e** ☹️ **f** 🙂

2

TODAY	WHEN ANNA WAS IN PORTUGAL	WHEN ANNA'S FRIENDS WERE IN PORTUGAL	WHEN ANNA WAS IN DUBAI	LAST WEEK	NEXT WEEK
~~windy~~	~~boiling~~ hot sunny	~~cloudy~~	~~really sunny~~ absolutely boiling	~~windy~~ ~~chilly~~ ~~cloudy~~ cold wet	~~sunny~~ warm

Listening 2: A conversation about a holiday
1 Yes
2 a one week **b** The Statue of Liberty, The Brooklyn Bridge, The Metropolitan Museum of Art, Museum of Modern Art, Times Square, The Empire State Building, Central Park **c** 4 hours **d** No **e** No

Speaking: Talking about a holiday
1 and 2
a Have you got any recommendations? **b** Are there any guided tours of the city? **c** Would you recommend eating in the hotel or going out? **d** Is hiring a car a good idea? **e** What's the weather like? **f** Have you got any other tips?
4 You should visit the Museum of Modern Art. I'd recommend going to Central Park. Going on a guided tour is a great way to see the main sights. It's well worth visiting the Empire State Building. Most nights we went out. I think that's the best idea.

Reading: A tourist information leaflet
1 a National Gallery and Hyde Park **b** National Gallery and Portobello Market **c** Portobello Market and Oxford Street **d** Portobello Market and Hyde Park
2 a F **b** F **c** T **d** F **e** F

Writing: Describing a holiday

1 Yes **2** This is to tell you about our visit to Scotland. We **spent** three days in the Highlands and it **was** absolutely beautiful. We **stayed** in a small guest house and **spent** most of the time walking. I **wanted** to see Ben Nevis, the **tallest** mountain in Scotland, but it **was** cloudy and it **rained** for the first two days. Then on our last day the weather **was better**, the rain **stopped** and we **saw** Ben Nevis. I **didn't climb** to the top but we **walked** for about three hours! I **was** really tired! We **met** some lovely people and they **told** us about a little pub in the village so we **went** there for dinner on our last evening and **had** a fantastic time. I really **enjoyed** it.

Edinburgh **was** also lovely but it **was busier** than the mountains (and **more expensive**!). We **spent** two days there. I **forgot** my driving licence so we **didn't hire** a car but **travelled** by bus. In fact, using public transport **was** probably **easier** than driving. I **lost** my bag on the second day and I **was** really worried but someone **found** it in the hotel bar and **took** it to the hotel reception. We also **visited** Edinburgh Castle and I **took** a lot of photos and I **got** some great pictures. Someone **told** me the view from Edinburgh Castle **was** well worth seeing and he **was** right. It **was** amazing.

Test yourself

1 Good weather: What a lovely day! It's really sunny. It's a beautiful day. It's hot. It's boiling. It's warm. Bad weather: It's really wet. It's quite windy. It's pouring with rain. What terrible weather! What miserable weather! It's raining. It's showery. It's cloudy. It's stormy. It's very cold. It's absolutely freezing. It's snowing. It's chilly.

2 a went **b** had **c** enjoyed **d** was, were **e** wanted **f** got **g** did **h** came **i** arrived **j** took

3 a Did you go to Scotland last year? **b** I didn't see him yesterday. **c** They weren't here last week. **d** Were you on holiday last week? **e** I was / We were in New York. **f** I took a lot of photos. **g** Did you lose your passport? **h** I forgot my money. **i** He didn't buy any souvenirs. **j** I spent a lot of money. **k** We really enjoyed it. **l** I tried to learn Spanish.

4 a hotter **b** colder **c** better, the best **d** worse **e** more expensive

5 a visiting **b** visit **c** doing **d** Travelling **e** tired **f** boring **g** disappointing **h** excited

UNIT 9: RESTAURANTS AND FOOD

Food in the UK
1 a 3 **b** 1 **c** 2
2 a roast beef **b** a cheese sandwich **c** fish and chips **d** a Chinese meal **e** a cream tea **f** a packet of crisps

Vocabulary 1: Types of food
1 b apple **c** orange **d** strawberry **e** tomato **f** carrot **g** cabbage **h** salad **i** egg **j** cheese **k** yoghurt **l** butter **m** chicken **n** beef **o** lamb **p** fish **q** bread **r** rice **s** pasta **t** potato **u** sugar **v** biscuit **w** cake **x** chocolate
2 1 Fruit 2 Vegetables 3 Dairy foods 4 Meat and fish 5 Carbohydrates 6 Sugary foods
3 fruit, ba<u>na</u>na, <u>ap</u>ple, <u>or</u>ange, <u>straw</u>berry, <u>veg</u>etables, to<u>ma</u>to, <u>car</u>rot, <u>cab</u>bage, <u>sal</u>ad, <u>dair</u>y foods, egg, cheese, <u>yog</u>hurt, <u>but</u>ter, meat, fish, <u>chic</u>ken, beef, lamb, carbo<u>hy</u>drates, bread, rice, <u>pas</u>ta, po<u>ta</u>to, <u>sug</u>ary foods, <u>sug</u>ar, <u>bis</u>cuit, cake, <u>choc</u>olate
4 The following foods are *usually* uncountable: g cabbage, **h** salad, **j** cheese, **k** yoghurt, **l** butter, **m** chicken, **n** beef, **o** lamb, **p** fish, **q** bread, **r** rice, **s** pasta, **u** sugar, **w** cake, **x** chocolate, fruit, meat, vegetables, dairy foods, carbohydrates, sugary foods
5 b apples **c** oranges **d** strawberries **e** tomatoes **f** carrots **i** eggs **t** potatoes **v** biscuits
If a word ends in *y*, we change the *y* to **i** and add **es**.
If a word ends in *o*, we add **es**.
6 a an **b** plural **c** some **d** some, some
7

A PACKET OF ...	A PIECE OF ...	A SMALL/BIG PORTION OF ...
crisps	cake	rice
biscuits	chocolate	pasta
sugar	apple	potatoes
	cheese	fish
	orange	chicken
	chicken	beef
	fish	meat
	fruit	lamb
	meat	salad
	bread	vegetables
		carrots
		cabbage

Vocabulary 2: Drinks
1, 2, 3

	a Do we usually drink it hot?	**b** Is it an alcoholic drink?	**c** Is it good for you?	**d** Bottle	**e** Can	**f** Cup	**g** Glass	**h** Pint (UK)/ litre
milk	no	no	yes	yes	no	no	yes	yes
coffee	yes	no	no	no	no	yes	no	no
tea	yes	no	no	no	no	yes	no	no
orange juice	no	no	yes	yes	no	no	yes	yes
coke	no	no	no	yes	yes	no	yes	yes
water	no	no	yes	yes	no	no	yes	yes
beer	no	yes	no	yes	yes	no	yes	yes
wine	no	yes	no	yes	no	no	yes	yes

Pronunciation: Containers and quantities
1 packet, piece, portion, glass, bottle, cup, can, pint, litre, milk, coffee, tea, orange juice, coke, water, beer, wine
We pronounce a /ə/ and of /əv/. We stress the container and the food or drink.
a /ə/ packet of/əv/biscuits
a /ə/ glass of/əv/milk
a /ə/ piece of/əv/cake
a /ə/ cup of /əv/tea

Conversation 1: Countable and uncountable nouns + *much/many*
1 orange juice, a cup of coffee, some yoghurt, some strawberries, an egg, some (two pieces of) toast, chicken, (a small portion of brown) rice, salad, (three) biscuits
2 a much **b** many **c** much **d** much **e** many
3 a many **b** many **c** much **d** many **e** much **f** many
4 with uncountable nouns: much; **with plural, countable nouns:** many
5 a I'd like some salad but not too **much,** please. **d** I'm on a diet. I can't have too **many** potatoes. **e** The restaurant was very good but there weren't **many** people there. **g** We haven't got **much** time. Is the restaurant near here? **h** I don't want **many** carrots, thank you. Just some cabbage. **k** I didn't eat **many** biscuits, really!

Conversation 2: Phrases to use in a restaurant

1 g, e, a, f, h, c, b, d. The waiter says: Good evening. Certainly. Come this way.
Here's the menu and the wine list. Someone will be with you shortly to take
your order. Can I get you any drinks while you look at the menu? Are you
ready to order? What would you like? Certainly. Good choice. Would you
like any side orders or salads? I'm so sorry. I'll sort it out immediately. I'm so
sorry. I'll see to it straight away. Here you are. I'm sorry about the mistake.
No, people can leave a tip if they think the service was good.

2 a Yes **b** a burger, fish/salmon, a green salad and some extra chips

3 a What are you having? What do you fancy? **b** I fancy … I'm having …
c How about (a burger); Why don't you (have a burger) **d** I'd prefer to have;
I'd rather have … **e** good, lovely, delicious; great, nice, amazing, fantastic,
excellent, awful, expensive, cheap

4

   a   We'd like a table for two, please.
   b   What are you having?
   c   Can I have + (the food). I'd like + (the food).
   d   How was + (the food)?
   e   Excuse me … I'm sorry but … + (the problem).
   f   Can I have the bill, please?
   g   Is service included?
   h   I'm sorry but I think there is a mistake with the bill.
   i   I'm so sorry.
   j   That's OK. Never mind.

5

   a   The table is too near the kitchen. The table is too near the toilets.
   b   This/It is too salty. This/It is too sweet.
   c   This/It is not hot enough.

6 We'd like a/ə/ table for /fə/ two please. This table is too near the kitchen.
What do /də/ you fancy? What would /wəd/ you like? What are/ə/ you
having? I fancy the salmon. I'd like the salmon. Can /cən/ I have the steak?
How about steak and/ən/ chips? Why don't you have steak and/ən/ chips?
I'd prefer to/tə/ have fish. I'd rather have fish. How was /wəz/ your/jə/
salmon? Excuse me, I'm sorry but … This is too salty. This is too sweet. It isn't
hot enough. My glass is dirty. The food is lovely. The chips are/ə/ really good.
Can/cən/ I have the bill please? Is service included? I'm sorry but I think
there is a/ə/ mistake with the bill. I'm so sorry. That's OK. Never mind.

Listening 1: In a café
1 They want a snack.
2 a F **b** T **c** T **d** F **e** F **f** F **g** T **h** F **i** F

Listening 2: In a restaurant
1 No

2 a They usually have a takeaway. **b** Two glasses of champagne, chicken pasta, salmon with vegetables, a green salad and some extra chips. **c** The food is cold (not hot enough) and they didn't bring the salad. Jenny's glass is dirty. **d** Nothing. **e** At home.

Speaking: In a restaurant
3 a Excuse me, I'm sorry but the table is too near the toilets and my glass is dirty. **b** Excuse me, I'm sorry but the salad is too salty and the soup isn't hot enough. **c** Excuse me, I'm sorry but we ordered white wine. This is red wine. **d** Excuse me, I'm sorry but we ordered some bread. We haven't got it yet. **e** Excuse me, I'm sorry but I think there is a mistake with the bill. You charged us for two burgers. We only had one.

Reading 1: Restaurant descriptions and reviews
1 b The King's Head **c** The Red Lion **d** City Deli
2 a City Deli **b** Coffee Time **c** The King's Head **d** The Red Lion
3

	THE RED LION	KING'S HEAD	COFFEE TIME	THE CITY DELI
Where is it?	in the city centre	ten-minute walk from the city centre, by the river	a ten-minute bus ride from the city centre, near the college	in the city centre in the main shopping area
What kind of food is there?	traditional British meals	sandwiches, bar snacks	cakes, biscuits sandwiches, hot snacks	European food, either eat-in or takeaway, snacks and sandwiches or a meal
What's the food like?	good quality/ traditional	delicious	good, home-made	great, European
When is it open?	Tuesday–Sunday	every day	Mon–Sat until 7 p.m.	Monday–Saturday 11a.m.–late

What's it like?	fantastic, busy, excellent and quick service, very friendly staff	small, traditional, country-style, quiet	friendly, busy	fantastic, modern, not very friendly
Is it cheap or expensive?	not cheap	reasonably-priced (not very expensive)	very cheap	expensive

4 a The Red Lion **b** King's Head **c** The City Deli **d** The City Deli **e** King's Head **f** The City Deli **g** Coffee Time **h** The Red Lion

Reading 2: A restaurant website
2 a T **b** T **c** T **d** F **e** F **f** T **g** F **h** F

3 a soup, mushroom omelette, green salad, garlic bread, all of the desserts

Test yourself
1

FRUIT AND VEGETABLES	SNACKS	DRINKS	CARBOHYDRATES	MEALS
salad, tomatoes, an apple, a banana	a cheese sandwich, chocolate, a biscuit, a packet of crisps (an apple, a banana)	milk, beer, tea, water	bread, rice, pasta, potatoes	a hamburger, roast beef, fried chicken, fish and chips

2 a, b, f, g, h, j, l

3 a I'd like a table for five, please. **b** Can I have steak and chips?/I'd like steak and chips. **c** How is your fish? **d** Excuse me, I'm sorry but this isn't hot enough. **e** Can I have the bill, please? **f** Is service included? **g** I'm sorry but I think there is a mistake with the bill. **h** That's OK. Never mind. **i** How many millilitres are there in a pint? **j** How much is an Americano?

4 a My soup is not hot enough. **b** This portion is too small. **c** The service isn't quick enough. **d** The restaurant is too expensive.

5 a I don't want many potatoes. **b** They can't have much rice. **c** There wasn't much wine. **d** He hasn't got many biscuits. **e** I ate too much pasta.

UNIT 10: SHOPPING AND MONEY

Shops and shopping in the UK

1 a chemist **b** supermarket **c** shopping centre **d** newsagent **e** market
f department store

2

	IS IT CHEAP?	CAN YOU BUY FOOD AND DRINK?	CAN YOU BUY CLOTHES?	CAN YOU BUY HEALTH AND BEAUTY PRODUCTS?
shopping centre	no	yes	yes	yes
department store	no	sometimes	yes	yes
market	yes	yes	sometimes	no
supermarket	sometimes	yes	sometimes	sometimes
chemist	no	no	no	yes
newsagent	no	yes	no	no

Vocabulary 1: Clothes and colours

1 and 2 a a pair of black jeans **b** some gold rings **c** a brown skirt **d** a pink
jacket **e** a purple shirt **f** a green dress **g** a blue T-shirt **h** a blue and yellow
jumper **i** a pair of red shoes **j** a pair of white trousers **k** a grey coat **l** a silver bag
3 before the noun

Vocabulary 2: Shopping online

1 a health and beauty **b** clothing **c** technology **d** sport and leisure
e jewellery and watches **f** flowers and gifts **g** food and wine **h** baby and
child **i** home and garden **j** entertainment and books
2 a some green soap **b** a pair of red trousers **c** a black laptop **d** a blue
football **e** a gold ring **f** some yellow flowers **g** some red wine **h** a pair of
white shoes **i** some pink towels **j** a green and red book

Vocabulary 3: In the supermarket

1 a basket **b** trolley **c** aisle **d** shelf **e** checkout **f** barcode **g** carrier bag **h** pay
for **i** change **j** receipt

Vocabulary 4: Money

1 a purse **b** get some money out/use a cashpoint **c** credit card **d** cash
e gift card **f** coins **g** wallet **h** debit card
2 cash, coins, credit card, debit card, gift card, purse, wallet, get some
money out, use a cashpoint

Vocabulary 5: Special offers
1 a £24 **b** £27 **c** £24 **d** £28.80 **e** £18 **f** £24 **g** £27 **h** £24
2 e

Listening 1: Buying souvenirs
1 souvenir shops, supermarkets, clothes shops, department stores, museum shops
2 a souvenir shop **b** supermarket **c** supermarket **d** supermarket or clothes shop **e** department store

Listening 2: English money
1 a Incorrect. There are £5, £10, £20 and £50 notes. **b** Incorrect. There are 1p, 2p, **5p,** 10p, 20p, 50p, £1 and £2 coins. **c** Incorrect. £1 coins are gold in colour. (Two pound coins are gold and silver in colour.) **d** Incorrect. A *fiver* is the same as £5. **e** Incorrect. A *tenner* is the same as £10. **f** Correct.

Audioscript 10.05
a *Forty-one quid* **b** *forty-one p* **c** *four hundred and twenty-eight pounds*
d *twenty-eight p* **e** *four quid* **f** *a tenner* **g** *ten p* **h** *ten pounds and twenty-eight p*
i *forty-two p* **j** *four pounds twenty-eight* **k** *four pounds ten p* **l** *twenty-eight quid*
2 a £41 **b** 41p **c** £428 **d** 28p **e** £4 **f** £10 **g** 10p **h** £10.28 **i** 42p **j** £4.28 **k** £4.10
l £28

Audioscript 10.06
a *a fiver* **b** *Six quid* **c** *Seven quid* **d** *a tenner* **e** *Seven p* **f** *Sixty-one p* **g** *Seven pounds fifty* **h** *Six pounds sixty*
3 a less **b** less **c** more **d** more **e** less **f** less **g** more **h** more
4 a £5 **b** £6 **c** £7 **d** £10 **e** 7p **f** 61p **g** £7.50 **h** £6.60

Conversation 1: Buying clothes
1 a 8 **b** 2 **c** 5 **d** 3 **e** 4 **f** 6 **g** 1 **h** 7
2 a–e I'm looking for some red trousers (some sports shoes/a jumper). Is there a supermarket (chemist/market) near here? Have you got any umbrellas (sports shoes/belts)? Have you got this in a bigger (smaller) size? Have you got this in a different colour (in red/in black)? **f–h** Where are the fitting rooms? Can I try this on? It doesn't fit. **i, j** How much is this? Can I pay by gift card?

Speaking and pronunciation 1
1 I'm <u>look</u>ing <u>for</u> a /fər ə/ <u>dress</u>. Is there a /ðərə/ <u>chem</u>ist's near <u>here</u>? Have /həv/ you <u>got</u> any <u>T</u>-shirts? Have /həv/ you got this <u>in</u> a /ə/ <u>small</u>er <u>size</u>? Have /həv/ you got this <u>in</u> a /ə/ <u>bigg</u>er <u>size</u>? Have /həv/ you got this <u>in</u> a /ə/ <u>diff</u>erent <u>col</u>our? <u>Can</u> I /kən/ <u>try</u> this <u>on</u>?

Where are the /əθə/fitting rooms? It doesn't fit. How much is this? Can I / kən/ pay in dollars? Can I /kən/ pay in euros? Can I /kən/ pay in cash? Can I /kən/ pay by card?

2 a I'm looking for a dress. **b** Is there a bank near here? **c** Have you got any trousers? **d** Have you got this in a smaller size? **e** Have you got this in a different colour? **f** Can I try this on? **g** Where are the fitting rooms? **h** The shirt doesn't fit. **i** How much is this? **j** Can I pay in dollars? **k** Can I pay by card?

3 a Where are the men's clothes?/I'm looking for the men's clothes. **b** Is there a cashpoint near here? **c** Have you got this jacket in a bigger size? **d** Have you got this coat in a smaller size? **e** Have you got this jumper in black? **f** Can I try this on? **g** How much are the shoes? **h** Can I pay in euros? **i** Can I pay by credit card?

Vocabulary 6: Customer services
1 a get a refund **b** get a replacement **c** get an exchange **d** get a credit note

Conversation 2: Taking things back to the shop
1 the receipt
2 Customer 2 There is a problem and she gets an exchange. **Customer 3** There is a problem and she gets a refund. **Customer 4** There isn't a problem and she gets a credit note.
3 Customer 2 It doesn't fit./It's too big. **Customer 3** It's damaged. **Customer 4** She (just) changed her mind.
4 a I'd like a replacement, please. **b** Can I get a refund, please? **c** I'd like to exchange it for a bigger/smaller/red one, please. Can I exchange it for a bigger/smaller/red one, please? **d** I just changed my mind.
5 Part B

Speaking and pronunciation 2
1 I bought this but it isn't /bət/ working. I bought this but it's /bət/ damaged. I bought this but it /bət/doesn't/dəznt/fit. I bought this but I / bət/don't want it now. I changed my mind. I'd like a /ə/ replacement. I'd like a /ə/ refund. I'd like to exchange this for a /fər ə/ bigger one. I'd like to exchange this for a /fər ə/ smaller one. I'd like to exchange this for a /fər ə/ black one. Can I /kən/ get a /ə/ replacement? Can I /kən/ get a /ə/ refund? Can I /kən/ exchange this for a /fər ə/ bigger one? Can I /kən/ exchange this

for a /fər ə/ smaller one? Can I /kən/ exchange this for a /fər ə/ black one?
2 b I bought this last week but it's damaged. I'd like a refund, please./Can I get a refund, please? **c** I bought this on Monday but it's too big/it doesn't fit. I'd like an exchange, please./Can I get an exchange, please?/Can I exchange it for a smaller one, please? **d** I bought this last weekend but I don't want it now. I changed my mind. I'd like a refund, please./Can I get a refund, please? **e** I bought these yesterday but they're too small/they don't fit. I'd like an exchange, please./Can I get an exchange, please?/Can I exchange them for a bigger pair, please?
3 a No, I just changed my mind. **b** Yes, here you are. **c** Yes, here you are. **d** I'd like a refund, please. **e** A credit note is fine, thanks.

Audioscript 10.11 and answers to Exercise 4

Is there anything wrong with it?
No, I just changed my mind.
Have you got the receipt?
Yes, here you are.
Have you got the card you paid with?
Yes, here you are. *Would you like a refund or a replacement?*
I'd like a refund, please.
We can do an exchange or give you a credit note. Which would you prefer?
A credit note is fine, thanks.

Reading 1: A social media post
1 yes
2 a F **b** F **c** T **d** T **e** F **f** T **g** F **h** F **i** T **j** T **k** F **l** T **m** F

Reading 2: Taking things back to shops
1 a, c
2 a can usually **b** can't usually **c** can't usually **d** can sometimes **e** can usually **f** can usually **g** can usually
3 a No **b** Yes **c** Yes

Writing: Complaining to a shop
1 No

Test yourself

1 a F **b** T **c** T **d** T **e** F **f** T **g** T **h** F **i** T **j** T

2

IN THE SUPERMARKET	ONLINE	BOTH
aisle	click on the section you	checkout
shelf	want	receipt
barcode	fill in your card number	add to your basket
pay cash		pay for shopping with a
pay with coins		gift card
get change		pay by debit card
carrier bag		pay by credit card
add to your trolley		
use a purse		
use a wallet		

3 a 9 Our Sports department is on the fifth floor. **b 6** Yes, the fitting rooms are over there. **c 2** Try a bigger size. **d 10** I'm afraid that's the smallest size we've got. **e 4** It's £40. **f 3** Yes, of course you can. **g 8** Would you like a refund or a replacement? **h 7** No, I just changed my mind. **i 1** OK, a credit note is fine. **j 5** Have you got a receipt?
4 b Correct. **c** Not correct. The correct amount is £7.50. **d** Not correct. The correct amount is £10. **e** Correct.

Review 2

1 Good weather: any five of: It's warm, It's hot, It's a (really) nice day, What a nice/lovely day, It's a nice/lovely/beautiful day, isn't it?
Bad weather: any five of: It's chilly, It's cold, It's (absolutely/really) freezing, It's cloudy, It's stormy, It's windy, It's snowing, What terrible/miserable weather, It's terrible/miserable/awful weather, isn't it?
2 a any three of: gold, white, silver, black, grey, pink, purple, brown, yellow, orange
b any three of: underground (in London, 'tube'), plane, coach, taxi (or mini cab), car, bicycle (bike), foot
c any three of: a double room, a twin-bedded room, a family room, an en suite room, a room with a view
d room only, half board, bed and breakfast
e any three of: a pair of trousers/shoes/jeans, a bag, a coat, a ring, a dress, a skirt, a T-shirt, a jumper

3 a The train arrives in London this evening. **b** We are travelling to Italy by train. **c** I am going on foot. **d** She is visiting London next year. **e** What time do you usually get home? **f** Where's my passport? I left it on the table. **g** The taxi rank is on the left in front of the cinema. **h** The bus stop isn't far. It's about two minutes from here. **i** Can I pay for the tickets in cash? **j** I paid by credit card.

4 a cheaper, cheapest **b** more expensive, most expensive **c** hotter, worse **d** best, more beautiful **e** quickest, easier.

5 a tiring **b** bored **c** disappointed **d** excited **e** amazing

6 a vacancies, hotels **b** passport, travelling **c** comfortable, hotels **d** reception, hotels **e** boarding card, travelling **f** hand luggage, travelling **g** wdelayed, travelling **h** central, hotels **i** en suite, hotels **j** security, travelling

7 a You can't smoke here. **b** We weren't in London. **c** She didn't go to France. **d** I wasn't tired. **e** It isn't very interesting.

8 They stayed in a small hotel with a view of the sea and when **they arrived** the weather **was** lovely. On Saturday morning, **they spent** a little time shopping at a local market. **She bought** some souvenirs and then **they walked** down to the sea and **found** a lovely little café. **They ate** lunch outside and **went** for a walk on the beach. It **was** beautiful. **She took** a lot of photos and **they visited** a castle just outside the town. The tourist office **said** it was the oldest castle in the area. On Sunday **they got** up late. After a fantastic breakfast, **they hired** two bikes and **went** cycling. It was lovely but after about an hour it **started** raining so **they didn't go** very far. The views **were** amazing!

9 a felt **b** flew **c** forgot **d** got **e** gave **f** knew **g** left **h** lost **i** made **j** saw **k** asked **l** enjoyed **m** tried **n** travelled **o** used **p** enrolled **q** wanted **r** worked **s** looked **t** did

10 a Excuse me. I'm afraid the Wi-Fi isn't working. **b** Excuse me. I'm afraid there aren't any pillows. **c** Excuse me. I'm afraid the rice is too salty. **d** Excuse me. I'm afraid the soup isn't hot enough. **e** Excuse me. I think there's a mistake with the bill. We didn't have any wine.

11 a How far is it? **b** How much is a (return) ticket? **c** What time does the train leave? **d** How long does it take? **e** What's the best way to get there? **f** Where is the train station? **g** Have you got any vacancies? **h** Does the price include dinner? **i** What time is checkout? **j** What's the weather like? **k** Where was he yesterday? **l** What did you buy? **m** How much is this T-shirt? **n** Can I pay by credit card? **o** Have you got this in a smaller size

12 a packet **b** piece **c** can **d** portion **e** cup

13 a Could you tell me where The Rex Hotel is? **b** I'd like to make a reservation, (please). **c** I'm afraid the TV isn't working. **d** Could you book theatre tickets for me, (please)? **e** We'd like a table for two, (please)./Could we have a table for two, (please)? **f** I'd like a steak. **g** Can I have a refund, (please)? **h** Can I have the bill, please? **i** (Excuse me/ I'm sorry but) I think there is a mistake with the bill. **j** Can you help me, please?

14 a C, biscuits **b** U, cheese **c** C, eggs **d** C, tomatoes **e** C, burgers **f** U, butter **g** U, meat **h** U, broccoli **i** U, bread, **j** U, fruit

15 a It's well worth going on a guided tour. **b** I'd recommend hiring a car. **c** How much pasta would you like? **d** I don't want many vegetables. **e** Can I have some rice/a portion of rice? **f** Can I try this on? **g** I'm looking for a pair of jeans./I'm looking for some jeans. **h** Have you got this in a different colour? **i** It doesn't fit. **j** Can I have a replacement?